I.B.TAURIS SHORT HISTORIES

I.B.TAURIS SHORT HISTORIES

I.B.Tauris Short Histories is an authoritative and elegantly written new series which puts a fresh perspective on the way history is taught and understood in the twenty-first century. Designed to have strong appeal to university students and their teachers, as well as to general readers and history enthusiasts, *I.B.Tauris Short Histories* comprises a novel attempt to bring informed interpretation, as well as factual reportage, to historical debate. Addressing key subjects and topics in the fields of history, the history of ideas, religion, classical studies, politics, philosophy and Middle East studies, the series seeks intentionally to move beyond the bland, neutral 'introduction' that so often serves as the primary undergraduate teaching tool. While always providing students and generalists with the core facts that they need to get to grips with the essentials of any particular subject, *I.B.Tauris Short Histories* goes further. It offers new insights into how a topic has been understood in the past, and what different social and cultural factors might have been at work. It brings original perspectives to bear on the manner of its current interpretation. It raises questions and – in its extensive bibliographies – points to further study, even as it suggests answers. Addressing a variety of subjects in a greater degree of depth than is often found in comparable series, yet at the same time in concise and compact handbook form, *I.B.Tauris Short Histories* aims to be 'introductions with an edge'. In combining questioning and searching analysis with informed history writing, it brings history up to date for an increasingly complex and globalized digital age.

www.short-histories.com

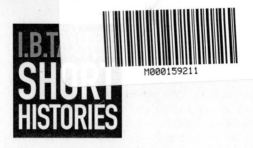

'It is remarkable how much information Michael Prestwich manages to include in his Short History. Fast-paced yet comprehensive narrative chapters are interspersed with illuminating discussions of subjects such as the composition and development of armies, changing battle tactics, diplomacy, chivalry and the balance-sheet on each side of profit and loss. All of this is illustrated with a telling array of statistics, entertaining anecdotes and judicious character sketches. Drawing on a lifetime of research into the conduct, logistics and implications of medieval warfare, Prestwich shows himself to be up to date with recent literature on the war and has the expert knowledge to challenge long-accepted but questionable assumptions. This is a complex story told with admirable clarity and is the ideal – manageable yet well-informed – volume to put in the hands of students, while also containing much that will make established scholars think again.'

– Chris Given-Wilson, Emeritus Professor of Medieval History, University of St Andrews

'*A Short History of the Hundred Years War* is a masterpiece of compression by one of our leading military historians.'

–Jonathan Sumption, author of The Hundred Years War volumes Trial by Battle, Trial by Fire, Divided Houses *and* Cursed Kings

'Michael Prestwich's introduction to the Hundred Years War can be very highly recommended. As a master of this complex history, he provides the reader with a brilliant narrative account. In addition, he offers sophisticated chapters on wider themes like military recruitment, logistics, chivalry and the economic impact of the war, all drawing upon the very latest scholarship and supported by short bibliographical essays that are worth the price of admission on their own.'

– Craig Taylor, Reader in Medieval History, University of York

A Short History of . . .

the American Civil War	Paul Anderson (Clemson University)
the American Revolutionary War	Stephen Conway (University College London)
Ancient China	Edward L Shaughnessy (University of Chicago)
Ancient Greece	P J Rhodes, FBA (Durham University)
Ancient Rome	Andrew Wallace-Hadrill (University of Cambridge)
the Anglo-Saxons	Henrietta Leyser (University of Oxford)
Babylon	Karen Radner (University of Munich)
the Byzantine Empire	Dionysios Stathakopoulos (King's College London)
Christian Spirituality	Edward Howells (Heythrop College, University of London)
the Crimean War	Trudi Tate (University of Cambridge)
English Renaissance Drama	Helen Hackett (University College London)
the English Revolution and the Civil Wars	David J Appleby (University of Nottingham)
the Etruscans	Corinna Riva (University College London)
the Hundred Years War	Michael Prestwich (Durham University)
Irish Independence	J J Lee (New York University)
the Italian Renaissance	Virginia Cox (New York University)
the Korean War	Allan R Millett (University of New Orleans)
Medieval Christianity	G R Evans (University of Cambridge)
Medieval English Mysticism	Vincent Gillespie (University of Oxford)
the Minoans	John Bennet (University of Sheffield)
the Mongols	George Lane (SOAS, University of London)
the Mughal Empire	Michael H Fisher (Oberlin College)
Muslim Spain	Amira K Bennison (University of Cambridge)
New Kingdom Egypt	Robert Morkot (University of Exeter)
the New Testament	Halvor Moxnes (University of Oslo)
Nineteenth-Century Philosophy	Joel Rasmussen (University of Oxford)
the Normans	Leonie V Hicks (Canterbury Christ Church University)

the Ottoman Empire	Baki Tezcan (University of California, Davis)
the Phoenicians	Mark Woolmer (Durham University)
the Reformation	Helen Parish (University of Reading)
the Renaissance in Northern Europe	Malcolm Vale (University of Oxford)
Revolutionary Cuba	Antoni Kapcia (University of Nottingham)
the Risorgimento	Nick Carter (Australian Catholic University, Sydney)
the Russian Revolution	Geoffrey Swain (University of Glasgow)
the Spanish Civil War	Julián Casanova (University of Zaragoza)
the Spanish Empire	Felipe Fernández-Armesto (University of Notre Dame) and José Juan López-Portillo (University of Oxford)
Transatlantic Slavery	Kenneth Morgan (Brunel University London)
Venice and the Venetian Empire	Maria Fusaro (University of Exeter)
the Vikings	Clare Downham (University of Liverpool)
the Wars of the Roses	David Grummitt (University of Kent)
the Weimar Republic	Colin Storer (University of Nottingham)

A SHORT HISTORY OF THE HUNDRED YEARS WAR

Michael Prestwich

I.B. TAURIS
LONDON · NEW YORK

Published in 2018 by
I.B.Tauris & Co. Ltd
London • New York
www.ibtauris.com

ISBN: 978 1 78831 137 3 (HB)
ISBN: 978 1 78831 138 0 (PB)
eISBN: 978 1 78672 326 0
ePDF: 978 1 78673 326 9

A full CIP record for this book is available from the British Library
A full CIP record is available from the Library of Congress

Library of Congress Catalog Card Number: available

Typeset by Free Range Book Design & Production Limited
Printed and bound by T.J. International, Padstow, Cornwall

FSC
www.fsc.org
MIX
Paper from responsible sources
FSC® C013056

Contents

List of Tables, Maps and Illustrations		ix
Acknowledgements		xii
Preface		xiii
Timeline		xvii
Chapter 1:	The Causes of the War	1
Chapter 2:	The First Phase, 1337–45	9
Chapter 3:	Crécy and Calais	20
Chapter 4:	Poitiers and Brétigny	32
Chapter 5:	Peace and War, 1360–77	49
Chapter 6:	New Kings, 1377–99	61
Chapter 7:	English Forces in the Fourteenth Century	76
Chapter 8:	French Forces in the Fourteenth Century	91
Chapter 9:	The Logistics of War	101
Chapter 10:	Agincourt	112
Chapter 11:	The Conquest of Normandy	127
Chapter 12:	The Maid and the English Collapse	138
Chapter 13:	Armies in the Fifteenth Century	155
Chapter 14:	Profit and Loss	168
Chapter 15:	Chivalry and War	181

Conclusion 189

Further Reading 195
Notes 205
Index 220

List of Tables, Maps and Illustrations

GENEALOGICAL TABLES

Table 1: The English Royal Family, 1327–1471 xxii
Table 2: The French Royal Family, 1270–*c.*1380 xxiii
Table 3: The French Royal Family, 1350–1461 xxiv

MAPS

Map 1: Major campaigns of Edward III and the Black Prince xxvi
Map 2: English lands in France according to the treaty of Brétigny, 1360 xxvii
Map 3: English lands in France after the death of Charles VI, 1422 xxviii
Map 4: English lands in France after 1436 xxix

FIGURES

Fig. 1: The capture of Caen by the English, 1346. From *Sir John Froissart's Chronicles of England, France, Spain and the Adjoining Countries*, 2 vols, trans. Thomas Johnes (London, 1839). 24
Fig. 2: A fifteenth-century interpretation of the Battle of Crécy. The English, with their archers, are on the 27

right. From *Sir John Froissart's Chronicles of England, France, Spain and the Adjoining Countries*, 2 vols, trans. Thomas Johnes (London, 1839).

Fig. 3: The slaughter of the peasant rebels at Meaux, 1358. From *Sir John Froissart's Chronicles of England, France, Spain and the Adjoining Countries*, 2 vols, trans. Thomas Johnes (London, 1839). 43

Fig. 4: The Chateau de Vincennes. The central tower was largely built by Charles V. Public domain. 45

Fig. 5: A knight bearing Bertrand du Guesclin's arms. From A. Parmentier, *Album Historique. Le Moyen Age* (Paris, 1896). 50

Fig. 6: An imaginative interpretation of the death of John Chandos, 1369. From *Sir John Froissart's Chronicles of England, France, Spain and the Adjoining Countries*, 2 vols, trans. Thomas Johnes (London, 1839). 56

Fig. 7: The Black Prince, lying sick in his litter, at the sack of Limoges, 1370. From *Sir John Froissart's Chronicles of England, France, Spain and the Adjoining Countries*, 2 vols, trans. Thomas Johnes (London, 1839). 57

Fig. 8: The tomb effigy of Bertrand du Guesclin, in the basilica of Saint-Denis. Public domain. 63

Fig. 9: The Earl of Buckingham crossing to Calais, 1380. From *Sir John Froissart's Chronicles of England, France, Spain and the Adjoining Countries*, 2 vols, trans. Thomas Johnes (London, 1839). 64

Fig. 10: The Battle of Aljubarrota, 1385. British Library, Royal 14 E IV f. 204 r. 73

Fig. 11: A mid-fourteenth-century French knight in full armour. From A. Parmentier, *Album Historique. Le Moyen Age* (Paris, 1896). 94

Fig. 12: A late fourteenth-century French knight. From A. Parmentier, *Album Historique. Le Moyen Age* (Paris, 1896). 97

Fig. 13: Charles VI and his queen, Isabeau of Bavaria. From *The Chronicles of Enguerrand de Monstrelet*, trans. Thomas Johnes (London, 1840). 113

Fig. 14: An imaginative engraving showing Henry V and his standard-bearer, with a prisoner kneeling before him. From *The Chronicles of Enguerrand de Monstrelet*, trans. Thomas Johnes (London, 1840). 125
Fig. 15: John, duke of Bedford. From *The Chronicles of Enguerrand de Monstrelet*, trans. Thomas Johnes (London, 1840). 135
Fig. 16: The French victory in the battle of Castillon, 1453. From Martial d'Auvergne's, *Les Vigiles du Charles VII*. Bibliothèque nationale de France, MS Français 5054, fol. 229v. 152
Fig. 17: A mid-fifteenth-century mounted knight. From A. Parmentier, *Album Historique. Le Moyen Age* (Paris, 1896). 161
Fig. 18: A fifteenth-century French crossbowman. From A. Parmentier, *Album Historique. Le Moyen Age* (Paris, 1896). 163
Fig. 19: *Dulle Griet*, a fifteenth-century bombard now in Ghent. Public domain. 165
Fig. 20: A nineteenth-century reconstruction drawing of a bombard. From A. Parmentier, *Album Historique. Le Moyen Age* (Paris, 1896). 166
Fig. 21: The execution of the notorious *routier* Mérigot Marchès in 1391. From *Sir John Froissart's Chronicles of England, France, Spain and the Adjoining Countries*, 2 vols, trans. Thomas Johnes (London, 1839). 172
Fig. 22: The tomb effigy of Olivier de Clisson, in the basilica at Saint-Denis. Public domain. 175
Fig. 23: Sir Kenneth Branagh rallies the troops in *Henry V* (1989). Renaissance/BBC/Curzon/Kobal/REX/Shutterstock. 192

Acknowledgements

I am very grateful to Alex Wright for suggesting that I should write this book, and for being so helpful during the process. I also owe much to Paul Tompsett, Ronnie Hanna, David Campbell and all the production team. I owe thanks to Durham University for providing me with continued access in my retirement to its library facilities, both in printed and electronic form. The process of research has been transformed in recent years by the availability of sources in electronic form, and it would not have been possible to write this book without the Internet Archive, the Hathi Trust and Gallica. As ever, I owe a huge debt of gratitude to my wife for her help and advice.

Preface

In 1435 a French official in English service, Jean de Rinel, explained that it was universally acknowledged that 'for one hundred years, by battles and other deeds, evils and irreparable damages have continually multiplied both by sea and on land'. This war was 'over the right and title to the crown of France'.[1] However, the term Hundred Years War did not come into use until the nineteenth century. It was employed initially in France, as a chapter-heading in a history textbook published in 1820.[2] English historians then adopted it in the second half of the nineteenth century. Modern historians have very understandable doubts about the term. The war comprised a number of distinct conflicts, extending north to Scotland and south to Spain, which were punctuated by periods of truce. The start and finish dates of 1337 and 1453 can be questioned; there is a good case for seeing the Anglo-French war of the 1290s as marking the start of hostilities. It was not until 1558 that the last English possession in France, Calais, was lost. Nor was it until the start of the nineteenth century that British monarchs ceased calling themselves kings of France. However, for all the undoubted complexities, the term Hundred Years War provides a convenient and unavoidable description of a lengthy period dominated by war. For the purposes of this book, I have taken a traditional view, that the core of the war was the conflict between England and France which lasted, with intermissions, from 1337 to 1453.

The Hundred Years War has been subjected to many different interpretations, and there have been significant recent developments in the historiography of so wide-ranging a subject. My debt to the historians who have worked on this period is immense. However, rather than identifying the contributions of individual scholars at this stage (with two notable exceptions), these will, I hope, become clear in the suggestions for further reading. The endnotes have largely been used to identify the sources of quotations, rather than to credit the work of historians.

Questions of military strategy and tactics have always been central to study of the war. For long, there was a consensus among historians that commanders had more sense than to fight battles, unless this was absolutely unavoidable; the French in the later fourteenth century achieved considerable success without taking such risks. However, this orthodoxy has been powerfully challenged, with arguments suggesting that the English, particularly under Edward III and Henry V, deliberately sought battle. The longbow has been at the centre of much of the debate about what can be seen as a tactical revolution in the fourteenth century, when forces fighting on foot gained mastery over cavalry. Discussion of the way in which archers were deployed on the battlefield have proved somewhat sterile; more interesting is the question of 'technological determinism', which asks how far the outcomes of the war can be explained in terms of military technology, with the development of both bow and bombard.

The history of war is much more than a study of strategy and battles, as the seminal work of the French historian Philippe Contamine demonstrated. The administrative efforts that went into campaigning created a huge volume of records, which provide detail about recruitment, supply and finance. The English archives are particularly full, but the evidence for both English and French forces has given historians a far deeper understanding than the chronicles can supply. Analysis of muster rolls, horse valuation lists and other records, assisted by the use of relational databases, has provided a new understanding of the composition of armies and the nature of military careers.

The war was brutal. Towns were sacked, villages were burned, crops were destroyed. Political life was punctuated by assassinations. Yet there was a different side to it, which exalted honour and noble deeds. This was the age of orders of knighthood, of grand tournaments and magnificent display. Chivalry was an aristocratic ethos, which with its emphasis on honour and its glorification of individual deeds of arms had significant implications for the conduct of war. Yet war was far more than a matter of knights on gaily caparisoned horses, inspired by their lady-loves to perform honourable deeds. For many, it was a business, with the potential of making huge profits from ransoming prisoners. Recent work has brought this aspect of the conflict into sharper focus.

The need to finance the war, and to provide the necessary manpower, had its economic impact. So too did the destructive strategy of English raiding, and the vicious activities of mercenary bands. People invested in building defences, rather than in profitable enterprises. At the same time, there were some who profited from the war, building up huge fortunes. Yet it remains hard to determine how far change was due to the war, and how far to other factors, such as the advent of bubonic plague in the mid-fourteenth century.

The range of work in recent years has meant that it has become possible to bring these various themes, and others, together in a considered, extensive narrative of the war as a whole. For much of the twentieth century, this type of history was out of fashion among academic historians, but this is no longer the case, as Jonathan Sumption has magnificently demonstrated with his volumes on *The Hundred Years War*, which provide both a broad sweep and unparalleled detail.

NOTE ON MONEY

The basic system of account was that a pound was made up of 20 shillings, with 12 pence to each shilling (in France, the terms were *livre*, *sous* and *denier*). An alternative method in England used the mark. This was two-thirds the value of a pound, and so consisted of 13 shillings and 4 pence. Coins might be silver or gold; in France gold coins were in use throughout the period of the Hundred Years War, while in England a gold coinage was first minted in 1344. Different currencies had different values, primarily as a result of the varying amounts of silver or gold in the coins. It is not possible to give meaningful equivalents in modern currency, but it may be helpful to note that a knight's wage normally amounted to £3 a month, and that he could buy an adequate horse for about £20. A mounted archer's pay for a month came to 15 shillings.

NOTE ON TITLES

I have chosen not to refer to English knights as 'Sir'. This is not because of any egalitarian objections I might have to such honorifics, but because it is not normal practice to acknowledge French knights as 'Sire', and it seems right to treat English and French equally.

Timeline

1327	Accession of Edward III in England.
1328	Accession of Philip VI in France.
1329	Death of Robert Bruce, king of Scots. David II succeeds him.
1337	Philip VI declares Gascony confiscate.
1338	Edward III sails to Flanders.
1339	The Thiérache campaign. Abortive battle at Buironfosse.
1340	Edward III formally claims the French throne.
	English victory in naval Battle of Sluys.
	Siege of Tournai.
	Truce of Esplechin.
1342	English intervention in the disputed succession in Brittany.
	Battle of Morlaix.
1343	Truce of Malestroit.
1345	Henry of Lancaster victorious at Auberoche.
1346	English victory in the Battle of Crécy.
	English victory in the Battle of Neville's Cross. David II of Scots taken prisoner.
1346–7	English siege and capture of Calais.
1347	Battle of La Roche-Derrien
1348	Advent of the Black Death in England.
	Foundation of the Order of the Garter.
1349	Charles, count of Evreux, becomes king of Navarre.
1350	Defeat of Castilian ships off Winchelsea.
	Death of Philip VI of France; accession of John II.

1351	Battle of the Thirty in Brittany.
1352	English victory in the Battle of Mauron.
1355	Black Prince's *chevauchée* to Narbonne.
1356	Black Prince's victory at Poitiers; capture of John II.
1358	Popular rebellion in France, the *Jacquerie*.
1359–60	Edward III's campaign to Reims and Burgundy.
1360	Treaty of Brétigny.
1362	*Routier* forces win the Battle of Brignais.
1364	Death of John II of France; accession of Charles V.
	Du Guesclin's victory at the Battle of Cocherel.
	Charles of Blois killed in the Battle of Auray.
1367	Black Prince's victory at Nájera in Spain.
1369	Reopening of war between England and France.
1370	Robert Knollys' unsuccessful *chevauchée*.
	Black Prince's sack of Limoges.
1372	English naval defeat off La Rochelle.
1375	English surrender of Saint-Sauveur-le-Vicomte.
	Truce of Bruges between England and France.
1376	The Good Parliament in England.
	Death of the Black Prince.
1377	Death of Edward III; accession of Richard II.
1380	Death of Charles V; accession of Charles VI.
	Death of Bertrand du Guesclin.
1382	French victory over the Flemings at the Battle of Roosebeke.
1385	Franco-Scottish invasion of the north of England.
	Portuguese victory over Castile at Aljubarrota.
1386	Planned French invasion of England abandoned.
1388	Scottish victory at Otterburn.
1392	Charles VI goes mad for the first time.
1396	Defeat of the largely French crusading army at the Battle of Nicopolis.
1399	Deposition and death of Richard II; accession of Henry IV.
1407	Assassination of the Duke of Orléans.
1413	Death of Henry IV; accession of Henry V.
1415	Siege of Harfleur, and English victory in the Battle of Agincourt.
1417	Start of Henry V's conquest of Normandy.

1418	Massacre of Armagnacs in Paris.
1419	Conclusion of the successful English siege of Rouen.
	Assassination of the Duke of Burgundy at Montereau.
1420	Treaty of Troyes. Henry V accepted as heir to Charles VI.
1421	English defeat in the Battle of Beaugé.
1422	Death of Henry V; accession of Henry VI.
	Death of Charles VI; accession of Charles VII.
1423	Anglo-Burgundian victory in the Battle of Cravant.
1424	English victory in the Battle of Verneuil.
1428	Siege of Orléans begins.
1429	Relief of Orléans by Joan of Arc.
	English defeat at the Battle of Patay.
1430	Capture of Joan of Arc.
1431	Trial and death of Joan of Arc.
1435	Treaty of Arras; Burgundy abandons support of the English.
	Death of John, duke of Bedford.
1436	Charles VII takes Paris.
1444	Truce of Tours.
1445	French military ordinance issued.
1448	*Franc-archers* established in France.
1450	French victory in the Battle of Formigny.
1453	French victory in the Battle of Castillon.

Genealogical Tables

THE ENGLISH ROYAL FAMILY, 1327–1471

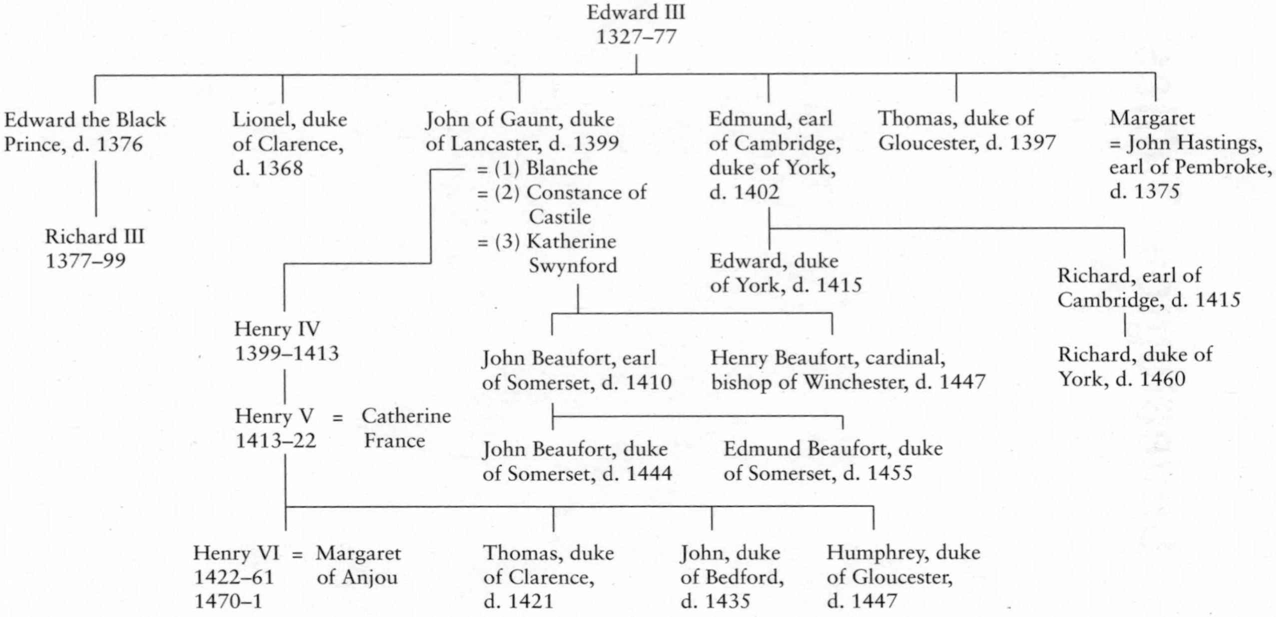

THE FRENCH ROYAL FAMILY, 1270–*c.*1380

Isabella of Aragon (1) = Philip III 1270–85 = Mary of Brabant (2)

- Philip IV 1285–1314
  - Louis X 1314–16
    - John I, 1316
    - Jeanne, queen of Navarre = Philip, count of Evreux, d. 1343
      - Charles II, king of Navarre, 1349–87
  - Isabella = Edward II, king of England, 1307–22
    - Edward III, king of England, 1327–77
  - Philip V 1316–22
  - Charles IV 1322–8
- Charles, count of Valois, d. 1325
  - Philip VI 1328–50
    - John II 1350–64
      - Charles V 1364–80
      - Louis, duke of Anjou, d. 1417
      - John, duke of Berry, d. 1416
      - Philip the Bold, duke of Burgundy, d. 1404
- Louis, count of Evreux, d. 1319 (son of Mary of Brabant)
  - Philip, count of Evreux, d. 1343
    - Charles, king of Navarre, d. 1387

THE FRENCH ROYAL FAMILY, 1350–1461

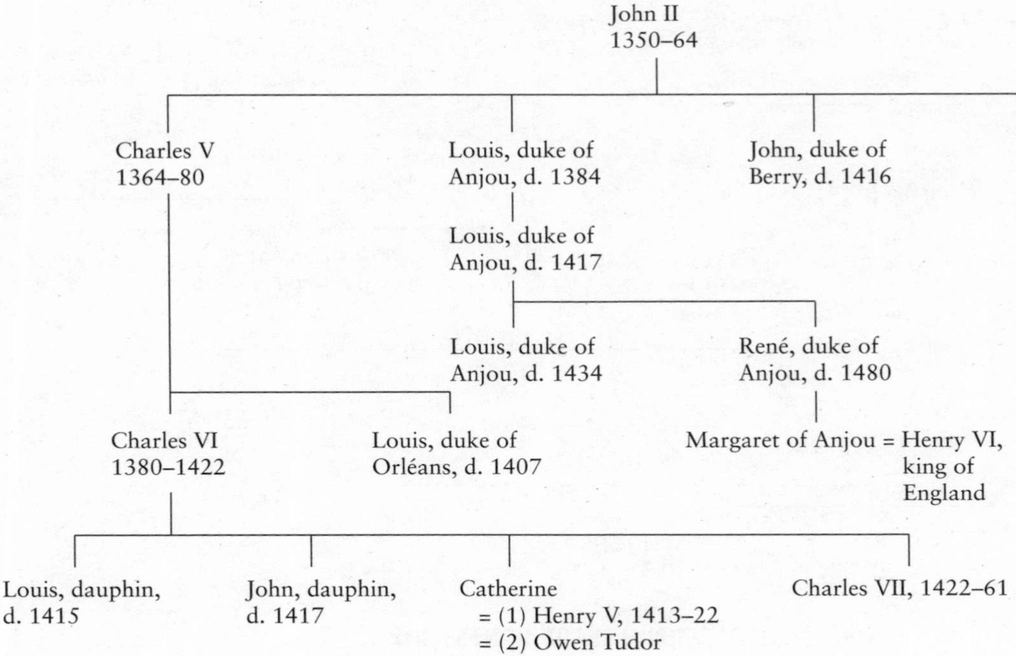
John II
1350–64
Charles V
1364–80
Louis, duke of
Anjou, d. 1384
John, duke of
Berry, d. 1416
Philip the Bold,
duke of Burgundy,
d. 1404
Louis, duke of
Anjou, d. 1417
John the Fearless,
duke of Burgundy,
d. 1419
Louis, duke of
Anjou, d. 1434
René, duke of
Anjou, d. 1480
Charles VI
1380–1422
Louis, duke of
Orléans, d. 1407
Margaret of Anjou = Henry VI,
king of
England
Philip the Good,
duke of Burgundy,
d. 1467
Louis, dauphin,
d. 1415
John, dauphin,
d. 1417
Catherine
= (1) Henry V, 1413–22
= (2) Owen Tudor
Charles VII, 1422–61

Maps

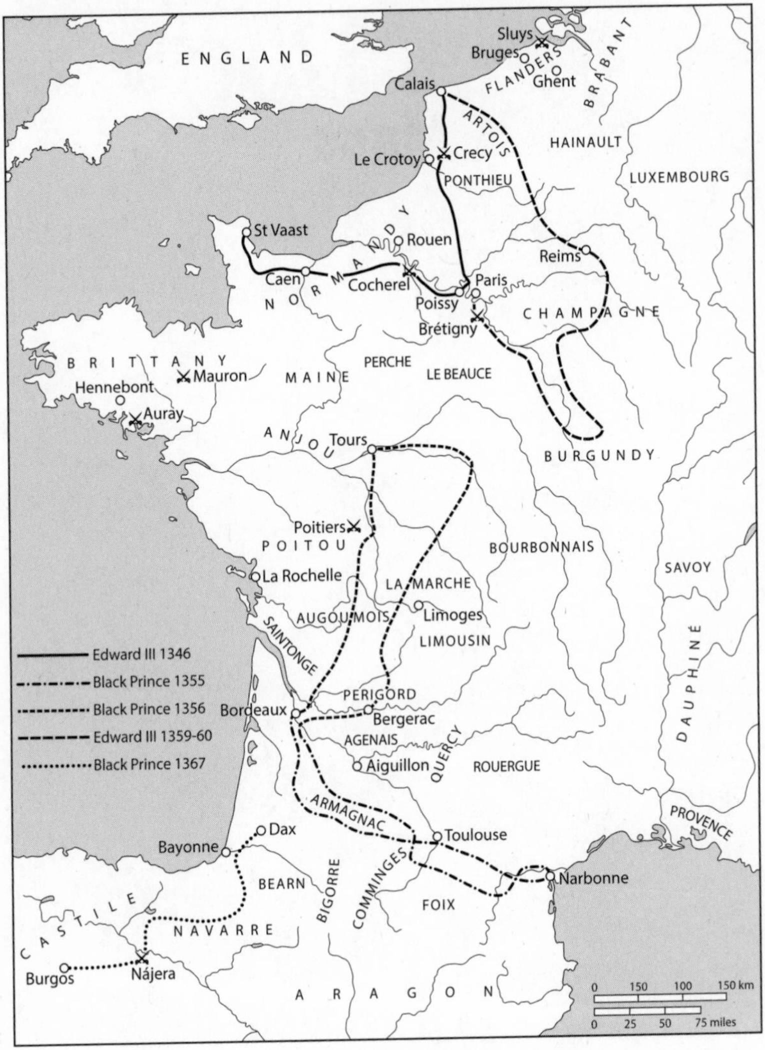

Map 1: Major campaigns of Edward III and the Black Prince

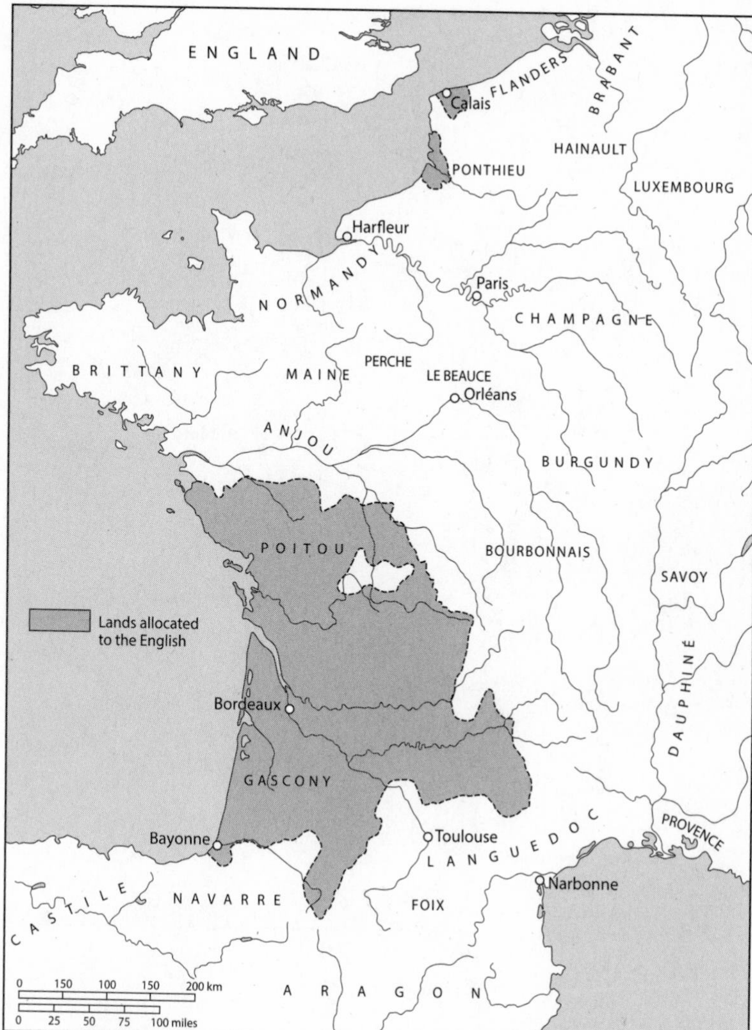

Map 2: English lands in France according to the treaty of Brétigny, 1360

Map 3: English lands in France after the death of Charles VI, 1422

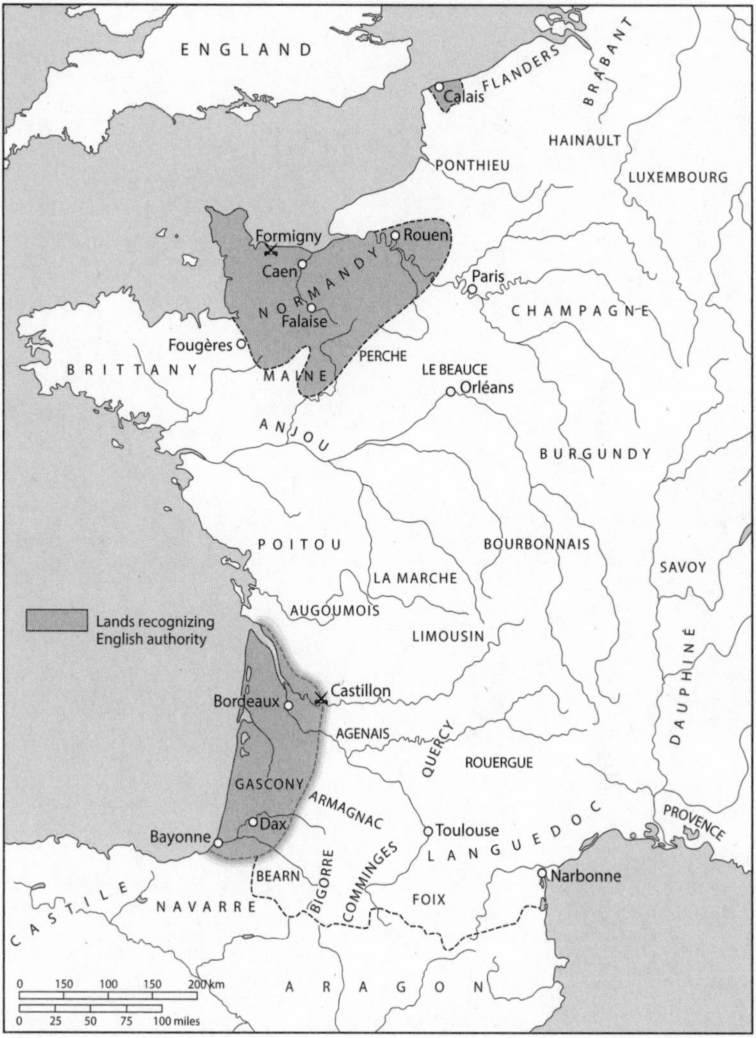

Map 4: English lands in France after 1436

1

THE CAUSES OF THE WAR

A small band of determined men made their way through the tunnels beneath the rock on which Nottingham Castle stands. It was October 1330, and among the group was the young king, Edward III. With his companions, he burst into the chamber occupied by his mother, Queen Isabella. The room had probably been designed by her late husband Edward II. Since his deposition in 1327, England had been ruled by the queen and her lover Roger Mortimer. Now, Mortimer and two of his advisors were seized. The personal rule of Edward III began. The coup revealed him as bold and determined, a man ready to take a dramatic gamble. He had much to do to restore the power and prestige of the monarchy after his father's disastrous rule.

Two years before the Nottingham coup, Philip VI of Valois became king of France. The previous king, Charles IV, was the last of the Capetian line that had ruled since 987. The dynasty had been astonishingly successful in producing male heirs in a direct line of descent until the death of Louis X in 1316. He was succeeded by his brother, Philip V, who was followed by his younger brother Charles IV in 1322. He died in 1328. Philip of Valois, grandson of Philip IV, was the closest heir in the male line; there was little argument over his succession to the throne. However, for the chronicler Froissart, it was Philip's accession that led to 'great war and great devastation.'[1] War did not come immediately; it was in 1337 that Philip ordered the confiscation of Edward III's duchy of Gascony.

GASCONY, SCOTLAND AND THE LOW COUNTRIES

There were long-standing issues regarding the duchy of Gascony, which had been acquired by the English through Henry II's marriage to Eleanor of Aquitaine in 1152. In the Treaty of Paris of 1259 the English acknowledged that their king owed homage to the French ruler for the duchy. Although the treaty was followed by over 30 years of peace between England and France, a situation in which one king was obliged to do homage to another for some of his lands was a recipe for trouble. In 1294 war broke out when the French *parlement* condemned Edward I to lose Gascony; this lasted until a truce was agreed in 1297. There was a brief war again in 1324. The French monarchy was eager to extend its rights of jurisdiction, and encouraged appeals by Gascons to the *parlement* of Paris. There were arguments over the foundation of new *bastides*, small defended towns. Ambitious Gascon nobles, anxious to build up their own power, played off the English against the French. There were also important disputes over the Agenais, to the east of Gascony. Seemingly endless diplomatic sessions failed to resolve the many issues. One of the accusations in Edward II's deposition articles was that the king had lost lands and lordships in Gascony. For Edward III, their recovery was an important task.

Even though no English king after Edward I visited the duchy, the question of Gascony and its status continued to be crucial throughout the Hundred Years War. To hold Gascony freely, without any form of French suzerainty, was a key English aim. The duchy was not, however, closely integrated with England. Gascon nobles did not hold lands in England, nor was the reverse the case. Gascon merchants did not always have an easy time in England, for royal favours to them provoked hostility, in particular from Londoners. However, the wine trade provided a strong economic link. In the early fourteenth century up to a quarter of Gascon wine exports, amounting to over 20,000 tuns a year, were sent to England in fleets of up to 200 ships.

Scotland was another point of friction. War between England and Scotland had broken out in 1296, dominating Edward I's later years. A Scottish alliance with France, though it achieved little, presaged the country's later alignment. Edward II's reign saw the disastrous English defeat by Robert Bruce at Bannockburn in

1314, and the ignominy of the king's near capture by the Scots in Yorkshire in 1322. The situation changed dramatically in 1332 when a small English army defeated the Scots at Dupplin Moor. Edward III was not openly involved; this was a victory for Edward Balliol, son of John Balliol, briefly king of Scots in the 1290s, and rival to the Bruces. In 1333 Edward III entered the war in support of Balliol, and was victorious at the Battle of Halidon Hill. This led to a protracted series of expensive campaigns against the Scots. The French gave refuge in 1334 to the young king David II, son of Robert Bruce. In 1336 an intelligence report provided the English with information about French plans to support the Scots, and to attack Portsmouth. In the event, French assistance to the Scots did not extend beyond diplomacy, but it was clear that If Edward were to succeed in Scotland, French support for the Bruce monarchy would have to be neutralized.

There were significant rivalries between France and England in the Low Countries. Edward III was married to Philippa, daughter of the count of Hainault. Commercial interests were important; the wealthy towns of the region depended on imports of English wool. While some of the territories, such as Brabant, Hainault and Jülich, were part of the Empire, the counts of Flanders and Artois owed homage to the French. In 1302 Flemish townspeople, many of them armed with little more than primitive clubs, had defeated the French at the Battle of Courtrai, but In 1328 Philip VI took revenge at the Battle of Cassel. An increase in French authority and influence in the Low Countries followed. Yet the towns, notably Ghent and Bruges, and some of the princes looked to Edward III as an ally.

THE CLAIM TO THE FRENCH THRONE

Issues over Gascony and Scotland, together with rivalries in the Low Countries, had all been elements in the Anglo-French war which began in 1294. The new factor under Edward III was the English claim to the French throne. Through his mother Isabella, daughter of Philip IV, Edward was senior to the Valois line. His case was a good one in law. In 1328 English envoys had given notice of Edward's rights, though hardly surprisingly the French did not take this seriously. The next year saw Edward perform homage to

Philip at Amiens, so effectively acknowledging the latter's right to the throne. He went again to France in 1331, keeping the mission secret. Edward privately acknowledged that he owed liege homage to the French king. Nor was his claim to the throne significant when war broke out in 1337. Edward III used the title only once in that year, and referred to Philip VI as king of France in a manifesto. Yet when Edward sent a justification of the war to the papacy in 1339, he provided a lengthy explanation of his claim to the French throne. Because 'the realm should not be governed by female fragility, and because of this a female person was excluded, this did not exclude a male person descended from the excluded female'.[2] In January 1340 a formal proclamation announced that Edward was king of France. He took the title in a ceremony in Ghent. Its immediate purpose was to bolster Edward's alliances; those of his allies who owed homage to the king of France would no longer be considered rebels if Edward held the title. The claim to the French throne continued to be an element in English ambitions throughout the war. At some points it was little more than a bargaining counter; at others a realistic war aim.

IMMEDIATE CAUSES OF THE WAR

Gascony, Scotland, the Low Countries and the English claim to the French throne provided long-term issues in the war. There were more immediate causes for the conflict in the 1330s.

It was the presence of Robert of Artois in Edward III's court that led Philip VI in 1337 to declare Gascony confiscate. Robert was Philip VI's brother-in-law, a close associate of the king, who was disgraced when it was discovered that he had documents forged in support of his claim to the county of Artois, which his aunt had inherited. He fled to England, and his was one of the voices encouraging Edward to go to war. Edward must have realized that the favours he accorded to Robert would infuriate and provoke Philip VI.

The breakdown of plans for a joint crusade, led by Philip VI and Edward III, was significant. Philip was not prepared to meet Edward's conditions, and did not take full account of the complexities of funding and organizing an expedition to the East.

Distrust mounted, and the Pope cancelled the crusade in 1336. The fleet that had been assembled at Marseilles sailed, threateningly, for the Channel ports.

There was little military action in 1337, and many chroniclers did not see the date as particularly significant. Some, however, did; the Tournai chronicle by Giles le Muisit has a heading about the start of the war in that year. In his view it was begun 'without justice and contrary to reason' by Edward III.[3] The breach between France and England in 1337 was much more than another hiccup in the diplomatic process. The measures taken by Edward III in that year show that he was planning war on a large scale. In parliament in March, Edward III made his eldest son duke of Cornwall, and elevated six men to earldoms, five of whom would have commands in the war. A propaganda exercise took place in the summer, when the reasons for the coming war were expounded in English in county courts and meetings of the clergy. Measures were taken to finance the conflict: in September the commons agreed an unprecedented grant of taxation for three years, and the clergy soon followed. It is very clear that war on a large scale, at great cost, was being planned.

BROADER ISSUES

The problems presented by Gascony, Scotland and the Low Countries, together with the English claim to the French throne, continued to be important in different ways and degrees, but cannot alone explain the Hundred Years War, for this was made up of many different conflicts. Alongside the specific reasons for these, such as succession disputes in Brittany, there is also the question of whether there were elements and ideas in late medieval society which led to war with such frequency and on such a scale.

When Edward III made a speech before the Battle of Sluys, he is said to have referred to the justice of his war, divine support, and profit: 'He who for me today gives battle will be fighting in pursuit of a just cause, and will have the blessing of God Almighty, and each shall keep whatever he may gain.'[4] War was seen as a proper means of resolving disputes. By the end of the thirteenth century, theorists, particularly canon lawyers, had developed a clearly articulated doctrine of the just war. The cause of war should be legitimate, and other methods of resolving a dispute exhausted. Kings therefore had the right to declare a just war, and could appeal to necessity in the defence of their realms, and in the common good. In such circumstances, subjects were obliged to provide their consent to demands for the men and money needed to fight.

Many wars have been fought over issues of faith, in the Middle Ages notably with the Crusades. Differences over faith, however, had little part in the Hundred Years War. Yet religion had an important part to play. All sides claimed that God supported them, and saw prayer as one of the weapons with which war might be won. There was an understanding that battle was a form of trial, with the outcome determined by divine intervention rather than by the force of arms. Writing to his council in 1346, Edward III asked 'that you thank God devoutly for the success he has given us up to now, and pray assiduously that he will give us a good continuance'.[5] Challenges to meet the French king in single combat were made 'so that the will of Jesus Christ should be shown between us'. In the battle plan they drew up before Agincourt, the French appealed to 'God, Our Lady, and Monsire St George', the same trio that Henry V trusted would assist him.[6] Such sentiments, echoed throughout the wars, should not be dismissed as mere rhetoric. Nor at a personal level was piety incompatible with fighting. One of the great English commanders, Henry of Grosmont, earl of Lancaster, wrote a sophisticated devotional treatise, the *Livre de Seynts Medicines*.

Though the war was not explicitly fought to win profits, or to gain control of economic resources, it provided a means of acquiring wealth and power in a period when other opportunities were constrained. The war took place during a period of economic difficulty and uncertainty. A climatic downturn began around 1300. Winters were often cold, and grain yields poor. Incessant rain meant that 1315 and 1316 were particularly disastrous years. There was considerable variation, but some decades, such as the 1430s, were particularly difficult. The advent of bubonic plague, the Black Death, in 1348 had far-reaching consequences, as labour became more expensive and prices lower. Even though societies proved astonishingly resilient, long-established social and economic relationships were challenged by changed circumstances. While war added to the economic difficulties, for some, it offered a way out of them.

There were other elements that paved the road to war. 'Chivalry' is a term which sums up the aristocratic culture of the later Middle Ages. It was not new in this period; the origins of chivalric culture go back at least as far as the eleventh century. It was, however, in the period of the Hundred Years War that the defining treatises and chronicles were produced. Much has been written about a concept which is hard to define. To be considered chivalrous, men were expected to display skill in arms, and to demonstrate loyalty, courage and generosity. Honour was vitally important. With its emphasis on deeds of arms, chivalry exalted violence, albeit violence in a just cause. Ideally, that violence should have been directed to the Crusade, but it was just as acceptable in the service of a ruler fighting for his rights.

The capacity of states to fight wars on a large scale was important. There were no standing armies, but contracts with nobles and with military entrepreneurs provided a highly effective method of recruiting troops, though broader concepts of military obligation were not abandoned. Financing war was never easy, but rulers had a wide armoury of weapons. Direct taxation was one means; indirect taxes such as the English export duties on wool and French sales taxes provided another. For the French, currency manipulation proved a useful source of funds. Credit was available from Italian bankers and from other traders. For the English in particular, it was important to have a ready supply of shipping, and although there was no substantial royal navy, it was possible to call on large numbers of merchant vessels to transport expeditions to France.

While France and England shared a common culture, with their respective aristocracies speaking the same language (though with different accents), there was a clear awareness of nationality. Some English propaganda portrayed the war as being fought in defence of national identity. In 1295, Edward I had suggested that the French wished to extirpate the English tongue from the land. This was picked up by Edward III, and in 1343 parliament was informed that Philip VI 'firmly intends, as our lord the king and his council fully comprehend, to destroy the English language and to occupy the land of England, which God forbid'. In 1346 a captured French invasion plan was read out in parliament, as evidence of the enemy's intention 'to destroy and ruin the whole English nation and language'. However, Edward's war was also 'to recover his rights overseas'.[7] English nationality had no more than very limited relevance to the defence of Gascony and the claim to the French throne. Yet perceived national differences were an element in, and a reflection of, the tensions and distrust between the nations. A fifteenth-century Spanish commentator considered that the English were a warlike people, who 'have no wish to live at peace with any other nation, for peace suits them not'. If foreigners came to England, 'the English try to seek some way of dishonouring them, or of offering them an affront. Accordingly, as I have said, they are very different from all other nations.' In contrast, the French were 'wise, understanding and delicate in all matters that pertain to good breeding, courtesy and nobility', and 'they glorify themselves for being gay and amorous'.[8]

The reasons for the outbreak of war in 1337 are clear, but it is not so easy to explain the way in which the war was continued and renewed for so many years. Individual circumstances, often dynastic, underlay particular elements of the conflict, but there were broader reasons in the nature of late medieval society. Peace had its protagonists, but the will to go to war was all too often overriding.

2

THE FIRST PHASE, 1337–45

The English plan for the war was clear. There would be defensive operations in Gascony, while the main campaign against the French would be launched in the Low Countries, where they would have allies, bought by subsidies. This was similar to the strategy that had failed King John in 1214, and which ran out of momentum in 1297. Even in Edward III's capable hands it had little success, leading as it did to political crisis and virtual bankruptcy.

The alliance was, at least on parchment, impressive. The counts of Hainault and Guelders, the Margrave of Jülich, the Duke of Brabant, the Count Palatine of the Rhine and the German emperor, Ludwig IV of Bavaria, were all brought into Edward's complicated and extremely expensive web. By the end of 1337, Edward had promised at least £124,000 to the allies. Eventually Edward's obligations probably totalled some £225,000. The French countered the English efforts. They had the support of the Count of Flanders and the Bishop of Liège, and bought that of the King of Bohemia and of the Duke of Lower Saxony. The problems for Edward were how to pay the bills, and how to swing the grand coalition into action. The Earl of Salisbury, one of his most important councillors, argued that the alliance 'did not seem to be drawing to a profitable conclusion, and that the king would not have the resources to bear the costs'.[1]

THE LOW COUNTRIES

Edward's hopes of leading an expedition to the Low Countries in 1337 were in vain. Recruitment was slow, and many troops had to be diverted to deal with Scottish attacks. The only action in the Low Countries was led by Walter Mauny, a Hainaulter, who had come to England in 1327 as a squire to Queen Philippa, and who served with distinction in the Scottish campaigns of the 1330s. The king 'loved him greatly, for he served him in many dangerous exploits'.[2] Mauny commanded a fleet which attacked the island of Cadzand, close to Sluys, in November. His troops cleared the island with brutal use of bow, sword and fire. Guy, bastard half-brother of the Count of Flanders, was captured, and subsequently sold by Mauny to the king for £8,000. Even at this stage, the incident demonstrated some important characteristics of the war as it would develop. English archery was highly effective; there was also extensive destruction, and significant financial profit.

The English king eventually sailed for the continent in July 1338, landing at Antwerp. His force numbered no more than about 5,000, yet it had taken a huge effort to take this small army across the sea. Some 400 ships, manned by about 13,000 sailors, were needed to transport the soldiers, their horses and the necessary supplies. Costs were high; Edward had promised his men double wages as an inducement to serve. No fighting took place. The king went to the Rhineland to meet the German emperor Ludwig IV to finalize the agreement with him; Ludwig agreed to appoint Edward as his imperial vicar in the Low Countries. A bizarre incident took place when a man known as William le Waleys appeared at Cologne, 'who asserted that he was the father of the lord king'.[3] It is barely conceivable that Edward II had escaped from his imprisonment at Berkeley Castle, rather than being murdered there in a most unpleasant manner, and there is no indication that Edward III was particularly concerned by Waleys' claim. According to the chronicler Thomas Gray, Edward spent his time at Antwerp 'jousting and leading a high life', rather than fighting.[4] The stay was not happy for all. There were troubles within Edward's own household; a group of soldiers murdered the son of the seneschal of Gascony, Oliver Ingham.

The French failed to take advantage of Edward's weak position in 1338. Philip VI ordered a muster at Amiens, but this was repeatedly postponed, and he made no attempt to bring the English to battle. Plans were drafted for an invasion of England, but nothing was done to put them into effect. It was in only a small way that the war was taken to England, with raids on ports on the south coast. Portsmouth was attacked and burned, and Southampton was sacked in a larger and more destructive raid. Two of the king's greatest ships were captured. Plymouth was attacked in 1339, but the French were driven off. They had more success at Hastings, but there was no realistic threat of full-scale invasion.

Edward III's campaign in the Low Countries finally began in late September 1339, when he and his allies laid siege to Cambrai. Savage destruction of French territory followed. This was war on a new scale. Villages and their crops were set ablaze. In a newsletter Edward III announced that 'the land is completely destroyed, grain, animals and other goods'.[5] The English hoped that this would put pressure on Philip VI, and bring him to battle. This hope appeared to be realized when the English faced the French near Buironfosse on 23 October. Edward III 'made all his people dismount, on foot, and he arrayed his men, the archers flanking the men-at-arms and the Welsh with their spears next to them'.[6] This surprised his allies, but it was a method which had proved its worth in the wars against the Scots, notably at Dupplin Moor and Halidon Hill. However, it was a defensive formation, and Edward had no means of goading his rival, Philip VI, to fight. 'We waited all day on foot, in battle array, until towards Vespers it seemed to our allies that we had remained there long enough.'[7] At night, the allied army slunk away. The French view had been that they had far more to lose than did the allies, and so caution, not gallantry, won the day.

GASCONY

In Gascony the English barely held their own. The position of the English administrators was extremely difficult. Promised troops never arrived from England, as preference was given to the campaigns in the Low Countries. Financial resources were also inadequate. In July 1337 the Count of Eu led a full-scale French invasion. Three castles and some minor fortifications were taken. A raid along the Garonne caused much damage, though no major towns or castles fell. The English managed to send out a small force which arrived in September. The French abandoned their campaign and the English soon recaptured almost all the places they had lost. In November they even conducted a successful raid into Saintonge. Early in the following year they invaded the Agenais. However, from the autumn of 1338 the war in the south-west went well for the French. Bourg and Blaye, which commanded the route by river to Bordeaux, fell in April 1339. Elsewhere many towns and castles were surrendered to the French. Oliver Ingham, the English commander, was in a desperate plight, with few troops and no money. Yet the pendulum swung again, and in July 1339 Ingham's troops compelled the French to abandon an attack on Bordeaux, and in the autumn the English made an important gain, when they won over an important magnate, the lord of Albret.

FINANCING THE WAR

The French planned their military efforts with care. An estimate of troop numbers and their cost, produced in 1339, predicted a considerable financial shortfall, and suggested that new taxes should be negotiated on a local basis. One agreement, with Vermandois and Beauvaisis, specified that the grant made should not form a precedent, and that the money raised should all be spent on the payment of troops.[8] There were particular difficulties with southern towns, and objections from the nobility, many of whom obtained exemptions from payment. Among the varied fiscal burdens, there were hearth taxes, sales taxes, export taxes, and levies on Italian merchants. As early as 1337 the crown began to alter the coinage, reducing the silver content and profiting from the recoinage. Though there was considerable hostility to the new taxes demanded by Philip VI, this was on a local basis, and the French king did not face a political crisis such as Edward III had to deal with.[9]

The financial situation in England was more difficult than that in France. By 1339 the crown's finances were in a mess. Plans, such as they were, were grossly overoptimistic. In particular, hopes of raising large sums through manipulation of the wool trade proved a fiasco.

In 1337 the English wool merchants agreed that the government would collect 30,000 sacks of wool. These would be sold overseas, and the operation would yield about £200,000. In the event, far less wool was collected than had been anticipated. Some was exported to Dordrecht, and when the merchants refused to advance £276,000 to the king, the wool was taken over by royal officials in exchange for bonds. The Italian merchant bankers, the Bardi and Peruzzi, were increasingly unwilling to lend to the king; their advances up to Michaelmas 1338 totalled about £70,000. Edward was angry and frustrated with what he saw as the failure of the administration in England to provide him with the funds he needed. A scheme, the Walton Ordinances, drawn up before the king left for the Low Countries in 1338, aimed to provide ways of controlling the administration from abroad, but this proved impracticable. In the autumn of 1339 the Archbishop of Canterbury, John Stratford, became chief councillor to the king's son, who was the nominal regent. His task was impossible; he explained in parliament that the king was £300,000 in debt.

On 26 January 1340, Edward was proclaimed king of France, in Ghent. There was an immediate reason for this: his allies in the Low Countries would be in a far stronger moral position supporting a king with a strong claim to the French throne, than they were as rebels against Philip VI. Of particular importance was Jacob van Artevelde, who led the Flemish towns. In December 1337 there had been a popular revolution in Ghent; an English embargo on trade with Flanders had contributed to anger against the count. Van Artevelde had emerged as the leader of the movement; his initial policy was one of neutrality, but by late 1339 he sought an alliance with the English, and with it, a massive subsidy of £140,000. Edward's financial obligations were rising to unacceptable levels.

When Edward returned from the Low Countries in February 1340 a grant of a new tax was made, in return for reform. Payment would not be in coin, but in kind, with people handing over a ninth of their produce for sale by royal officials. The plan was a failure. In part this was because there was a serious shortage of coin in the realm; this shortage meant that people could not buy the produce at the expected prices. By June 1340, payment of about £190,000 had been promised out of the tax, which by November yielded no more than about £15,000.

Inevitably, there was popular anger at what was taking place. The indirect impact of war, through taxation and demands for foodstuffs and wool, was extensive. A change in taxation methods meant that the poorest no longer had any exemption. Until 1334, each tax had been based on individual assessments of the value of people's movable goods. Thereafter, local communities paid a standard sum, which meant that far more people contributed to the taxes. The position was made much worse by the shortage of coin in England. A contemporary poet complained that 'half of what is raised in the kingdom does not come to the king', and that men could give no more.[10] The compulsory levies of wool, and the forced purveyance of foodstuffs for the army, added to the burdens. The quantities of foodstuffs collected were not as great as in Edward I's reign, but records show that the process was riddled with violence and corruption. Rather than make the sheriffs responsible, as in the past, merchants and others were given commissions to collect supplies. Some undertook this task responsibly; others, notably the king's outrageously corrupt purveyor, William Wallingford, did not. Inquisitions into the tax of a ninth suggested that as a result of taxation much land had been abandoned, completely lost to cultivation.

THE BATTLE OF SLUYS AND ITS AFTERMATH

Matters did not go well for the English in the Low Countries while the king was in England from February to June 1340. Two of the earls, Salisbury and Suffolk, were captured during an ill-considered raid near Lille. John, duke of Normandy conducted a savage campaign of destruction in Hainault, in which some 50 towns and villages were burned. Edward was needed in the Low Countries, and despite his domestic difficulties, he left England on 22 June. On the next day his fleet was at the Zwin estuary, within sight of the French ships moored at Sluys. On 24 June, with wind and sun behind them, the English attacked. Most of Edward's fleet, probably numbering some 160 ships, was made up of merchant vessels, some converted for war by the addition of 'castles' fore and aft. Archers did some damage as the English closed in on the French fleet, which lay at anchor, the ships chained together. When the

English pretended to be about to turn and flee, the French released the chains, opening up their formations. Ships were grappled and boarded, and fierce hand-to-hand fighting followed. One squadron under the command of the Genoese admiral Barbavera managed to escape. The English, with their archers and men-at-arms, were a far more formidable force than the French sailors, but the fight was a long one. By evening, the French had lost most of their 200 ships, and about 15,000 men, mostly through drowning. There is no evidence that the English took any prisoners. This was probably because there were few nobles or knights among the French who would have been worth ransoming.

The victory at Sluys was important in putting an end to any French hopes of mounting an invasion of England, and it put a halt for many years to French attacks on the south coast. However, the English were unable to follow up their success at sea with victories on land. Robert of Artois was defeated in battle outside St Omer. Edward and his allies besieged Tournai. The siege lasted almost two months, and went badly for the English; all they achieved was the destruction of the surrounding countryside. Edward's ally the Count of Hainault burned the monastery of Saint-Amand, and ravaged its lands. Its losses were later put at 20 hamlets and 32 farms and granges. Bombardment by siege engines achieved little; the defenders were able to answer in kind. However, Philip VI was too cautious to risk battle when he led his army close to the besieged town. Even though those who could not contribute to the defence had been expelled from Tournai, supplies in the town were nearly exhausted, but Edward's allies had no enthusiasm for continuing, and English funds had run out. A truce was negotiated at Esplechin on 25 September. The English strategy had collapsed, and with it much of Edward's reputation. The defence of Tournai demonstrated how difficult it was to take a large town by a lengthy siege, and presaged future failures, such as that at Reims in 1359. The capture of Calais in 1347 and of Rouen in 1419 were rare successes.

In November 1340, Edward suddenly left the Low Countries with a small number of his closest associates. He arrived at the Tower of London completely unexpectedly, and embarked on a major purge of a government which he considered had completely failed him. His quarrel was especially bitter with John Stratford, the Archbishop of Canterbury, who had led the government when the king was in the Low Countries. The political crisis was acute, but the parliament that began in April 1341 eventually saw concessions made and compromises achieved. There was even agreement to collect a new tax on wool. A new expedition was carefully planned. The army would number about 13,500, and 12,000 sailors would man the transport fleet. The leaders of retinues were not to be paid in the normal way, but were to be assigned wool to cover their wages for the 40 days the campaign was expected to last. The document detailing the plans did not reveal where the force was to go; it was characteristic of Edward to keep this secret. It is likely, however, that the Low Countries were once again the intended destination. In the event, the expedition was cancelled, as Edward's allies wanted to extend the truce with France. It was clear that the expensive strategy that had shuddered to a halt in the autumn of 1340 could not be revived. The war would have to take a new course.

BRITTANY

That new direction of the war was prompted by the death of Duke John III of Brittany in May 1341. The succession was disputed between his half-brother, John de Montfort, and his niece Jeanne de Penthièvre, who was married to Charles of Blois, the French king's nephew. In the autumn of 1341, Edward agreed to support Montfort's cause. However, a swift French campaign saw Montfort surrender Nantes to his rival. He was then imprisoned in Paris. By early in 1342 virtually all of Brittany was in Charles of Blois's hands, though Montfort's courageous countess, Jeanne of Flanders, continued to resist, holding out at the siege of Hennebont. There she rode through the streets, fully armed and mounted on a warhorse, encouraging the women of the town to take stones to the walls, and to hurl them at the besiegers. Initially she received scant help from the English. A small mounted force under Walter Mauny achieved little, though when he and his followers attacked the besiegers, the countess kissed him, and all the others, two or three times, on their return. 'You could well say that this was a valiant lady.'[11] An expedition under the Earl of

Northampton landed in August and laid siege to Morlaix. When Charles of Blois attempted to relieve the garrison there, the English drew up their troops in a defensive formation, protected by pits and ditches which they covered with brushwood. Accounts of the battle are brief, but it is clear that the French cavalry were unable to break the English line. The fighting was exceptionally fierce. Edward III landed in Brittany at the end of October, with a small army of some 3,800 men. He had great initial success, as towns and castles were surrendered. However, he was halted at Vannes, and in mid-December a French offensive began. Winter was not suitable for campaigning, and though the French recaptured some places which had fallen to the English earlier, they avoided battle. They were clearly unaware of the small size of the English army, and the army was suffering from disease and the cold. In January 1343 the Truce of Malestroit was agreed. Hostilities were to cease for three years. Each side was to keep the territory it held, though Vannes was handed to the papacy.

The Countess Jeanne was the heroine of the war, one of the very few women to take up arms. After the truce was agreed, this Amazonian sailed for England with the English king. Soon afterward she was confined, on royal orders, in Tickhill Castle. It may be that she had become insane, and that the stresses and trauma of war contributed to her condition. Alternatively, it may be that she was an inconvenient obstacle to Edward III's ambition to control Brittany. She lived on in captivity until 1374.

The Truce of Malestroit provided an opportunity for peace negotiations, though the English were not enthusiastic participants in them. In 1343 Edward did all he could to delay sending his ambassadors to Avignon, where talks took place under papal supervision. They ended without agreement early in 1345, largely thanks to the obduracy of the English negotiators. Papal attempts to find common ground between the two sets of negotiators failed. In England, parliament was told that the French had executed prisoners savagely, and that:

> the said enemy, in every way he knows or can, strives to take and occupy all the lands and possessions which our said lord the king has overseas, and to remove his allies from our lord the king, in Brabant and Flanders as well as in Germany; and

> thus he firmly intends, as our lord the king and his council fully comprehend, to destroy the English language and to occupy the land of England, which God forbid, if forcible remedy is not provided against his malice.[12]

Edward III was determined to take the war further, and the truce ended a year early.

Given the very limited English successes in these years, it was not easy to build support for the war. Edward was very aware of the difficulties involved in persuading his subjects to fight in France, as the decision to pay double wages shows. In 1337 bishops, earls and important barons had been appointed to meet county communities, to explain the decisions that had been taken and to set out the king's plans. In the next year, 'all men of religion and women' were requested to pray 'for a safe journey for the king in his expedition beyond the sea'. [13] This was no doubt expected to yield divine assistance for the king, but also to help build up popular support for the war. The bishops were sent an explanation of the origins of the war, which stressed the generous offers made by the English, and the unreasonable attitude of the French, who aimed to conquer not just Gascony, but all of Edward III's lands. The French had committed 'arson, homicides, robberies and other horriblenesses'.[14] Not everyone was persuaded by such propaganda. There were inevitable criticisms. A poem explained that it was wrong for 'The king should not go to make war outside the realm, unless the community of his land is prepared to consent.' It went on to condemn the taxes and seizures of wool, blaming not the king, 'a young bachelor', but his councillors.[15]

This first phase of the war, up to the Truce of Malestroit, was indecisive for both English and the French. Philip VI's troops had not gained control of Gascony, while Edward and his allies had achieved virtually nothing in the Low Countries. Some French territory had suffered appalling destruction, and some English south-coast ports were damaged. The siege of Tournai had demonstrated the difficulties that armies faced when confronted by stone fortifications. In Brittany, it had not proved possible to follow up the initial English successes. The costs of war had proved unmanageable for the English: Edward III even had to pawn his own great crown.[16] The credit mechanisms provided by the Italian bankers had not been sufficient, and, for a range of reasons, the two great companies of the Bardi and Peruzzi were approaching bankruptcy. The political crises had meant that Edward was compelled to make unwelcome concessions.

3

CRÉCY AND CALAIS

Battle was not always to be expected. In 1300 Philip IV had been advised that 'Nowadays your Majesty's enemies no longer dare follow the old methods of warfare: they neither dare nor can risk a straightforward battle, fought out with sword, shield, and lance.'[1] Yet the story was very different in 1346 when the might of the French army was brought down by Edward III's troops at Crécy. The English victory was extraordinary. It was followed up by the siege of Calais, the fall of which provided the English with a base in France a short sea journey from Dover. These events changed the course of the war dramatically.

THE CAMPAIGNS OF 1345

Edward III's plans when the war restarted in 1345 were highly ambitious. The Earl of Northampton was to take one force to Brittany. Another, led by Henry of Lancaster, was to be sent to Gascony. The destination of the main army, to be led by the king himself, was not disclosed, but it was to sail from Sandwich, and was probably intended for Flanders.

Northampton achieved little in Brittany. The English position was weakened by the death of John de Montfort, and all that was achieved by the end of the year was the capture of La Roche-Derrien on the northern coast of the duchy. The troops were delighted at the seizure of 1,600 tuns of Spanish wine there, but in military terms the place was of limited value. The king's own expedition, intended to number some 20,000 men, achieved nothing. It was delayed in July by a crisis threatening the alliance with the Flemish towns of Ypres, Bruges and Ghent. Edward's ally Jacob van Artevelde was murdered. Despite this, agreement was reached with the towns, and all seemed set for the major expedition to sail. The weather intervened. A violent storm scattered the fleet, and the plans were abandoned.

In contrast, Lancaster was astonishingly successful in Gascony. His expedition arrived at Bordeaux in August, where it was reinforced with locally recruited troops. Bergerac was swiftly taken by storm, and from there Lancaster led his force to Périgeux. He did not capture the town, but took a number of nearby places, including Auberoche. When the French attempted to recapture Auberoche by siege, Lancaster moved swiftly to attack. The English caught the besiegers by surprise. Their archers did a great deal of damage, and the French commander, Louis of Poitiers, was taken prisoner in the course of the hand-to-hand fighting. Louis died of his wounds, but many other nobles and knights were captured. There were rich prizes for the English in ransom payments, which were estimated at £50,000. The triumph at Auberoche was followed by the capture of the town of La Réole on the Garonne. The citadel held out for a time, but terms were agreed with the garrison; if no French army came to relieve the place within five weeks, it would surrender. It duly did. Success engendered further success in Gascony, as families and communities abandoned the French cause. In December 1345 Aiguillon in the Agenais was swiftly taken, and within a few months most of the region was under English control. Lancaster's campaign had been a remarkable triumph.

THE 1346 PLANS

In 1346, Edward's army assembled for embarkation not at Sandwich, as in the previous year, but at Portsmouth. It was far larger than any force the English had deployed earlier in the war. Numbers can only be approximate, but in all, there were probably about 2,500–3,000 knights and men-at-arms and 10,000 or more archers

The huge fleet of about 750 ships made a landing at Saint-Vaast-la-Hougue in Normandy on 12 July. Why Edward took this course has been much debated. Bartholomew Burghersh, one of the English commanders, writing five days after the landing, explained that the original destination was Gascony, but that unfavourable winds led the fleet to sail for Normandy. Recent historians have given this account of an accidental invasion of Normandy short shrift. Yet it is not easy to be sure what the king's intentions were. One problem is that, as with another landing in Normandy, D-Day in 1944, there was complete secrecy. Edward took every precaution to ensure that the destination of his expedition was not revealed.

An expedition to Gascony, as suggested in Burghersh's letter, would have made sense. After a number of successes, John, duke of Normandy, Philip VI's son, laid siege to Aiguillon in April 1346. This was a major operation, and although the French siege engines had little success, Lancaster was under considerable pressure; his achievements of the previous year were now threatened by a large French army. His terms of service had provided that in the event of his being besieged or threatened by a larger force than he could deal with, the king was obliged to come to his assistance. There were therefore strong reasons why Edward should make Gascony the destination for his expedition. There was, however, an alternative way to bring the siege of Aiguillon to an end. An attack on Normandy would draw the besieging forces away, and this is indeed what happened. When Duke John had news of the English landing in his own duchy, he requested a truce. On 20 August the siege was hastily abandoned.

According to the chronicler Jean le Bel, it was a minor Norman noble, Godfrey of Harcourt, who persuaded the English king of the advantages of an invasion of Normandy: the duchy was rich and undefended. Godfrey had rebelled in 1343, for entirely personal reasons. He fled initially to Brabant, and then to England in 1345. No doubt he provided some useful intelligence, and very probably also misinformation about the support Edward was likely to receive in Normandy. Yet it is hard to credit that such a man as Godfrey was responsible for the new English strategy.

The traditional view is that Edward intended a destructive raid in Normandy, a *chevauchée*, which would put pressure on the French. He was not seeking battle, but had no option other than to fight at Crécy when the English, retreating northwards, could no longer outrun the French. Jonathan Sumption argued that Edward's initial intention was to win Norman support for his cause, and establish an English occupation of the duchy. When it was clear that this was impracticable, destruction and devastation followed. Clifford Rogers presented a persuasive alternative scenario, arguing that Edward's strategy was battle-seeking from the first. His march northwards was not an attempt to escape the French, but was rather intended to put him at a clear advantage when he came to confront Philip VI.[2] It is tempting to assume that the outcome of a successful expedition was planned from the outset, but it is more likely that as the campaign developed, so did its aims. It is likely that the initial plan was both to divert French attention from the siege of Aiguillon and to conquer Norman territory, but that as the campaign developed, battle became a clear objective. The campaign was punctuated by challenges from either side to battle; Edward expressed his readiness to fight, but 'we do not consider it advisable to be cut off by you, or to let you choose the place and day of battle'.[3] These challenges can be dismissed as little more than exercises in propaganda, a conventional ritual which never led to agreement on the time and place for the fight. It is, however, likely that Edward was genuinely keen to face Philip in battle. Before the campaign, as part of his propaganda effort, he explained that the French were threatening his lands, 'wherefore the king judges it better to make a speedy passage and place himself in the hands of God'.[4] Battle could be seen as a form of trial, in which God would ensure that right would triumph. Edward's readiness to face the French in battle no doubt reflected this.

Events showed that any hopes the English may have had of taking control of Normandy were little more than fantasy. Bartholomew Burghersh optimistically wrote that 'the commons of the land come in numbers to the obedience of the lord king', but there was no move on the part of local lords to accept Edward's lordship.[5] Nor did the English behave in a way calculated to win support. A royal proclamation protecting the old, women and children, and forbidding the robbing of churches and the burning of buildings, did little to restrain the English troops. Destruction marched alongside the English army as it advanced toward Caen. Ports were ravaged by the fleet. Caen was taken with surprising

Fig. 1: The capture of Caen by the English, 1346

ease, and an orgy of rape and plunder followed. A plan for the invasion of England was found there, which provided excellent propaganda.

Edward planned to march north from Normandy: a royal letter sent from Caen ordered ships and reinforcements from England to come to Le Crotoy, on the Somme estuary. He probably intended to move from there on to Calais. However, when the army reached Rouen, the bridge over the Seine was broken. The English were forced to continue their advance upriver, and finally halted at Poissy, close to Paris, to wait to see if the French were prepared to do battle, and to repair the bridge. 'When the king of England saw that his enemy did not wish to come to do battle with him, he had the countryside around burned and pillaged.' Edward himself explained that after crossing the Seine, 'in order to better draw our enemy to battle, we headed for Picardy'.[6] The army marched north, managing up to 15 miles a day, a good deal faster than in the early stages of the campaign, even though there was a substantial baggage train of carts and sumpter horses. On reaching the Somme, a local revealed the existence of a ford at Blanquetaque. Though the crossing was guarded, the English forced their way over with surprising ease. On 26 August they halted at Crécy, and prepared for battle.

THE BATTLE OF CRÉCY

The Battle of Crécy is not easy to interpret, for the various sources cannot be reconciled. The accounts by English and French chroniclers have their problems, and for the most part differ radically from Italian versions of what took place. The contradictions are manifest, and reflect the difficulties that contemporaries had in understanding what happened.

The site of battle cannot be easily identified from the contemporary sources, but local tradition places a gentle hillside close to the village of Crécy as the position where Edward drew up his forces. On the opposite side of the valley the slope was interrupted by a long escarpment or bank, six feet or more in height. This would have prevented the French from advancing directly on the English position; instead, they would have had to come along the valley before turning to face their enemy.[7]

Interpretations of the way the English were drawn up vary. There is no doubt that their knights and men-at-arms were dismounted, rather than being ready to make a cavalry charge. Many battles in the half-century prior to Crécy had demonstrated the vulnerability of cavalry to well-armed men on foot; among them were the Scottish victories at Stirling Bridge in 1297 and Bannockburn in 1314. The English response had been to dismount the cavalry. They planned to fight on foot against the Scots in 1327, had their foes been willing to engage. In 1332 a small English force, fighting on foot in a defensive position, with archers on the flanks, was victorious at Dupplin Moor. Many of the Scots were crushed to death as huge piles of dead and wounded men built up on the front line. In the following year a much larger army commanded by Edward III himself triumphed at Halidon Hill. There were three English divisions of dismounted knights and men-at-arms, with archers in support. Similarly, at Crécy there were three such divisions. How they were drawn up, however, is not clear; they may have been abreast, or one behind the other. The way in which the English archers were positioned on the battlefield at Crécy has proved more controversial than the way the knights and men-at-arms were organized. It seems likely that most of the archers were in formations on the flanks, some hidden in a wheatfield. Froissart described them as being *en herse*, a term which has given rise to much debate. It may refer to a harrow, to a hedgehog or to a triangular candelabrum used in churches. It is likely that it refers to a wedge-shaped formation.

Most problematical is the way in which the English used a defensive circle of carts. The Italian chronicler Villani, and an anonymous Roman account, made much of this, stating that the entire English army was surrounded by carts, with a single opening in the circle. Guns as well as archers defended this formation. In contrast, the chronicle written at St Omer described a 'great hedge' of carts which protected the king's division from any surprise attack from behind. The *Chronique Normande* interestingly suggests that Edward had camped at Crécy, with his army enclosed by the carts, thinking that battle was unlikely. This account suggests that it was in the initial phase of the battle that the English came out from behind the defensive formation of carts.[8] Alternatively, just one of the English divisions may have been protected by carts, while a circle of carts to the rear guarded the baggage and horses.

It is possible that a few guns added to the strength of this defence provided by the carts. The earliest evidence for the use of guns is from 1326; by the late 1330s, English-held castles in Gascony were equipped with gunpowder weapons. In 1338 a French shipmaster was issued with a gun, two dozen bolts for it to fire, and a small amount of sulphur and saltpetre for gunpowder.[9] Guns at this time were largely for defensive purposes; their use on a battlefield was highly unusual, and given the very slow rate of reloading, probably largely ineffective. It used to be thought that the 100 'ribalds' referred to in English accounts were multi-barrelled guns, but Thom Richardson has shown that they were in fact small carriages, each fitted with ten spears.[10]

There are no accurate figures for the size of the French army, but it undoubtedly far exceeded Edward's force. In addition to the French

Fig. 2: A fifteenth-century interpretation of the Battle of Crécy. The English, with their archers, are on the right

troops, there were foreign allies such as John of Luxembourg, king of Bohemia, and the Duke of Lorraine, bound by treaty to provide Philip VI with soldiers in return for subsidies. A further source of troops was Italy; a large troop of Genoese crossbowmen added a different dimension to the army. Like the English, the French army was divided into three main divisions of knights and men-at-arms, drawn up one behind the other.

The French deployed the Genoese crossbowmen first of all; they had no time to gather their large defensive shields, and they were unable to shoot effectively; their feet slipped on the muddy ground which made reloading difficult. Wet bowstrings added to their problems. Impatiently, the French cavalry charged through the Genoese ranks. English arrows rained down on them, maddening the horses. As the battle proceeded, successive waves of French cavalry drove towards the English formations. They almost achieved a great success, when they broke through the Black Prince's lines. It is very possible that the prince was briefly captured. The battle was hard-fought, but went the way of the English. King Philip fought bravely; two horses were killed under him, and he was wounded by an arrow in the face. It seems likely that a quarter of the French knights and men-at-arms were killed. A tragic sight was that of the blind King of Bohemia, found slain, his knights around him. One report had it that just one of the English knights and two of the squires lost their lives.

Most explanations of the English success at Crécy give pride of place to the English longbowmen. They played a vital role in halting the initial French cavalry charges. Yet once the mêlée began, archery was of little use, as friend might be hit as well as foe. At least as important as the archery was the success of English men-at-arms fighting on foot. In the hand-to-hand fighting, sheer courage played its part, and Edward III's men had no lack of that. There was courage too among the French, but also panic as cavalry charges were broken by the hail of arrows, and individual bravery was overtaken by general fear.

Normally, success in battle would result in the capture of prisoners, who could then be ransomed at a high price. Crécy was different. The French deployed their sacred banner, the *Oriflamme*, indicating that this was a battle to be fought to the bitter end, with no quarter given. Edward's dragon standard sent out a similar message. This was a brutal fight. The list of French casualties was headed by the King of Bohemia, the Duke of Lorraine, the Count of Alençon and the Count of Flanders. English propaganda made much of the losses. It was astonishing that so many great men should have been killed, not captured. The flower of French chivalry had wilted.

CALAIS, BRITTANY AND SCOTLAND

Following the triumph at Crécy, Edward moved on to besiege Calais. Any hope that this might be a swift action like the capture of Caen was in vain. The siege was a waiting game of 11 months. The English were unable to blockade the town by sea until the spring of 1347. Assaults on the walls came to nothing: stone-throwing trebuchets, with their high trajectories, could not batter down the fortifications. Dysentery reduced troop numbers and morale. It was not until July 1347 that Philip VI advanced with his army to relieve the town. The terrain, however, was unsuitable for battle. Negotiations achieved nothing, and the French army withdrew. The garrison, exhausted and starving, offered to surrender. Edward demanded total unconditional submission. Walter Mauny argued 'If you put these people to death, as you say, the same may be done to us in similar circumstances.'[11] In the event, in a stage-managed performance, the six leading townsmen were allowed to go free. The town was cleared of its people, and pillaged. Edward set about turning the place into an English town. In October some 180 properties, mostly inns, were granted to English tenants.[12] Calais was to be extremely important, providing as it did an easy cross-Channel route, and a highly convenient entry into France. At the same time, it was difficult and expensive to maintain.

Elsewhere, the war continued. In the south-west, in the autumn of 1346, Henry of Lancaster led a raid to Poitiers. His troops killed, burned and pillaged at will. In Brittany in 1347 La-Roche-Derrien was besieged by Charles of Blois. The English, led by Thomas Dagworth, attacked by night. In a confused engagement, Dagworth was first captured, then freed when the besieged troops sortied. Charles was taken prisoner, and many nobles slain. The battle was won by vicious hand-to-hand fighting, rather than by English archery. English successes were not limited to France. In the autumn of 1346 David II of Scotland, encouraged by the French, invaded England. At Neville's Cross, just outside Durham, on 17 October a scratch English army led by the Archbishop of York defeated the Scots in a hard-fought battle. The English archers were once again highly effective in the early stages; as the battle proceeded, the fighting at close quarters was hard and exhausting. In the aftermath of the battle, King David was taken. His capture transformed relations between England and Scotland. Negotiations were complex. A huge ransom was eventually set at £66,666, and terms negotiated for David's release. English support for the claim of Edward Balliol to the Scottish throne was a complicating factor. It would not be until 1357 that David would be freed from a far from unpleasant captivity.

THE AFTERMATH

There had been little that was chivalrous about Edward's campaigning in 1346–7. Quarter had rarely been given, reducing the opportunity to take men for ransom. The tedium of the months encamped outside Calais was not lightened by knightly encounters. If, however, the war was not fought in a chivalric spirit, the same could not be said of the aftermath. After his return from Calais in the autumn of 1347, the king held a series of tournaments and festivities, appearing on one occasion in blue armour, with a crest of a pheasant with flapping wings. The culmination came with the creation of a chivalric order, the Garter. Earlier, in 1344, Edward had planned to establish an order of 300 knights, and the construction in the upper bailey of Windsor Castle of a great round house to house their Round Table had begun. Perhaps because it was too elaborate and too expensive, the scheme was abandoned. Revived in a different form, 1349 saw the first formal meeting of his new Order of the Garter. This consisted of a close-knit group of just 24 knights, selected for their distinction in the war. Though there were Castilian and Hungarian precedents for a knightly order, it was the Garter above all which set a fashion followed throughout much of Europe.

In its early stages the war had proved extremely expensive for the English because of the cost of the foreign alliances. This was no longer the case in 1345–7. Nevertheless, the burden of the war on England was heavy; in 1347 Edward was again forced to pawn his great crown. However, new arrangements to farm out the customs duties for £50,000 a year to English merchants proved highly effective. Direct taxes were granted for two years in 1344 and in 1346. There were none of the vicious political arguments of earlier years; in 1343, parliament had acquiesced in the repeal of the statutes that Edward had conceded two years earlier. Even so, had Edward not won such a resounding victory at Crécy, the demands he placed on the nation might have led to a new political crisis.

The situation was different in France. Complex negotiations for taxes and troops from local assemblies were long-drawn-out, and grants proved hard to collect. Ministers were dismissed, but their successors were unable to rescue the government from its plight. Loans from the papacy helped the crown, but the situation was desperate. The abbey of Saint-Denis lent silver plate worth over 1,200 *livres parisis*. By early 1347, Phillip VI had to resort to an arrest of Italian bankers, and a confiscation of the debts owed to them. There was further debasement of the coinage. The war was hard on the French nobility, and by the late 1340s many had incurred substantial losses and were heavily in debt to Italian moneylenders. The military defeats ensured that the regime was thoroughly discredited.

The English triumphs of 1346–7 were astonishing. Under Lancaster, the English were dominant in Gascony. Philip VI's army had been defeated in battle at Crécy. The king of Scots had been taken prisoner, and the French commander in Brittany captured. A major port, Calais, lay in English hands, providing them with a new and highly convenient gateway into France. What no one could have expected was the disaster about to strike all of Europe.

4

POITIERS AND BRÉTIGNY

In 1348 a pandemic, the Black Death, reached France and England. Scientific examination of the teeth of plague victims has settled arguments over the nature of the disease, for it has shown that the outbreak was caused by the bubonic plague bacillus, *Yersinia pestis*. The level of mortality varied from place to place, and between social classes, but in broad terms about half the population of Europe died.

People were terrified by the epidemic. Lancaster, Arundel and the Archbishop of Canterbury refused to travel to Avignon to negotiate an extension to a truce, for they were too fearful. In London it was feared that the air itself was infected, for the streets 'are so foul by filth that is thrown out of the houses both by day and by night', and this was leading to 'mortality by the contagious sickness which increases daily'.[1] Walter Mauny's reaction was that of the practical soldier: he leased land 'for a cemetery of poor strangers and others, in which sixty thousand bodies are buried, and built there a chapel'.[2] Despite the horror and the misery, plague-struck society showed astonishing resilience in the face of the cataclysm. Social order did not break down. Governments continued to operate. The war was not halted. Yet it was impossible to continue to maintain a military effort on the scale of 1346–7, and no major campaign took place until 1355.

In 1350, at the start of the year, a French attempt to regain Calais was thwarted. Plans by both sides for a major campaign came to nothing. Edward, no doubt frustrated, engaged instead on little more than piracy when he intercepted a Castilian fleet, packed with merchandise, off Winchelsea. The English justification was that the Spanish vessels had been engaged in hostile activity in the Channel. Froissart described how with great merriment the king, wearing a black velvet jacket and a beaver hat, made John Chandos sing a tune he had brought back from Germany. 'Ho, I spy a ship, and I think it's Spanish', came the cry. Trumpets were sounded, and the ships were readied for battle. The Castilian vessels, far larger than the English, met the challenge. The king's own ship almost sank during the fight, but Froissart claimed a great English victory, with the Spaniards losing 14 ships out of 40.[3] More plausibly, the French chronicler Giles le Muisit despaired of finding the truth of what had happened, beyond that 'many were killed and many were drowned on both sides'. He noted sardonically that the Spanish were merchants, not nobles, in complete contrast to the English, and concluded that in all probability the English lost more than the Spanish.[4]

Philip VI died in the summer of 1350, to be succeeded by his son John, duke of Normandy. A cultured man, keen on music, John suffered from ill health and had no great skill in the use of arms. The new regime looked very different from the old. The arrest and immediate execution of Raoul d'Eu, the Constable, was a major shock. The French nobility did not expect to see such treatment of a man who had returned from captivity in England to arrange payment of his ransom. The new king hoped to win support when in 1351 he announced the formation of the Company of the Star, akin to Edward III's Order of the Garter. He expected that with this new order of 500 knights, French chivalry would bloom.

Financial problems in France at this time were acute. Knightly wages rose by a third. The main forms of tax were aids, the salt tax known as the *gabelle*, and the *fouage*, or hearth tax. There were also sales taxes. Central assemblies of the estates-general were less fruitful than local assemblies, which provided grants at a rather higher rate than in the past, but it proved impossible to negotiate any grants from Burgundy. Manipulation of the currency continued. According to Gilles le Muisit, in 1351 everyone complained about the money, and he 'could never remember such scarcity of all things as in that year'.[5] In contrast, post-plague England saw no such difficulties. A recoinage in 1351 meant a mild debasement, but there was no brutal manipulation of the currency along French lines. In 1352 Edward III conceded that he would not repeat the experiments in military obligation of the 1340s. There were also concessions over purveyance (the requisitioning of food supplies). In return, parliament granted a tax for three years. A boom in wool exports also brought in welcome customs revenues. Efficient management and budgeting by the treasurer, William Edington, was a huge contrast to the way in which debts had built up in the early stages of the war.

CALAIS AND BRITTANY

Inconclusive fighting continued after John's accession to the French throne, punctuated by interludes of truce. Calais was defended, but in 1351 the French were successful in one skirmish, in which both sides 'dismounted on foot, each against the other, and they joined battle most harshly'.[6] The French were learning from English battle tactics. In Brittany, Thomas Dagworth, the victor of La-Roche-Derrien, was killed in 1350. His successor, Walter Bentley, faced considerable difficulties; freebooting captains and castellans were impossible to control. Living off the land meant taking ransom payments, or *appatis*, from hard-pressed villages. When he returned to England, expecting royal gratitude for his service, Bentley was imprisoned for allegedly disobeying orders; it took a year or more for him to be exonerated. Some of the great names of the war began their careers in these confused, lawless conditions, notably the two Cheshire men, Hugh Calveley and Robert Knollys, and the Breton Bertrand du Guesclin. In 1351 Calveley and Knollys both took part in an organized fight, 'the Battle of the Thirty', seen by Froissart and others as a great chivalric event. It provided an opportunity to display courage and skill in brutal combat, if not to exercise such virtues as courtesy and liberality. The outcome was victory for the French, and death or imprisonment for their English opponents. What was happening in Brittany, with gratuitous violence and the exploitation of villagers by warrior bands, presaged what would happen on a much wider scale as the war developed.

At Mauron in 1352, Walter Bentley, with a small force, defeated a French army. Once again, the English employed the tactics tried and tested in the Scottish wars of the 1330s. There were archers on each wing, and dismounted men-at-arms in the centre. As in the previous year near Calais, the French emulated their opponents, and dismounted the majority of their force. The advance to the English position was tiring and the fighting exhausting. French cavalry had some success against the archers, 30 of whom were later beheaded for abandoning their position. Bentley was badly injured, but the French commander, Guy de Nesle, was killed. Along with him there fell many knights of the Company of the Star, a disaster from which the order never recovered.

Fighting in the south-west achieved little for either side. In 1351 the English won a victory near Saintes, while the French took St Jean d'Angély. Neither French nor English gained a decisive advantage; it was local marauding bands who gained most from the situation.

PEACE NEGOTIATIONS

Given the near stalemate, it made sense for both sides to try to reach a negotiated settlement. Discussions began at Guines early in 1354 and continued at Avignon into 1355. At Guines, a preliminary agreement was reached, that in exchange for abandoning his claim to the French throne, Edward would hold Aquitaine and lands up the Loire, together with Calais, in full sovereignty. Normandy and Brittany were not included in the deal. There was enthusiasm in the English parliament for a peace, but the negotiations fell through. The English certainly took them seriously: headed by Lancaster, Arundel and a couple of bishops, the embassy was over 630 strong, outnumbering the papal entourage. The cost was also substantial, at £5,648. Lancaster's instructions made it clear that Edward was prepared to give up the claim to the throne in return for Gascony and the other lands in France, provided they were held freely, not subject to French suzerainty. Yet a well-informed chronicle account has it that at the end of the discussions, the Duke of Lancaster stated that 'the king bore the arms of France upon the advice of his liege men of France, and that he would not give them up for anyone alive'. This has led historians to assume that 'the duke refused specifically to give up Edward's claim and title to the throne of France'. However, bearing the *fleur de lis* quartered with the English lions was not quite the same thing as claiming the French throne; indeed, Edward would continue to display the French symbol on his great seal in the years after 1360, when he no longer termed himself king of France. Lancaster was offering a retort to the French demand that the king of England should do homage to the king of France for Gascony. It did not mean that Edward considered his claim to the French throne to be a sticking point; it was the French requirement for homage that led to the breakdown of the negotiations. One account explained that 'The French wholly rejected the peace, saying it had not been arranged together in this way, nor would they consent to this kind of peace in any way whatsoever.'[7]

Charles the Bad, king of Navarre from 1349, provided a major complication. An ambitious, clever and disloyal troublemaker, he inherited Navarre through his mother, but it was the title he obtained from his father, that of count of Évreux in Normandy, that represented his main interests. Like Edward III, he had a claim to the French throne through a female line. Married to King John's daughter, he was in a powerful position. He was responsible for the murder of Charles de la Cerda, Constable of France, in 1354, accusing him of slander, and of 'great damages, annoyances and impeachments against myself and my friends'.[8] He then entered into negotiations with the English. However, Charles and John were subsequently reconciled. Consistency was one of the many qualities the maverick Charles lacked, and at Avignon he held discussions with Lancaster. The English were once again tempted by the prospect of a deal with him, and this may help to explain why the negotiations with the French broke down.

THE BLACK PRINCE AND THE CAMPAIGNS OF 1345–6

The English had overambitious plans for the resumption of hostilities after the failure of the negotiations at Avignon. Henry of Lancaster would campaign in Normandy, the king would lead an expedition from Calais, and the Black Prince would campaign in the south-west. Lancaster's fleet set off down the Thames on 10 July, but contrary winds meant that it got no further than Portsmouth by the end of August, one of many demonstrations of the problems faced by broad-beamed vessels rigged with a single square sail. When news came that Charles of Navarre had once again changed sides, and had come to terms with King John, the expedition was abandoned.

The weather that had delayed Lancaster meant that it was not until the end of October that Edward himself eventually landed at Calais. He led a quick march south, accompanied by the usual horrors of destruction and burning, and by the conventional and ineffective challenges to battle from both sides. After a couple of weeks, the king returned to England.

The Black Prince's expedition arrived in Gascony in late September, a couple of months later than had been hoped. He had full powers as the king's lieutenant in Gascony and commanded a force of some 2,600 men, of whom 1,000 were fully equipped men-at-arms. He led his army south-eastwards. French forces came close, but the English claimed that they were unwilling to engage them in battle. The prince's men burned Carcassonne, and stormed part of Narbonne, close to the Mediterranean, before returning to Bordeaux. John Wingfield, the prince's chief administrator, wrote triumphantly, 'Know for certain that, since this war began against the king of France, there has never been such loss or destruction as there has been in this raid.'[9] Wingfield went on to explain, with some exaggeration, the impact of the consequent losses on the funding of the war by the French. This was not destruction for its own sake; the pillaging had purpose, putting pressure as it did on French finances, as well as bringing terror to towns and villages. The strategy was deliberate; it echoed advice that had been given to Philip IV in 1300, that 'all the vines, fruit trees, and plants must be destroyed'. Opposition would collapse 'when the whole year's hay, straw, and grain have been destroyed by fire'.[10]

Late in 1355, Scottish affairs came briefly to the fore. Edward III had abandoned his support of Edward Balliol and attempted to negotiate a settlement with the Scots that would have seen them acknowledge one of his sons as heir to David II. This was unacceptable to the Scots. In October 1355 a small Scottish force invaded Northumberland. Even worse for the English, Berwick was captured in a surprise dawn attack. Edward retaliated. The Scots in Berwick surrendered in January 1356, and there followed a swift campaign, known as the Burnt Candlemas, which brought all the brutality the English had practised in France to the Scottish Lowlands. Winter storms, which made it impossible for the English ships to bring urgently needed supplies to the army, forced an end to the expedition.

The campaigning in France in 1356, which culminated in the English victory at Poitiers, again raises the question of whether there was a carefully thought out strategy, or whether the English commanders did little more than react to events, seizing opportunities as they arose. One event certainly transformed the situation in Normandy and changed English plans. The French king's son Charles gave a banquet in Rouen, at which Charles of Navarre was present. In the middle of the meal King John entered, fully armed, backed by impressive force. Navarre was seized and led off to imprisonment in Paris. The Count of Harcourt, two other magnates and Navarre's squire were executed. John may have been right in thinking that the unstable Charles of Navarre was plotting against him, but the Rouen coup had disastrous results. Navarre's brother Philip led resistance to John, and sought English assistance.

Edward III's original intention had been to send Lancaster to Brittany, but the situation demanded that he go to Normandy. In a deliberate propaganda policy, newsletters were sent home to tell of the successes of English campaigns. One provided a detailed account of Lancaster's expedition. His force was composed of 900 men-at-arms and 1,400 archers. 'Each day the men took various fortresses, and a great quantity of prisoners and pillage, and on their return they brought with them 2,000 of the enemy's horses.' The raid reached as far as Verneuil. The French challenged Lancaster to battle, but received the response that the duke had completed his business and that if 'King John of France wished to disturb his march, he would be ready to meet him'.[11] This was one of the many occasions when no battle took place. In August, Lancaster moved on to Brittany and then to the Loire valley.

The Black Prince had received reinforcements from England, and on 4 August set out northwards from Bordeaux, with 6,000–7,000 men, advancing at about ten miles a day. The prince later explained that he intended to encounter the Count of Poitiers, King John's son, at Bourges, and expected to hear that Edward III had landed in France. The count was not to be found, and the prince marched on toward the Loire, hoping to join Lancaster. The Loire, however, could not be crossed, and the French king's army was close by. The manoeuvrings that followed saw both armies move south, until the French drew up their forces ready for battle near Poitiers, and the English did likewise.

THE BATTLE OF POITIERS

As with the Crécy campaign, a key question is whether the English were trying to avoid battle or were deliberately seeking it. The former is the traditional view; the latter was argued by Henri Denifle at the end of the nineteenth century, and more recently by Clifford Rogers.[12] One issue is whether the route taken by the prince suggests that he was trying to avoid the French army. It seems likely that the English were not in headlong retreat towards Gascony, but were manoeuvring in the hope of bringing the enemy to battle. Food and water were running low, and further delay was out of the question.

Another part of the argument hinges on the negotiations that took place immediately prior to the battle. The Pope had appointed Cardinals Talleyrand and Capocci to try to broker an agreement. Talleyrand conducted lengthy talks prior to the battle, and if Jean le Bel and some other chroniclers are to be believed, he obtained agreement from the prince that he would give up all the places he had taken, release all his prisoners and promise not to bear arms against the French for seven years. If the prince did agree such terms, it suggests that he was desperate to avoid a battle in which his forces would be severely outnumbered. Yet although the cardinal may have suggested terms along these lines, there is no evidence from English sources that the prince was prepared to accept any such agreement. It is more probable, as the English chronicler Baker reported, that a truce until Christmas was the most he was ready to agree to. In the event, the French were not prepared to agree any terms, and demanded unconditional surrender.

On 19 September the two armies faced each other. The French, said to be acting on the advice of the Scot William Douglas, dismounted most of their men-at-arms. This was a tactic they had adopted previously, at Mauron. Their vanguard was flanked by cavalry wings; three divisions were drawn up behind the van. The Anglo-Gascon army was likewise in three divisions, most probably formed up along a road and protected by hedges and a ditch. Numbers estimated by contemporaries are rarely reliable, but Bartholomew Burghersh provided plausible figures in his report of the battle, putting the number of men-at-arms in the French army at 8,000, with 3,000 infantrymen. He put the Black Prince's army at 3,000 men-at-arms and 2,000 archers, with a further 1,000 infantry he termed sergeants.[13] The proportion of archers in the English army was lower than had been the case at Crécy, but their role was nonetheless vital. As the Norman chronicle noted, the French had men-at-arms, but 'few other combatants such as archers and crossbowmen, and because of this the English archers shot more safely when it came to battle'.[14]

The terrain was very significant. Hedges, ditches, vineyards, marshy areas and woodland favoured the defensive tactics the English used. In contrast to Crécy, the battle began early, and lasted most of the day. 'There were far more fine feats of arms there than there had been at Crécy,' wrote Froissart.[15] Initial French cavalry assaults were driven back; the armoured horses proved vulnerable from the flanks, as the arrows plunged into their rears. The French men-at-arms, advancing on foot, were exhausted by the march toward the English positions. As the battle proceeded, the archers ran out of arrows and were reduced to pulling used ones out of the dead and dying, as well as throwing stones. Whereas, it was said, you would know who was winning after an archer loosed no more than six arrows, here the outcome was still unclear after a hundred. The fight was fierce as the successive French divisions attacked. That led by the 20-year-old Duke of Orléans broke, fleeing the field. The Black Prince had ordered the Gascon Jean de Grailly, the Captal de Buch, to take his force around the French army. When he was in place, he raised the banner of St George. His mounted charge into the rear of the French was an appalling shock to an increasingly demoralized army. The French king was captured, and in the rout that followed the English pursued the remnants of his army to the gates of the city of Poitiers.

The reasons for the English victory were many. The prince's army may have been tired and hungry, but it was a coherent force that had been together since early August. There was considerable experience among its commanders, men such as the earls of Warwick and Salisbury and John Chandos. In contrast, the French army had only come together in the days before the battle. Some of its leaders, notably Orléans, lacked experience. There was no effective co-ordination between the French divisions, whereas the Black Prince's generalship was very evident. While it made sense to adopt the English tactics of fighting on foot, the French had limited experience of this. The role of the English archers was perhaps less crucial than it had been at Crécy, but once again, their capacity to terrify horses was important, and their role at the start of the battle was crucial.

Casualties were heavy. The French lost one of their Marshals, Jean de Clermont, in the early stages of the fighting; the Constable, Jean de Brienne, was also killed. The deaths of the Duke of Bourbon and the Bishop of Châlons were serious blows, as was that of one of the most notable knights of the age, Geoffroi de Charny. Bartholomew Burghersh put the French losses at 2,000 men-at-arms and 800 others. English casualties were much lighter. At Crécy, both sides had decreed that no quarter would be given. At Poitiers only the French made such a declaration by displaying a red banner; the English took an astonishing number of prisoners, notably King John himself and his son Philip. The Black Prince in a newsletter gave a list of 42 important prisoners, and claimed that a further 1,993 had been taken.[16]

THE AFTERMATH OF POITIERS

The capture of so many prisoners created problems as well as opportunities. For individuals, there was the expectation of big financial profits; for the crown, political as well as financial advantage beckoned. Many of the lesser captives were released promptly after the battle, after promising payment. Thirteen important prisoners, however, were bought from their captors by the crown at a cost of about £44,000. Later, Edward III bought a further three from his son for £20,000. It does not seem that the king made any significant profits from ransoming these men; rather, he aimed to hold them as a means of putting pressure on the French in any negotiations. The noble prisoners were well treated. The

Duke of Bourbon's son, according to his biographer, impressed all by his manner and his lineage. Full of gracious words, 'he could not bear to be anywhere where ladies or young women were ill-spoken of'. At court, he would enjoy a game of dice with the queen.[17]

The capture of King John himself was a prize the English can only have dreamed of. Yet though it transformed the situation, it did not bring Edward III all he might have expected. Instructions to the Prince of Wales in December 1356 had made it clear that a fundamental requirement in any agreement would be 'remaining firm in every way on the point of having perpetual liberty' in the lands the English held in France. The issue of Edward III's claim to the French throne was not mentioned, though King John was merely referred to as 'the adversary'.[18] There was a difficulty, as with David II of Scotland, of negotiating the release of a ruler whose right to his throne the English refused to recognize. The ransom of King John was set at four million écus, about £666,666. Two draft treaties were agreed at London in 1359. While Edward did not specifically state that he would renounce the title of king of France, this was the clear implication. The English lands in France were to be held in full sovereignty. According to the second treaty, Edward would hold a vast swathe of territory in western France, from Normandy to the Pyrenees, as well as Calais and Ponthieu in the north. Furthermore, the French would cease their support of the Scots.[19]

It was one thing to negotiate in London, but quite another to persuade the government in France to agree to the terms. The issue of King John's release was the least of the problems that the Dauphin, Charles, faced. There were difficult discussions with the estates-general. In Paris the provost of the merchants, Étienne Marcel, led opposition to him, supporting the claims of the King of Navarre. Early in February 1358, Marcel and his supporters, wearing red and blue, forced entry to the palace, and murdered the Marshals of France and Normandy in the Dauphin's presence. He claimed that they were evil councillors, slain for the good of the realm. Later in the month, Charles of Navarre entered Paris. The country was moving rapidly towards civil war.

THE *JACQUERIE* AND THE *ROUTIERS*

In May 1358 a peasant revolt, the *Jacquerie*, broke out to the north of Paris. This was not a region that had suffered badly from the depredations and pillaging of war; the anger of the peasants there was directed at their lords. Froissart told of a knight roasted on a spit, whose wife was forced to eat his flesh. After being gang-raped, she was killed. There were close links between the rebels and the Parisians; Étienne Marcel lent them his support. The rising barely lasted a month, Charles of Navarre doing much to restore order. In June he faced a peasant army at Mello. Interestingly, Jacques Cale, the rebel leader, drew up his men in a manner which suggests he had experience of Crécy. The *Jacques* 'made two battles, putting 2,000 men in each. They put those who had bows and crossbows in front, and the carts in front of them.'[20] Another division was formed of 600 horsemen. The armies faced each other for three days; no

Fig. 3: The slaughter of the peasant rebels at Meaux, 1358

battle took place. Cale was invited to discuss a truce, but was seized and taken off to be executed. The peasant army was routed. A bloodbath followed, as the nobility took revenge. A massacre took place at Meaux. In June, Charles of Navarre entered Paris, to general acclaim. He became captain of the city, but his triumph did not last. Étienne Marcel, suspected of pro-English sympathies following the release of some English prisoners, was killed on 31 July. Two days later the Dauphin Charles entered Paris by the very gate where Marcel had been assassinated.

France faced yet more problems. Bands of soldiers known as *routiers*, under no control, marauded, robbed and raped their way through a countryside already ravaged by the darkest aspects of war. Arnaud de Cervole, a renegade minor cleric known as the Archpriest, had fought at Poitiers. In May 1357 he struck out on his own, leading a brigand band into Provence, to the great alarm of the papacy. By 1359, the force he led was known as the Great Company. It included Gascon and English soldiers as well as French. The Archpriest was completely out of control, and his men had no regard for the chivalric conventions of war. Troops loyal to Charles of Navarre conducted a reign of terror in northern France. Eustace d'Auberchicourt, a Hainaulter long in English service and a knight of the Garter, led a powerful band. 'We are enough to fight all of Champagne; let us ride out in the name of God and St George.'[21] However, at Nogent-sur-Seine his force was defeated in battle, in a rare instance of English archers breaking formation.

Castle-building was one response to the chaos. Local communities responded to the menace presented by the English and the *routiers* as best they could, with an explosion of small-scale fortification. Tower-houses combined residence with protection. A great many church towers were fortified. No doubt some marauding bands were deterred by such fortifications, but some defences proved to be a threat for the local populace, serving as engines of oppression rather than as a protection. There was also some building on a grand scale. Magnificent towers, the most notable being Charles V's impressive six-storied one at Vincennes, were an expression of royal and lordly prestige, rather than being the product of a defensive strategy.

These were hard times for the French populace. According to Jean de Venette, 'The wretched peasants were oppressed on all

Fig. 4: The Chateau de Vincennes. The central tower was largely built by Charles V

sides, by friend and foe alike, and could cultivate their vineyards and fields only by paying tribute to both sides.'[22] A pardon issued to the Archpriest explained that he and his men had 'taken and ransomed men, towns and places, beaten, distressed and put to death men and women, raped matrons, maids and nuns, burned and destroyed towns, manors and houses, both property of the church and of others'.[23] Parts of France suffered more than others, but in general the rural economy was hard hit, though it proved capable of surprising recovery later in the century. Towns suffered less than the countryside, but they had to bear the cost of building and restoring their walls, a particularly heavy burden in the 1350s.

THE 1359–60 CAMPAIGN AND THE TREATY OF BRÉTIGNY

With France apparently prostrate, it is not surprising that it proved impossible to pay the first instalment of King John's ransom. Nor were those around the Dauphin prepared to accept the peace terms agreed in London. The estates-general agreed on fresh taxation to finance a renewed war. Weak as the Dauphin's position was, amidst all the bad news there was one remarkable volte-face in the summer of 1359. In August, negotiations took place with Charles of Navarre. Declaring his patriotism and loyalty to the Valois dynasty, of which he was of course a part, Charles changed sides. 'I will be a good Frenchman henceforth, your subject and friend and close supporter and defender against the English and all others.'[24]

For Edward III, a new campaign was the obvious option. There seemed little hope that King John's ransom would be paid, or the terms negotiated in London accepted by the Dauphin. The recruitment of archers was ordered in January 1359. In July the exchequer was ordered to be ready to pay the soldiers' wages for three months, and orders went out to take ships and crews into royal service.[25] It was not until October that Lancaster, with about 1,000 men in his personal retinue, led a swift *chevauchée* from Calais, in advance of the main army. This departed early in the next month, in three main divisions. The nobility of England were out in force, with a duke, ten earls and 70 bannerets in the army, which numbered almost 12,000. In addition, many men-at-arms from the Low Countries and elsewhere joined the army. If Edward was seeking battle, however, he had a problem, for there was no French army for him to fight. The Dauphin's strategy was to avoid engagement. Further, French intelligence was good. The regent wrote to the authorities at Reims in July, warning them that trustworthy people had informed him that Edward III was preparing an expedition, and that there was a list of cities he aimed to besiege, 'among which Reims is especially named'. Edward's aim was indeed to take Reims, where by tradition kings of France were crowned. He hoped to make good his claim to the kingdom.

The march was grim, for it poured with rain, and food was hard to find in areas ravaged by war. The army, with its huge baggage train, averaged less than six miles a day. Nor was Reims captured. Earlier, there had been worries about its defences. Instructions to Gauchier de Chatillon, captain of the city, issued earlier in 1359, pointed out that 'the enemy could easily descend into the castle's ditches, and then climb into the town without being hindered by any appropriate and defensible walls or palisades'.[26] By the time the English arrived, the defences were in a better shape. The city was blockaded for over five weeks, with no success. The army then moved to Burgundy. In March an agreement was reached with the young Duke of Burgundy, who promised to support Edward should he be crowned king of France, and to pay a huge ransom of 200,000 *moutons d'or* (£40,000) to be free of English troops. Edward evidently still had genuine hopes of a French coronation. The army then marched towards Paris, burning and pillaging. Challenges to do battle were ignored by the Dauphin. Edward then turned his forces south-west. On Monday, 13 April a ferocious storm lashed the army. There was no defence against huge hailstones, and many horses died, no doubt panicked. The effect on morale was more serious than the physical damage; the storm was regarded as a sign from God. By 8 May peace negotiations at Brétigny had been concluded.

The agreement reached at Brétigny was not very different from what had been agreed in London. King John's ransom was reduced to 3 million écus, and was to cover the other French prisoners held by Edward. The English were to hold an enlarged Aquitaine, Poitou, Saintonge and Angoumois, with Ponthieu, Calais and the county of Guines in the north. Normandy and Brittany, however, were not to be English. Edward was to renounce his claim to the French throne. The French would cease supporting the Scots, and the English abandon support of the Flemings. Historians have put very different interpretations upon the treaty, some seeing it as a victory for the French, and some for the English.[27] The 1359–60 campaign had been a failure for Edward, in that he had not been crowned at Reims and had not defeated the Dauphin in battle. On the other hand, he had apparently achieved his fundamental aim, that of holding his possessions in France in full sovereignty. In addition, England would not be exposed to French attacks; there were very real fears over this, which had seemed fully justified when a French fleet raided Winchelsea in March 1360.

Agreeing peace terms was one thing, implementing them quite another. King John's release took place on 24 October 1360, later than had been agreed. The major problem was over the transfer of territories, which could not be achieved quickly. Following an English suggestion, the relevant clauses of the treaty were shifted to a separate agreement, setting a final deadline of November 1361. This was impractical, and the failure to carry out the terms agreed at Brétigny meant that the French could still claim sovereignty over the lands the English held in France. Also, though Edward ceased using the title of king of France, he was within his rights to resume it. Nor did he cease using the French arms, quartered with those of England. It is likely that neither the French nor the English appreciated the complexities of putting the Brétigny agreement into effect, and that both were content to see that there would be ways of going back on it in the future.

Though the negotiations that followed the Treaty of Brétigny were not completed, almost half of King John's ransom, about £166,600, was paid by early 1364. English finances were transformed; this sum was the equivalent of five annual subsidies. There was more to come, with at least £50,000 paid after 1364. Further, Edward III had the proceeds of the ransoms of King David of Scotland and Charles of Blois, together with the payment from Burgundy, at his disposal.

In one sense, payment of King John's ransom was disastrous for French finances. Yet it resulted in a transformation of fiscal structures, strengthening the monarchy in the long run. An ordinance promulgated late in 1360 set out the system of direct and indirect taxation, as well as attempting to stabilize the currency. Though there was no fiscal uniformity across all France, the precedents were set for the establishment of an effective financial system, with both indirect and direct taxes. The *fouage*, or hearth tax, of 1363, agreed by the estates-general, was particularly significant, for it was paid both by towns and countryside, without the need for local ratification. Further negotiations over the treaty and the payment of the ransom saw King John permitted to return to France. In January 1364 he returned to England, in an attempt to achieve a settlement and to deal with the fallout from the breaking of parole by his son, the Duke of Anjou. In April, John died. He had been an ineffective king and a poor soldier; in his son, Charles V, the English would face a very different kind of opponent.

5

PEACE AND WAR, 1360–77

By 1360 war had become a way of life for many. The *routiers* who pillaged the French countryside, the captains who hoped to profit from ransoms, the knights who hoped to win glory through great feats of arms: such men had little to gain from the peace which so many others desired to see. While England and France were temporarily at peace, other disputes offered employment to those eager to exercise their military skills. There was little sign of war-weariness.

For many in France, the peace agreed at Brétigny ushered in worse times. It was not simply that the payment of King John's huge ransom necessitated the payment of highly unpopular taxes every year. Much of central France could make no contribution to the ransom, because of the costs of local defence and the payment of protection money. Many English captains, such as James Pipe and Mathew Gournay, continued their operations, pillaging, burning and taking ransoms from villages. There were Gascon, Navarrese, Breton and German companies causing chaos, particularly in central France. In 1360 many of these bands came together in the Great Company, and in 1362 they combined with yet other groups and defeated a royal army in the Battle of Brignais, near Lyon. A surprise attack won the day. The Archpriest was on the losing side, but promptly turned his coat following the defeat. The *routiers*, however, soon broke apart, to continue to terrorize the populace in individual bands. Some leaders, such as the notable

Fig. 5: A knight bearing Bertrand du Guesclin's arms

John Hawkwood, were tempted away from France by the wealth and wars of Italy.

Almost inevitably, the perennial troublemaker Charles of Navarre caused renewed disturbance in France. He had a claim to the duchy of Burgundy, which was dismissed in 1361. In retaliation, he planned a rising in Normandy, with the tacit support of the English. The Dauphin's forces pre-empted him, moving against the Navarrese supporters in the spring of 1364. Disaster came when Charles's ally, Jean de Grailly, marched north from Gascony, joined forces with some English soldiers of fortune, and was engaged in battle at Cocherel. The French army, led by Bertrand du Guesclin and including the Archpriest, was victorious in a hard, brutal fight. The Anglo-Navarrese army was outflanked and attacked from front and rear. Casualties were high on both sides. Even this defeat did not end Charles of Navarre's ambitions in Normandy, but events soon meant that he had to direct his attentions to his Pyrenean kingdom.

There was also war in Brittany, where the Montfort cause had not been forgotten. John de Montfort, whose claim Edward III had backed earlier in the war, had died in 1345. His son, also John, was brought up in the English court. In 1362 he returned to Brittany, to challenge Jeanne de Penthièvre and her husband Charles of Blois. In 1364, after diplomacy had failed, Montfort laid siege to the little port of Auray. On 29 September Charles of Blois arrived to relieve the place, and the two sides engaged in a fierce battle. Many of the great names of the war were involved. John Chandos commanded the Montfortian army; Hugh Calveley, Robert Knollys and Eustace d'Auberchicourt served under him, Calveley unwillingly taking charge of the rearguard. Olivier de Clisson, future brother-in-arms of Bertrand du Guesclin, armed with an axe, fought with the English (and lost an eye). Bertrand himself was with Charles of Blois. The English archers did not have their normal success against the French, who were armed with lances cut down to five feet, and battle-axes. By forming up tightly, and interlocking their shields, they were able to prevent the hail of arrows from doing much damage. However, after fierce hand-to-hand combat, the French broke. The discipline of the Anglo-Breton army was an important factor, while Calveley's division, held on the flank, played a vital role in the final stages. Charles of Blois himself was killed, and a host of prisoners, including du Guesclin, was taken. The Breton civil war had come to an end.

SPAIN

In the 1360s the war spilled over into Spain. Dynastic issues, with disputes for the Castilian throne, were one reason for this. The English were also concerned by Castilian naval strength, while it was important to secure Gascony's southern border. The history of the Castilian monarchy at this time is an extraordinary one of intrigue, betrayals, executions and assassinations. In 1350 Alfonso XI of Castile died, to be succeeded by his son, Pedro the Cruel. Alfonso also had illegitimate twin sons, Enrique of Trastamara and Fadrique, by his mistress, Leonor de Guzmán. She was executed in 1351, and Fadrique was assassinated in 1358. Enrique had designs on the throne, and found backing from the French and the *routier* companies. Pedro turned to the English for support, concluding an alliance in 1362.

In December 1365 a huge *routier* force advanced into Spain. It was headed by du Guesclin, whose ransom after his capture at Auray had been paid with money from the Pope, the King of Aragon and Enrique himself. Anglo-French rivalries were set aside, for alongside du Guesclin was Hugh Calveley; the two men entered into a contract to be brothers-in-arms. Matthew Gournay and Eustace d'Auberchicourt were also in the company. King Pedro put up little resistance, and fled by sea to Gascony. Enrique was crowned in his place.

In 1362 the Black Prince had been granted Aquitaine (which included Gascony) as a principality. After Enrique's seizure of the Castilian throne, it made sense for him to intervene to restore Pedro's rule. Negotiations with the ever-unreliable Charles of Navarre were successfully concluded; the Prince would have safe passage across the Pyrenees. In February 1267 his army arrived in Pamplona, and then marched to Castile. The usual challenges to battle took place, but Enrique's French advisors recommended caution. On 2 April at Nájera the armies faced each other. There are no pay records to reveal the size of either army, but the chronicler Ayala was clear that the 'flower of Christian cavalry' were in the Prince's army, which totalled 10,000 men-at-arms, whereas Enrique's army was no more than 4,500 strong.[1] The Black Prince's army surprised Enrique by advancing early in the morning, taking a route which brought it round to attack from a flank. As usual, the English dismounted, and the archers loosed 'volleys thicker than rain ever fell', to devastating effect. 'They killed and wounded a large number of horses, despite their armour, and King Enrique and his men fell back.'[2] The Prince's army was victorious. The rout saw the enemy chased to the river Ebro; more were drowned than were killed in the battle.

Nájera, like Poitiers, saw an exceptional number of prisoners taken; in a letter to his wife, the Black Prince overstated their number at 10,000 men of quality. The unpleasant King Pedro wished to see his opponents executed; the Black Prince would not allow this save in isolated cases. Arguments over the captives show how the laws and conventions of war operated. There was much argument over Arnoul d'Audrehem, Marshal of France, who had fought with Enrique. The Black Prince was furious that he had been in the battle, for as his ransom agreed after Poitiers had not all been paid, it was dishonourable that he had fought. Arnoul argued that 'I did not take up arms against you, but against King Don Pedro, who is the chief captain of your party.'[3] The case was put to a commission of twelve, which decided in Arnoul's favour. In the case of the Count of Denia, the issue of who should receive his ransom of about £29,000 led to complex litigation which continued into the next century.

Though Nájera was a clear-cut victory, the battle was far from decisive. Pedro could not pay the Prince the huge sums demanded for his services. Disease took its toll; the Prince returned to Gascony, his health broken. Enrique began to recover his position in Castile. In 1369, after victory in the Battle of Montiel, he murdered his half-brother King Pedro and so secured his position on the Castilian throne. The foray into Spain had proved disastrous for the English; it would not, however, end their ambitions in the Peninsula.

TOWARDS REOPENING THE WAR

The *routiers* continued to cause problems. Following the Battle of Nájera, most of them returned to France. They caused havoc as they pillaged their way northwards towards Burgundy, and on to Champagne and elsewhere. Many were English and Gascons who had fought with the Black Prince; whether they had his tacit consent is open to question. One English band even reached Normandy, capturing the town of Vire by subterfuge. Some *routiers* came close to Paris; others brought their savage brand of warfare to Anjou and the Loire valley. The bands eventually broke up, after demonstrating that although this was may have been a period of peace between

England and France in formal terms, in reality these were years of continued war.

In Gascony the financial position was becoming more difficult. The Black Prince met the estates, and it was agreed that he should levy a hearth tax for five years, and in return maintain the currency, both silver and gold, without any devaluation for the same period. A long list of concessions, reminiscent in some ways of Magna Carta, made it clear that traditional rights and liberties would be respected. The Count of Armagnac bluntly refused to pay the tax; he was impoverished by war, and had a daughter to marry off. He appealed to Edward III, and without waiting for an answer, also appealed to the French king. Armagnac's nephew Amanieu d'Albret also acknowledged Charles V as his liege lord.

English attempts to negotiate with the French came to nothing. King John had been committed to the peace agreed at Brétigny; his son Charles V was not. Physically unimpressive, Charles suffered from ill health. Froissart implausibly attributed this to poison administered in his youth by Charles of Navarre, which had caused his hair and nails to fall out, and rendered him dry as a stick. The weakness of his left arm is documented; though he was no inactive invalid, he was a man incapable of feats of arms. A cultured king, Charles possessed a huge library. His military strategy was a cautious one, in which the English were not to be engaged in battle as they had been under Philip VI and John. This approach yielded rich dividends.

The French had not formally conceded sovereignty over Aquitaine, though they had not attempted to exercise it since the Brétigny agreement. In 1369 legal opinions, carefully harvested, favoured Charles V's claims over the duchy. The Black Prince was summoned to appear before the *parlement* of Paris in May. He did not attend, and was declared to be a contumacious vassal. In northern France, French troops began to move into Ponthieu. Plans for the renewal of war were discussed in the English parliament, and Edward III resumed use of the title of king of France.

THE FRENCH RECOVERY

This renewed war, which lasted from 1369 to 1380, was very different from the earlier conflicts. The English were now on the defensive. In the small and ugly Bertrand du Guesclin, the French possessed an experienced and charismatic commander. Du Guesclin's family was of the petty nobility. Warlike even as a child, Bertrand was said to have led a gang of marauding boys, who he persuaded to hold mock tournaments. He had to make his own way as a soldier, learning in the tough school of Breton warfare. Another Breton was du Guesclin's close associate Olivier de Clisson. He had been brought up in England, and probably fought with the English at Poitiers. He certainly did so at Auray, but by 1370 he had joined the French cause. He had full knowledge of English tactics, and knew how important archers were, for when he was setting out from England for Brittany in 1358, he was supplied with 500 bows, 1,500 bowstrings and 100 sheaves of arrows.[4] Well aware of the disasters caused by French eagerness to fight, he was influential in persuading them to adopt defensive methods, avoiding the risks of pitched battle. As for the English themselves, Edward III's energies in the bedroom were not matched by his campaigning efforts; from 1372 he withdrew from active warfare. The Black Prince was in no fit state to lead expeditions. Men such as Robert Knollys and Hugh Calveley had vast experience, but lacked the flexibility of mind to manage the new situation. Even the English belief that they controlled the seas proved to be a fiction; this was a period when naval warfare gained a new importance, as invasion threatened.

Froissart recorded a meeting of Charles V's council in 1373. Du Guesclin was asked for his advice. 'Sire, all those who talk of fighting the English do not think of the dangers which will come of it. I am not saying that they should not be fought, but rather that this should be to our advantage.' He reminded Charles of the defeats suffered at the hands of the English, 'which have gravely damaged your kingdom and the nobles present at them'.[5] The French campaigns were characterized by sieges, skirmishes and ambushes, by swift surrenders and remarkable success. English *chevauchées* were countered by emptying the land before them.

Fig. 6: An imaginative interpretation of the death of John Chandos, 1369

In 1369 there was no resistance when the French took Ponthieu, and under the Duke of Anjou they recovered much territory in the south-west. The king's son John of Gaunt, in his first independent command, took a force from Calais into Picardy and Normandy and back. At one point the English and French armies faced each other for a week. Discussions took place as to where a battle might be fought. This, however, was one of the many occasions when caution won. At the turn of the year John Chandos, recently appointed seneschal of Poitou and arguably the best English commander, was killed in a skirmish, slipping on icy ground. In 1370 the English countered continued French advances in traditional manner: Robert Knollys led a *chevauchée* from Calais to Poitou. His own retinue contained at least 1,400 men-at-arms and a similar number of archers. The financial arrangements were unusual: the crown was to pay for the first three months, and thereafter the expedition was intended to be self-financing. In the event, it cost the English government over £38,000. The raid went badly: no towns or castles were taken. Knollys drew up his men in order of battle outside Paris, but the French were not to be tempted into an engagement. The expedition concluded in complete disarray, with John Minsterworth (who would later turn traitor) in particular challenging Knollys' leadership in a rare example of mutiny. The dispirited remains of the force were finally crushed at Pontvillain by Bertrand du Guesclin. The defeat was disastrous, leading to the disillusionment and desertion from their cause of Charles of Navarre, who was reconciled with Charles V in the following year.

In September 1370 the Black Prince, ailing and carried in a litter, led an army to recapture Limoges, recently taken by the Duke of Berry. The sack of the city has been described as 'one of the worst atrocities in medieval European warfare'.[6] However, it was justified according to the laws of war, for it was taken by storm, rather than a negotiated surrender. The scale of the massacre there is open to question. Froissart made much of it, but his rhetoric did

Fig. 7: The Black Prince, lying sick in his litter, at the sack of Limoges, 1370

not match the reality. It was only the part of Limoges controlled by the bishop that was stormed; the other section, the *Chatèu*, was loyal to the Prince, who had made a number of important grants to it in the early days of his rule in Aquitaine. The number of those slain was probably around 300, a tenth of Froissart's figure.

The English regarded themselves as masters of the sea, but this conceit took a hard blow in 1372. The Earl of Pembroke sailed with a small flotilla of some 20 ships to take up his recently appointed post as royal lieutenant in Aquitaine. A Castilian fleet prevented their entry to La Rochelle, and was victorious in the ensuing battle. The use of fire was particularly terrifying at sea, and oil sprayed onto the English ships proved to be a decisive weapon. The horses panicked, breaking up the ships' timbers. 'It was horrible to hear the din of the fire and the noise made by the horses burning in the ships' holds.'[7] Though the numbers of men and ships involved were small, the defeat struck home hard. Edward III's response was to attempt a large-scale demonstration of naval power. In late August he boarded his flagship at Sandwich. As the winds were contrary, the fleet could do no more that crawl along the coast, reaching no further than Winchelsea before the expedition was abandoned. This fiasco was Edward's final campaign, a miserable contrast to the glories of the 1340s. As for Pembroke, he was harshly treated in prison in Spain before being sold to du Guesclin. He promised to pay him a huge ransom of 120,000 gold francs, but he died in France before he was released. The war was going increasingly well for the French. In 1372 the Duke of Brittany, John de Montfort, took refuge in England. The French took over his duchy with little resistance; only Brest remained in English hands. In the following year, plans to send John of Gaunt to Brittany were abandoned. Instead, he determined to reach Gascony overland, and led a *chevauchée* from Calais to Bordeaux. This took from August to December. Though the English drew up their troops outside Troyes for battle, the French stuck to their policy of avoiding a major confrontation. Later in the campaign, Olivier de Clisson slew an estimated 600 men in an ambush. Far more considerable losses came through the hardships of the journey, particularly during the crossing of the Massif Central. Contemporaries, French and English, saw the expedition as a failure, but it can be argued that Gaunt showed considerable qualities of leadership in keeping his force together on such an arduous expedition. However, the fact remains that the *chevauchée* achieved nothing.

The French were clearly in the ascendant. In 1375 the important castle of Saint-Sauveur-le-Vicomte in Normandy was surrendered after a lengthy siege, in return for substantial payments of 40,000 francs to the garrison, and 12,000 to its captain. Cognac in the south-west was lost, besieged by du Guesclin. Pope Gregory XI had been attempting to negotiate peace since 1370, and in 1375 it was agreed to hold a conference at Bruges. A truce, brokered by the papacy and negotiated at Bruges, finally came into effect in June. It was later extended for a further year.

In 1376 one of the great figures of the war, the Black Prince, died. He had shown his mettle as a young man, fighting at Crécy in the midst of the mêlée. His victories at Poitiers and Nájera had demonstrated his qualities as a commander. Importantly, he was consistently loyal to his father; there was no question of his adopting opposing policies in the way that Henry V would do before his accession to the throne. Nonetheless, there have to be some doubts about the Black Prince's potential as a ruler: his rule in Aquitaine created more problems than it solved. The introduction of a new central administration was resented by the Gascon nobility, and financial difficulties became increasingly acute. As a commander and a warrior, however, the Prince was peerless.

Edward III did not survive his eldest son for long. He died in 1377. The St Albans chronicler imagined a deathbed scene in which the king's mistress, Alice Perrers, 'furtively removed from his hands the rings that the king wore on his fingers as part of his royal dignity'.[8] Deserted by his courtiers, a single priest oversaw the king's final moments. Edward had been astonishingly successful. He was an inspirational leader in war, and was well served by able commanders. Council documents show how he was involved in the detailed planning of campaigns, with a close attention to detail. There may be some question marks over his strategic vision, particularly as to whether the way he conducted the war was ever likely to achieve his ultimate ambitions. The grand alliance of the initial phase of the war was far too expensive, and the subsequent *chevauchées*, successful as they were, were never likely to result in conquest, much less the acquisition of the French throne. Yet he displayed flexibility, taking advantage of new opportunities as they arose. By 1360 it appeared that he had succeeded in greatly extending English possessions in France, holding them freely, without doing homage to the French king. In his final years, after the renewal of the war in 1369, Edward lost his touch; he did not relate to a new generation of soldiers in the way he had to their predecessors in his days of glory.

6

NEW KINGS, 1377–99

The war reopened in 1377 on an indecisive course. There was a new king, Richard II, on the English throne; a boy incapable of providing the leadership that Edward III had given. The government adopted a new strategy, that of the 'barbicans'. Cherbourg was leased from Charles of Navarre in 1378, and Brest had been in English hands since 1342. These ports would give the English a good position to control the sea route to Gascony, and they would provide convenient bases from which their armies could operate. Calais and the Gascon ports were also seen as barbicans. The commons in parliament, dubious about the cost, were told, 'if the barbicans are well guarded, and the sea safeguarded, the kingdom shall find itself well enough secure'.[1] For the English, the war against the French was increasingly defensive, and increasingly expensive.

In 1378 there was a new element in the conflict, the papal schism. On the death of Gregory XI, the Roman candidate, Urban VI, was supported by the English. His rival at Avignon was Clement VII; he was backed by the French. The schism would continue to divide Europe until 1417; though there were no doctrinal differences between the two sides, a new dimension was added to dynastic and other conflicts.

Gascony was not given a high priority by the English in these years. James Sherborne calculated that the duchy received just 16 per cent of all of the funds spent on the war from 1369 to 1375, less than Calais with 29 per cent. It cost over £32,000 to send

John of Gaunt to the duchy in 1370, returning in the next year, but after 1372 very little was spent on the defence of Gascony. In 1377 a major French offensive under the Duke of Anjou captured, among other places, Bergerac and Saint-Macaire. The chief English commander, Thomas Felton, was taken prisoner in a skirmish. Yet the English were not to be driven out of the duchy. A new royal lieutenant, John Neville, had considerable success in 1378. Real power in southwestern France, however, lay increasingly in the hands of Gaston Phoebus, count of Foix, and the counts of Armagnac. The Duke of Berry proved to be an ineffectual French royal lieutenant, and little was done to dislodge the English. *Routier* companies, many claiming some allegiance to the English, found the region a good hunting ground. The Duke of Bourbon, given command alongside Berry in 1385, had some notable successes; at the siege of Verteuil he fought hand-to-hand in the mine that his engineers had dug under the walls of the castle, and duly received its surrender.

In 1378 the *parlement* of Paris condemned the Duke of Brittany, John de Montfort, in his absence. The duchy was declared confiscated. There was much hostility in Brittany to this move, and when the duke returned there in 1379, he found widespread support. However, when an English fleet set sail for the duchy in December it was destroyed by a fierce storm. The commander, John Arundel, was drowned; Hugh Calveley clung to some rigging, and was blown ashore onto a beach. For the chronicler Walsingham, the disaster was hardly surprising, for before the fleet had sailed, Arundel had insisted on billeting many of his men in a convent, where they 'subjected the nuns to their excesses, giving no thought to the infamy that would result from their sinful debauchery'.[2]

The year 1379 saw an extraordinary plan adopted, which suggests that some English ministers were living in a fantasy world. At Windsor the young Count of St Pol, who had been captured in 1374, met a seemingly adorable widow, Matilda Courtenay, half-sister to the king. His release was agreed on condition that he did homage to Richard II, held his castles for the English, and attacked the town and castle of Guise in Picardy. The plan failed dismally, but the count paid his ransom, and married Matilda. The wedding featured musicians and actors galore, but the chronicler Walsingham commented sourly that 'it gave joy to few and advantage to nobody, and indeed most people were upset by it, and found it hateful'.[3] The count would die at Agincourt.

A major loss for the French in 1380 was the death of du Guesclin, who fell ill at a siege in southern France. He was seen in his own lifetime as a chivalric hero *par excellence*, comparable with the Nine Worthies of legend, who included Charlemagne and King Arthur. He had been appointed Constable of France in 1370 in an acknowledgement of his military reputation. Until his death he was constantly active in French service against the English. His career, however, remains something of a puzzle. He experienced defeat as well as victory, and quite what it was that so impressed his contemporaries about his leadership abilities has been lost in the welter of adulation accorded him. For one French historian, Edouard Perroy, he was 'a mediocre captain, incapable of winning a battle or being successful in a siege of any scope', and was a man 'swollen with self-importance'.[4] He was, however, an inspirational leader, who had an excellent sense of strategy. It was not a matter

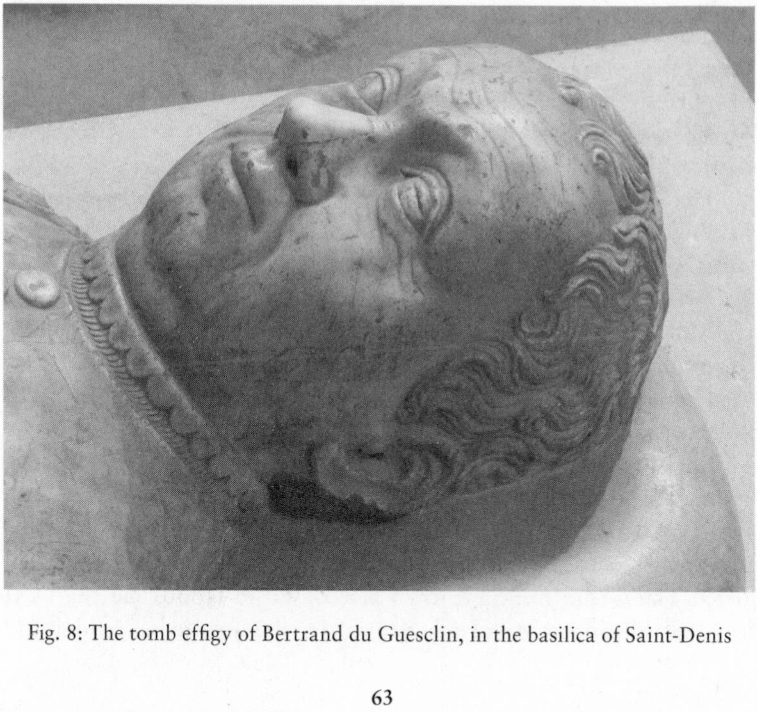

Fig. 8: The tomb effigy of Bertrand du Guesclin, in the basilica of Saint-Denis

Fig. 9: The Earl of Buckingham crossing to Calais, 1380

of glorious battles, but one of rapid marches and surprise attacks in what was almost guerrilla warfare. Together with Olivier de Clisson, he transformed the course of the war.

The English had ambitious plans in 1380. Initially, it was hoped to send a substantial force to Brittany, but there were insufficient ships. Instead, the Earl of Buckingham set out from Calais towards Reims and then Troyes. This traditional English strategy of the *chevauchée* was no longer as effective as in the past. The Duke of Burgundy refused battle, and the army proceeded on its destructive course to Brittany. The French might have blocked its route, had it not been for the news of the death of Charles V.

The new king, Charles VI, was almost 12; like England, France faced the problems of an underage monarch. The war with England was of less concern than the situation in Flanders. The towns of Ghent, Bruges and Ypres had risen against the count in 1379. The Ghent militia known as the White Hoods led the way; in 1382, Philip van Artevelde, son of Jacob, emerged as leader and was victorious at Beverhoutsveld over the Bruges militia. There, an initial artillery barrage proved highly effective. Artevelde sought English support, but no worthwhile assistance was forthcoming, and at Roosebeke a large Franco-Burgundian army, its strategy and tactics masterminded by Olivier de Clisson, defeated the townsmen. Artevelde himself was slain. The Flemish artillery proved ineffective against well-organized cavalry attacks. The Duke of Bourbon's biographer described the way his hero swung his axe left and right and 'plunged amongst the Flemings, and fell to the ground and was wounded, but was soon rescued by the good knights and squires'.[5] This was the first experience of battle for a future hero of chivalry, the 16-year-old Jean le Meingre, known as Boucicaut.

In 1383 English assistance to the Flemings finally arrived. It took an unusual form: Bishop Despenser of Norwich led an expedition which, taking advantage of the papal schism, took the form of a crusade supporting the claims of Urban VI against the supporters of Clement VII. Roosebeke had been a Clementist triumph. A crusade had advantages for recruitment, as Bishop Despenser could offer heavenly rewards: 'It was even said that some of his commissaries asserted that angels would descend from the skies at their bidding.'[6] His force did not lack experience; both Calveley and Knollys took part in the expedition. Initial success was deceptive. A siege of Ypres failed, and though a large French army did not engage Despenser in battle, the English lost all that they had taken at the start of the campaign. Despenser and three of his captains (though not Calveley or Knollys) were put on trial when they returned, thoroughly demoralized, to England. This dismal expedition to the continent was the last of Richard II's reign.

THREATS OF INVASION

These years saw England threatened by invasion, to much alarm. In 1371 the Chancellor, William Wykeham, told parliament that the French were stronger than in the past and had a sufficient army to conquer all the English possessions. Their fleet was sufficient to destroy the English navy, and then invasion would follow. There proved to be justification for his warning. In 1377 a French fleet, which included Castilian and Portuguese ships, raided the south coast. Ports from Rye in the east to Plymouth in the west were assaulted. After returning to Harfleur for resupplying, the notable French admiral, Jean de Vienne, sacked much of the Isle of Wight in a second raid. In 1380 the French took Jersey and Guernsey, and Castilian galleys attacked Winchelsea and Gravesend. There was real panic right across the south coast.

Measures were taken to deal with the invasion threat. At Southampton over £1,700 was spent on a new tower, which was started in 1378. Some new castles were built, notably Bodiam and Cooling, both licensed in the 1380s, and built respectively by the veteran soldiers Edward Dalyngrigge and John Cobham. No doubt personal glorification was one motive, but a sense of patriotic duty should not be dismissed. There was a very real fear that the war that had so ravaged France would come to England.

The renewal of the conflict with France in 1369 had brought with it an inevitable renewal of the Franco-Scottish alliance. David II died in 1371 and was succeeded by Robert II, a Stewart. Cross-border raids, and the fact that some of David II's ransom remained unpaid, were a cause of friction, but the truces largely held. In 1384, however, a small French force landed in Scotland, and joined in a raid into Northumberland. In the next year a larger French force of 1,300 men-at-arms and 300 crossbowmen sailed to Scotland in a fleet of some 180 ships. Orders were given for 'four of the largest ships in the army's fleet to be painted in a bright red colour, with the arms and emblems of Monseigneur Jean de Vienne, admiral of France'.[7] There was justified concern 'lest any riot or debate occur between any of the French and Scots'. Those who were disobedient were threatened: 'if he is a man-at-arms he will lose horse and harness, and if he is a valet, he will lose his fist or ear'.[8] Though the French reached Morpeth, well into Northumberland, the expedition ended in disarray, with bitter recriminations between the French and the Scots.

Meanwhile, Richard II had raised a large army of some 14,000 men. An old-fashioned feudal summons was employed, the first since 1327; there may have been a concern that if none was issued during the reign, the precedent would be entirely lost. Faced with a large-scale invasion, the Scots did as they had done in 1322, and simply pulled back, taking as much food away as they could.

The English army reached Edinburgh, and, increasingly short of supplies, rapidly withdrew.

The next year, 1386, saw by far the most serious threat of invasion, when a huge Franco-Burgundian fleet and army assembled at Sluys. Preparations included the construction of 'a palisade of marvellous contrivance, with towers and armaments, which they were to take with them, and which, wonderful to relate, could be assembled within three hours of their landing in England'.[9] One French writer estimated that there were 16,000 ships, of which half were large vessels with two sails. No finer fleet and army, he thought, had been assembled since the siege of Troy.[10] However, the winds were unfavourable, and the French army was diverted to recapture Damme, taken earlier in the year by the men of Ghent (with English assistance). The invasion of England was delayed and then abandoned when the weather turned in October, with contrary winds and torrential rain. This was a major turning point, for it was the closest that the French came to a large-scale invasion during the whole of the Hundred Years War. Had they managed a landing, they might well have succeeded in overthrowing Richard II's weak and unpopular rule. English preparations saw some 4,500 men recruited, but such a force would have been quite inadequate in face of a French army which may have numbered as much as 30,000.

In the following year the English had a rare success. A large Franco-Flemish fleet had been loaded with wine at La Rochelle. In March the Earl of Arundel, with a fleet of some 60 ships, larger and better equipped, defeated the Franco-Flemish in a running battle, initially off Margate, and finally near Cadzand. The earl's forces then engaged in a brief pillaging campaign, but were unable to follow their victory through. Arundel's attentions were then directed to domestic politics; he was one of the Lords Appellant who attacked the king's favourites in the Merciless Parliament of 1388.

The Scots continued to threaten; in 1388 they launched a double attack on the north, with one army in the east and one in the west. At Otterburn an English force under Henry Hotspur, son of the Earl of Northumberland, was routed, even though the leader of the outnumbered Scots, Douglas, was killed in the battle. In 1389 a truce was agreed, which lasted for the rest of the century.

POLITICS AND PEACE

After the failure of the planned invasion of England in 1386 there was little enthusiasm in France for a continuation of the war with England. In 1388 the young king Charles VI threw off the control exercised by his uncles, the dukes of Burgundy, Berry, Anjou and Bourbon. A group referred to sarcastically by their opponents as *marmousets* dominated government until 1392. These men were largely drawn from the middling nobility; Olivier de Clisson was among them. There were also some with bourgeois backgrounds. The *marmousets* had a clear, coherent and ambitious view of the nature of the state. A programme of reform was instituted, aimed at reducing administrative costs and taxes. Indirect taxes were reduced; the king should live off his own resources. Officials would be selected for their competence. However, when the king's mental instability became all too clear, the king's uncles moved against the *marmousets*. Clisson, who had survived an assassination attempt in the summer, was deprived of the office of Constable, and was fined 100,000 francs. Rather than renewing the war with England, the French became increasingly involved in the complex world of Italian politics. In 1396 the crisis-ridden city of Genoa decided to accept French rule. A further ambitious and difficult project was the crusade. In 1396 a large crusading army, largely drawn from France and including many veterans of the war with England, was crushed in the Balkans by the Turks at the Battle of Nicopolis.

The war, its expense and what was seen as its mismanagement provided the backdrop to the turbulent politics of this period in England. In 1376, in the Good Parliament, the commons had attacked the king's ministers, and his mistress Alice Perrers. Accusations over the loss of Saint-Sauveur and Bécherel were directed at Lord Latimer and Thomas Catrington. Richard II faced the anger of the Lords Appellant (the Duke of Gloucester and the earls of Arundel, Warwick, Derby and Nottingham) in 1388 in the Merciless Parliament. Many of the king's favourites and associates, notably the Duke of Suffolk, were summarily found guilty of treason. Suffolk escaped, but many were executed. Court intrigue, with an extreme dislike of Richard's favourites, does much to explain the crisis, but it is also the case that the Appellants wished to see a far more aggressive policy taken in the war, rather than the appeasement favoured by the young king.

Peace with England was one of the objectives of the *marmousets*, and a truce was agreed in 1389, though a final agreement remained elusive. In 1390, Richard II granted Aquitaine to his uncle John of Gaunt, to hold from him in his claimed position as king of France. This has given rise to much argument among historians. John Palmer argued that this was a first step towards a peace settlement, in which Gaunt would hold Aquitaine from the French king. His views have attracted much revision.[11] It is likely that this was among the many options discussed, but by 1393, with a different regime in control in France, the way forward was envisaged as agreeing on the one hand to settle the boundaries of English-held Aquitaine, and on the other, accepting that Richard would do liege homage to Charles VI. This, however, was unacceptable to the English parliament, and the peace process ground to a halt. In 1395, however, Richard married Charles VI's daughter Isabella, aged just six. Relations between the two countries were now on a very different footing, and in the following year a 28-year truce was agreed.

FINANCING WAR

A peace policy made sense, for the costs of war were high in these years. Even though there was no great campaign on the scale of Edward III's 1359 expedition in these years, military expenses following the renewal of hostilities in 1369 were very high. James Sherborne estimated that almost £1,100,000 was spent by 1381. Lancaster's *chevauchée* in 1369 cost £75,000, and that of 1373 at least £82,000. The 1381 expedition brought expenses of about £82,000. The war at sea was costly: in 1373, naval expenses approached £40,000. Arundel's expedition in 1387 was an exception, for it was relatively cheap, at about £18,000. It was also successful, with prizes and booty totalling about £16,500, a quarter of which went to the crown. Maintaining the Calais garrison, with associated expenses, cost £20,000 or more a year. Brest and Cherbourg, the barbicans, were also very expensive to maintain, at some £30,000 a year. In the years 1377 to 1381 about a third of English war expenditure was accounted for by these three ports.

The French also faced high costs, but ways were found to overcome the financial problems. In 1371, payment of officials' salaries was halted, and with tax revenues declining, Charles V had to borrow 10,000 francs from a syndicate of Italian bankers. Yet by continuing to levy taxes initially imposed in order to pay for King John's ransom, the position of Charles's government improved, with receipts probably worth double those of the English crown. However, a major crisis over taxation began in 1380, when the dying king, aware of the possibility of rebellion, abolished the *fouage*, the hearth tax. His successor, Charles VI, was only 12. Popular pressure led to the promised abolition of all taxes introduced since the early fourteenth century. A request to the estates-general for new grants met with a hostile response, but it was agreed that regional assemblies should be approached. Grants were made, but these were insufficient, and when a general assembly conceded a sales tax of 12 pence in the pound, the townspeople 'took no account of the ordinance, saying that if axes were used to compel them, they would never accept the decree without widespread slaughter'.[12] There was a violent reaction in many towns to the demands. In Rouen a local merchant was proclaimed king of the city, promising the abolition of all taxes, but the rebellion was soon put down. Victory in Flanders at the Battle of Roosebeke in 1382 strengthened the crown's position, and the traditional taxes were reimposed. In 1385 the familiar expedient of debasement of the coinage yielded substantial receipts, while a forced loan raised large sums. By 1390, French royal revenue was probably higher than at any other point of the Hundred Years War.[13]

For the English, the traditional means of raising revenue for war were no longer sufficient. It was not possible to raise loans on the imprudent scale of Edward III's borrowings in the initial years of the war, and the parliamentary subsidies, the fifteenths and tenths, were inadequate, as were customs revenues. Even a grant of a double subsidy in 1377 was not enough. A tax levied on parishes in 1371 was granted specifically as a one-off. The calculations for this tax were seriously out of line, as the government assumed there were far more parishes than was the case. Poll taxes, of which three were levied, were introduced in 1377. As in France, unpopular taxation led to popular rebellion, for this was a major cause of the Peasants Revolt of 1381.

ITALY

The fragile peace established at Brétigny, and the English lack of success when the war was renewed in 1369, led some English soldiers to look elsewhere for fame and fortune. Italy was tormented by war, with complex rivalries between wealthy cities. These conflicts provided splendid opportunities for ambitious men schooled in the Anglo-French wars. By 1369, Florence had 33 English captains in its forces, employing a new formation, that of the lance, which consisted of two men-at-arms supported by a squire and backed up with archers.

The most notable of the English who fought in Italy was John Hawkwood, whose career there began in the early 1360s, when he was one those who, following the Treaty of Brétigny, continued to fight. He joined the mercenary White Company, commanded by a German, Albert Stertz. Nothing is known of Hawkwood's experience in Edward III's armies, but he clearly had an excellent knowledge of the arts of war. His first real success came in 1369 at Cascina, where he dismounted his men-at-arms in a manner familiar from the battlefields of France. His forces soon became known as the English Company; some of his men were drawn from his own home neighbourhood in Essex. Over the years he fought for Pisa, Milan, the kingdom of Naples and the papacy, but above all he served Florence, where he became captain-general in 1380. Hawkwood's successes were many; one resounding triumph was at the Battle of Castagnaro in 1387, where he led forces from Padua against Verona. Dismounted cavalry, supported by archers, and a carefully chosen battle site were the key to victory, as had been the case at Crécy and elsewhere. In his final campaign, in 1391, Hawkwood succeeded in extricating the Florentine army when the Milanese appeared to have it at their mercy. It was his strategic and tactical awareness, his skilled surprise tactics and his use of intelligence that made Hawkwood such a notable commander. He was a loyal Englishman; both Edward III and Richard II employed him in their diplomacy in Italy, particularly in negotiations with Milan. There was no move, however, to employ him in the French war. Though Hawkwood sought a comfortable retirement in England, he died in 1394 before his planned return home, having lost most of the fortune he had won.

SPAIN AND PORTUGAL

One reason why the English were unsuccessful in the war with France in this period was the distraction provided by continuing ambitions in the Iberian Peninsula. John of Gaunt's marriage to King Pedro's daughter Constanza in 1371 gave him a claim to the kingdom of Castile. In the following year Edward recognized Gaunt as king of Castile. This was an obvious way to counter the French alliance with Enrique of Trastamara. It seems likely that the English optimistically hoped to detach Enrique from his alliance with France by withdrawing Gaunt's claim, but Enrique was not to be moved. Gaunt's alliance with the Portuguese ruler, Fernando I, came to nothing, nor did those with Aragon and Navarre. It was not until 1381 that an English force landed in the Peninsula. This was led by Gaunt's brother Edmund of Langley, later duke of York, who was married to Constanza's younger sister Isabel. The expedition was a failure. The English troops allegedly behaved disgracefully towards their allies, 'killing and robbing and raping women, haughty and disdainful to all as if they were their mortal enemies'.[14] Fernando made peace with Enrique's son, Juan I, who had succeeded to the Castilian throne in 1379.

In parliament in 1383 the Bishop of Hereford compared the prospects for campaigning in Flanders or Portugal and declared of the latter that 'there is no place on earth so likely to bring an end to the wars, swiftly and effectively concluding them, as is that place at present'.[15] Before Fernando's death in 1383, his queen had made an alliance with Juan of Castile, who married her daughter Beatriz. She was underage, and Juan took advantage of the situation to try to take over Portugal. A rebellion saw Fernando's illegitimate half-brother João of Avis first become regent, and then king in 1385. He sought an alliance with England, and achieved a striking victory over Juan at Aljubarrota. There were probably about 700 English troops present, mainly archers, part of an army of some 12,000. The Portuguese organized their forces along English lines, with dismounted men-at-arms in the centre in two divisions one behind the other, and cavalry on the wings with archers placed behind them. Nuno Álvares Pereira, the Portuguese Constable, had argued for a battle, in contradiction to most of João's council. The first position he chose was outflanked by the Castilians; the second proved ideal. The Castilian vanguard was decimated by archery and javelins; further attacks failed disastrously, though there was such alarm when the main Castilian division advanced that the order was given to kill the prisoners who had been taken, just as would happen at Agincourt. The argument was that 'It is better to kill than to be killed, and if we do not kill them, they will free themselves while we are fighting, and then kill us. No one should trust their prisoners.'[16] Eventually Juan fled, his army cut to pieces. Most battles in this period were not decisive; this one was, for it ensured the survival of the independent kingdom of Portugal.

Aljubarrota is particularly interesting because of the exceptional archaeological survivals, unique among battles of the Hundred Years War. Excavations revealed a defensive system of ditches and pits, clearly intended to protect infantry from cavalry attack. In

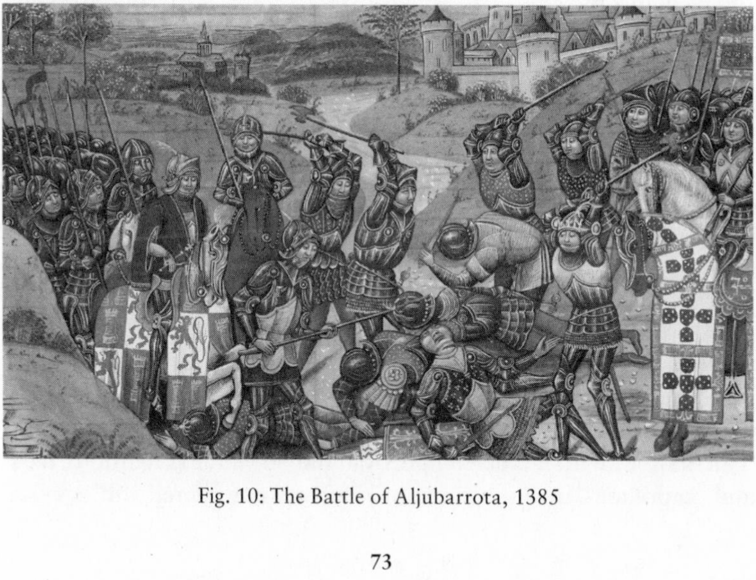

Fig. 10: The Battle of Aljubarrota, 1385

many cases pebbles were found in them, which fits with chronicle evidence that the infantry hurled stones at the start of the battle. Bones from some 400 individuals were discovered, which show the horrific effects of battle, with many savage cuts to the head, and evidence of wounds from crossbow bolts and longbow arrows.[17]

Following the Portuguese victory, John of Gaunt's claim to the kingdom of Castile looked more realistic. In parliament in 1385 the Chancellor 'argued by a variety of reasons and examples that the best and safest defence of the said kingdom would be to conduct and wage fierce war on the enemies of the king and kingdom in foreign parts, since beyond doubt to await war on home soil would be most dangerous and greatly to be feared'.[18] It was agreed that part of the taxes granted should go towards Gaunt's expedition, though the sum involved was well short of what was needed. When he sailed in 1386 it was with a force probably numbering about 1,500 men-at-arms and 2,000 archers. He landed in A Coruña, and conquered Galicia with surprisingly little difficulty; Juan was not concerned to protect a remote province, nor was he willing to risk the battle that Gaunt was ready to offer. Gaunt's position became more difficult in the following year. He was able to provide only limited assistance to the Portuguese invasion of Léon, and though Villalobos surrendered, the campaign was soon abandoned. Dysentery and desertion led to the disintegration of the English force. Juan's position was strengthened by French reinforcements. Gaunt cut his losses, and negotiated terms with the Castilian ruler. Each would work for peace between England and France; Juan's son would marry Gaunt's daughter. Gaunt would give up his claim to the Castilian throne, and his conquests in Galicia, in return for substantial sums. In 1389, further negotiations, aimed at establishing both a permanent peace and the end of the papal schism, ended in failure. Gaunt's involvement in Spanish affairs came to an inglorious end. His claim to the Castilian throne was extinguished, the Franco-Castilian alliance was not broken and the schism was not ended. Gaunt eventually died in 1399.

Richard II's reign closed with his deposition in 1399, and his life ended, somewhat mysteriously, in 1400. A complex character, he had an exalted view of kingship, but lacked military ambition. 'Fair-haired, with a pale complexion and a rounded, feminine face' and 'capricious in his behaviour', he was considered 'unlucky as well as faint-hearted in foreign warfare'.[19] Among his disastrous miscalculations in his final years, the most serious was his decision to exile John of Gaunt's heir, Henry Bolingbroke. Richard's power base of a narrow clique of councillors proved totally inadequate. The war with France was not a major factor in the crisis that led to his deposition, but a treaty between Bolingbroke and the Duke of Orléans, drawn up in 1399, threatened the amicable relationship between Richard and the French government. It was from France that Bolingbroke set out, to land at Ravenspur. With the support of the powerful Percies in the north, he swept to power, facing virtually no resistance. With the advent of a new dynasty, that of Lancaster, the war would take a new course.

7

ENGLISH FORCES IN THE FOURTEENTH CENTURY

Armies looked and sounded the part. When drawn up for battle, banners and pennons were displayed in magnificent pageantry. Battle cries invoked heavenly aid, while trumpets and kettledrums beat out a rhythm. Knights were splendidly arrayed. An inventory from 1378 shows that Robert Salle's armour was enhanced with cloth of gold. He had a red breastplate and a quilted golden surcoat with silver buckles. There was a silver-gilt chaplet for his bacinet (war helmet), and a crest for his great helm. A man of impressive size, he must have looked magnificent.[1] Formations of archers with their bows of six foot or more in length, many in parti-coloured uniform, presented a different, and formidable, threat.

A large army was normally divided into three divisions. The basic building blocks of the army were the retinues, provided by magnate and knights, which varied greatly in size. The largest of all was that of the king's household, consisting under Edward III of some 50 or more bannerets and knights, each of whom would have their own following. The retinues consisted of both men-at-arms and archers, most of whom possessed horses. The number of men-at-arms and archers in the retinues were roughly equal; other archers, recruited in the shires, were organized in units of twenties and hundreds. For campaigns in the Low Countries and northern France, armies were recruited in England. In Gascony, although

English expeditionary forces were important, the majority of troops were local.

Command naturally went to those at the top of society, the dukes and earls. These men were brought up to have such a role; there is no question of armies being led by aristocratic amateurs. Henry of Grosmont, earl and later duke of Lancaster, had great ability as well as all the advantages of birth. Robert Ufford, earl of Suffolk, was praised by the chronicler Geoffrey le Baker, who described his role in command at Poitiers in 1356. He went up and down the lines, 'encouraging and strengthening each man to do his best, cautioning the young not to advance too rashly, and telling the archers not to shoot in vain'.[2] There were some commanders who gained their position through experience and renown, not nobility. Walter Bentley was a case in point. A Yorkshire knight of no great standing, he showed his mettle leading his own *routier* band in Brittany, before being appointed by Edward III in 1350 to succeed Thomas Dagworth in the duchy. A memorandum he submitted to the king showed him to be a man who thought hard about the difficult situation he was in, with underpaid garrisons battening onto defenceless villages. Robert Knollys was a notable commander, of obscure origins in Cheshire, who probably began his career as an archer. His military abilities were such that he was the first man below the rank of earl to be given command of a major expedition.

There was no complex hierarchy of command, or trained professional officer corps. After the dukes and earls, the bannerets were the next highest rank. Normally of baronial standing, they bore rectangular banners. Theirs was a purely military status, which was not hereditary, unlike that of knight. Though a knightly title had strong military implications, it also indicated social standing, and was normally inherited. Below the knights were squires, a term which covered men of very differing status. Some might be aspirant knights, but many had no such ambitions. By the later fourteenth century some squires were of considerable standing, with their own coats of arms, but others were of no high position. They were often simply termed 'men-at-arms', with no indication of their rank. For convenience, the knights and men-at-arms are often referred to by historians as 'cavalry', though this is hardly accurate, for while they rode on campaign, they normally dismounted to fight.

Knights and other men-at-arms were well equipped. The chronicler Jean le Bel noted that on the campaign against the Scots in 1327 English armour was outdated, but that just over a decade later it was quite up to date. The evidence of memorial brasses shows that from the 1330s, plate armour was becoming far more common. Full protection was provided for arms and legs by rerebraces, vambraces, poleyns, greaves and sabatons, while for the torso there were 'pairs of plates', iron or steel plates riveted onto fabric, as well as mail shirts. By mid-century the visored bacinet was replacing the traditional 'great helm'. Fashion led to tight jupons replacing cumbersome surcoats.

RECRUITMENT

Traditional feudal obligation, whereby landowners were obliged to provide set quotas of knights, was largely irrelevant by the time of the Hundred Years War. There was a feudal summons in 1327 for the campaign against the Scots, but by this period such a request yielded a very limited response. There was no precedent for using such a summons for expeditions to France or the Low Countries. However, concerns over recruitment in England during the first few years of the war with France led to an ambitious new scheme for compulsory service. In 1344 a graduated system was introduced, for everyone with an income of £5 a year or more. A £5 landholder was to provide one archer, a £25 one a man-at-arms. Commissioners were accordingly appointed to assess people's wealth. In the following year, orders went out to recruit troops on this new basis. This was extremely unpopular. There were protests in parliament, and in 1346 the king conceded that he had acted out of necessity, and that this would not be a precedent. Finally, in 1352 he agreed that no one was to be obliged to perform military service, except by common consent in parliament. Compulsion was dead.

The alternative to compulsion was pay and persuasion. The normal rates of pay were 8*s*. a day for an earl, 4*s*. for a banneret, 2*s*. for a knight, and 1*s*. for a squire or man-at-arms. Because of concerns about recruitment for the Flanders campaign in 1338, higher wages, generally double the normal rate, were offered as an encouragement. This could only be afforded until the autumn of the following year. Later, high wages were occasionally offered, as in 1369 when John of Gaunt's force was paid at one-and-a-half times the standard rate, and in 1370, when Knollys was promised a double rate for his men. In addition, from the mid-1340s a bonus, known as the regard, was payable, usually on a three-monthly basis. The normal rate was 100 marks (£66) for 30 men-at-arms, but this could be doubled or even trebled.

One source that the crown could rely on to provide service was the royal household, particularly when the king himself was leading an expedition. The knights and others of the household were in receipt of fees and robes on an annual basis, as well as pay when on campaign. They were an experienced body, who provided essential administrative as well as military service. There were probably at least 50 household bannerets and knights on the Crécy campaign, all with their own retinues. These varied greatly in size, from about 150 men down to as few as three or four. In all, the king's household probably provided at least 1,700 men in 1346, forming the bulk of one of the three divisions of the army. There was a change in the 1350s, as a small body of a dozen or so emerged as 'knights of the chamber' rather than 'knights of the household'. A wider affinity was then developed under Richard II, of 'king's knights', men whose allegiance and service could be relied upon, but who were not expected to reside permanently at court. When Richard led an army to Ireland in 1394, out of a total of 89 bannerets and knights there were 39 king's knights and nine chamber knights.

The most convenient method of recruiting more widely was to use contracts. Thus in 1346, Thomas Dagworth agreed to hold Brittany with 200 men-at-arms and 600 mounted archers in return for 2,500 marks, customary wages and a regard. Two years later the Earl of Warwick entered into an agreement for life. He was to receive an annual fee of 1,000 marks, and was to serve the king with 100 men-at-arms, who would be paid wages and a regard. In 1372 the Earl of Salisbury contracted to serve for a year, on land and sea, with 20 knights, 100 men-at-arms and 200 archers. He was to receive wages, and a double regard. Two years later, Richard Adderbury agreed to serve at sea with 40 men-at-arms and the same number of archers, for wages and a regard at one-and-a-half times the standard rate.[3] English armies in Gascony depended to a very considerable extent on local recruitment; contracts were used there just as in England. In 1345 one of the Albret brothers, Bernard-Etz, provided 185 men-at-arms and 940 foot-soldiers, a huge force. However, for the king's own large expeditions to France, as in 1346 and 1359, contracts were not used, as the armies were directly administered by the officials of the royal household.

To fulfil their contracts with the crown, nobles would turn first to their permanent retainers, who received fees, robes and other benefits in return for service in war and peace. Thus the Earl of Warwick made an agreement in 1339 for Robert Herle to serve him for life. One of the earl's most important administrators, in wartime Herle would have a following of four men-at-arms. He duly fought with Warwick at Crécy, though later he had an independent career as captain of Brittany, captain of Calais, Admiral of the North and West, and Warden of the Cinque Ports. Other men would be hired for a specific campaign. In 1372 the Earl of Salisbury made a contract with Roger Maltravers, who was to serve for a year with two archers, and for overseas expeditions would have in addition three servants. He would provide his own horses and be properly equipped. He could keep two-thirds of any booty taken, with one third going to the earl.[4]

In the years up to 1360 the structure of retinues was reasonably stable. Men tended to serve with the same lord on successive campaigns. Out of 20 knights serving with the Earl of Warwick in 1346, 17 had been with him before on at least one occasion, and 12 had been on at least two earlier campaigns. The huge following that Lancaster took to Gascony in 1345 has been analysed in detail by Nicholas Gribit. This was more a small army than a retinue, and for many this was the only occasion they served with the earl. However, over a third of the knights had fought in his company previously, and about 80 per cent of the bannerets and knights who had been with him in 1344 were in his retinue in the following year. Many had family connections with Lancaster which went back to the time of the earl's uncle, Thomas of Lancaster, who had been executed in 1322. There was a solid core to the retinues, with men linked not only by their military experience but also by bonds of land tenure and kinship. The proportion of knights to other men-at-arms did not change much in these years. In 1338 almost a quarter of the Earl of Suffolk's retinue were knights, while the figure for Salisbury's contingent was 19 per cent. In Brittany in 1343, 22 per cent of Lancaster's retinue were knights. For the 1359 expedition, almost a quarter of the Black Prince's cavalry were knights.

The resumption of war in 1369 brought change. The crown contracted for much larger retinues, such as the 900 of Hereford's following in 1369, or the 700 two years later. There was, broadly, far less continuity in retinues, and presumably a consequent reduction in the sense of camaraderie. Just 19 per cent of those who served with the Earl of Arundel in 1388 had been with him in the previous year. With very large retinues, there was an increased reliance on subcontractors, who might themselves subcontract further. In 1374 the Earl of March, who had a contract with the crown, made an agreement with John Strother, who was to provide 30 men-at-arms and 30 archers for a year. Though Strother came from Northumberland, the men he recruited, again by contract, were mostly from East Anglia. He stood to make a profit, for the £40 a year he promised his men-at-arms was less than he was due to receive from March in wages for them.

There was a marked fall in the proportion of knights in the years following the renewal of the war. For Gaunt's *chevauchée* of 1373 the figure was 13 per cent, with leaders of retinues finding it impossible to recruit all the knights they had contracted to supply. In 1388 knights in Arundel's force were roughly 7 per cent of all the men-at-arms. This reflected wider changes in society, as men were increasingly reluctant to take up the burdens of knighthood. Whether this, in turn, was the result of a lack of enthusiasm for an increasingly unsuccessful war is questionable. It seems more likely that it was the burdens of knighthood in civil society that were unwelcome.

Military experience among the knights and men-at-arms was extensive, for soldiering was not exclusively for young men. A number of men gave evidence in the 1390s in a celebrated dispute over the coat of arms used by both the Scrope and Grosvenor families, detailing their military careers. Andrew Luttrell's service in war stretched from 1337 to 1388, over 50 years. Guy Brian's first campaign was against the Scots in 1327, and his last with John of Gaunt in 1369. William Lucy recalled the Battle of Sluys, the siege of Tournai, the battles of Crécy and Poitiers and the 1359–60 campaign. He also had experience of crusading in Prussia. John Rither, squire, had memories of the 1339 campaign. He had fought at Morlaix and at Crécy, and was on the 1359 expedition. His last battle was Nájera in 1367, his last expedition Gaunt's *chevauchée* in 1373. His fighting career therefore lasted at least 34 years. Normally, however, a military career might be expected to last up to 20 years, and in some cases far less than that. The grizzled veterans on campaign, however, will surely have preserved knowledge of terrain and tactics, and given valuable advice to their younger companions.

HORSES

A poet described knights on campaign, mounted 'on our swift war-horses, our shields at our necks and our spears lowered'.[5] Though English soldiers had learned in the Scottish wars that success in battle was best achieved on foot, horses were still crucial for knights and men-at-arms. Men fought on horseback in skirmishes, and rode in the rout that followed battle. Further, they were a vital element in chivalric identity. Noble deeds were best performed on horseback. On one occasion Knollys 'spurred on his horse in a very headstrong manner' and charged a group of Bretons, only to be knocked off his horse, so that he had to be rescued by his men.[6] In Spain, in 1367, William Felton 'spurred his courser down from the hill, his lance lowered. When he reached the Spaniards, he drove his spear so fiercely at a Castilian that the blow pierced his armour, so that his lance went right through his body, killing him.'[7]

Very large numbers of horses were needed. In 1340 the convention was that earls should have six each, bannerets five, knights four, and men-at-arms three. For the 1359–60 campaign the Black Prince took 1,369 horses to France. In all, 395 were lost on campaign, but these losses were more than compensated for by acquisitions, so that the Prince brought home 2,114 horses. Records show that almost 9,300 horses were brought back to England in 1360. In 1370 Knollys, with about 4,000 men, took 8,464 horses to France for his ill-fated *chevauchée*. The best horses, the *destriers*, needed a great deal of care, with a groom for each animal. They were given large quantities of oats, supplemented by hay and cut grass; these pampered animals were not accustomed to grazing. The requirements of an army for horse fodder and water were immense. The needs of the horses might be greater than those of the men; in 1360 the Black Prince had to take a different route through Burgundy than his father, 'for lack of fodder for the horses'.[8] Horses need to drink at least eight gallons a day; it proved disastrous when, on the Prince's 1345 expedition, they were given wine as no water was to be found.

Horses were a major investment, and until the 1360s it was normal practice for men to be compensated for the value of horses lost on campaign. Andrew Ayton studied the lists of horses that were drawn up by royal clerks, noting that the values in 1338–9 were almost double those of 1359–60. The proportion of high-value beasts fell dramatically as the war progressed: in 1338–9, 29 per cent were worth over £20, whereas in 1359–60 only 2 per cent fell into that category. In 1361 John Chandos claimed for the loss of 100 coursers, at a mere ten marks each. There are a number of explanations for this shift. The high valuations of 1338–9 may have been artificial, intended to encourage recruitment, just as the double wages of the time were. The practice of fighting on foot may have discouraged men from taking the best quality *destriers* on campaign. A top quality horse still cost a great deal in the 1360s; one bought for the king at Liège in 1362 cost over £100. In 1362 the Black Prince paid an impressive £232 for two *destriers* acquired in Flanders. There was a major change from the 1370s, for compensation for lost horses was no longer paid. Instead, the potential rewards men might receive from campaigning were raised. Rather than the king claiming half of the profits of war (from ransoms and booty), the proportion was lowered to a third.[9]

ARCHERS

There were normally more archers in Edward III's armies than any other type of soldier. In 1339 there were roughly equal numbers of knights and men-at-arms, mounted archers and archers on foot. Twenty years later the large royal army consisted of about 4,750 knights and men-at-arms, 5,500 mounted archers and 1,100 footmen. In 1369 John of Gaunt agreed to serve with 500 men-at-arms and 1,000 mounted archers.

A crucial development under Edward III was the use of mounted archers. These men fought on foot, but rode with the cavalry, so enabling faster movement of troops. They were first used in Edward III's Scottish campaigns; in 1334 there were 838 men-at-arms and 771 mounted archers in the retinues brought by great men. In the Low Countries in 1338 Henry of Lancaster had a retinue of 16 knights, 52 men-at-arms and 50 mounted archers.[10] Curiously, a plan for forces in 1341 included no mounted archers, but in 1342 there were approaching 2,000 such men in the English forces in Brittany.

There were two main ways in which archers were recruited. They might form part of a retinue, and be recruited by the retinue captains. By the time of the Battle of Crécy, about a third of the archers were incorporated in retinues alongside the knights and men-at-arms. Alongside this, archers were also recruited in the shires by specially appointed commissioners of array. This system was open to abuses of all sorts. In 1345 in Norfolk, 'the constables and under-constables levied large sums of money for the wages and clothing of the archers and the conductor of the same', but either failed to recruit any men, or refused to give them what they were due. Arrayers might themselves be assaulted, as when one official complained in 1346 that 'some malefactors by force prevented him from making the array'.[11] By 1359, only about 2,100 infantry, 1,000 of them from Wales, were recruited by commissions of array. The bulk of the archers were recruited by lords for their retinues. Recruitment was not always popular. When one William Fletcher was chosen to serve, his lord, the Abbot of Buckland in Devon, used force to prevent him being taken, saying that the king should never have William, nor any other of his men.[12]

Most explanations of the English success at Crécy and elsewhere give pride of place to archers. It was in the victory over the Scots at Halidon Hill in 1333 that the English archers had first shown Edward III their value. They could shoot at a fast rate, up to ten or twelve arrows a minute, at a range of up to 200 yards, crippling an advancing enemy. A single archer could probably loose two or three arrows as a horseman charged towards him. It used to be thought that there was a revolutionary transition from the 'short bow' to the longbow, but while the evidence does not support a dramatic change, it is likely that the bows used by Edward III's archers were longer and more formidable than those of earlier periods.

Partly inspired by the discovery of a large number of bows in the wreck of the *Mary Rose*, there has been a great deal of discussion and experimentation to try to determine how effective the longbow was. Kelly DeVries has argued that arrows were ineffective as killing weapons. With a high trajectory, they would have struck at an angle, ricocheting off armour rather than penetrating. This argument flies in the face of the evidence of the chroniclers, as Clifford Rogers has pointed out. Descriptions of battle after battle attest the impact of English arrows. [13] However, not all injuries inflicted by arrows were fatal. Philip VI was wounded in the face at Crécy, as was David II of Scotland at Neville's Cross, and as Henry V would be at Shrewsbury. All three were presumably not protected by lowered visors. Horses presented a larger target than men, and were particularly vulnerable to plunging arrows, which maddened them. Archers could bring a charge to a halt, with uncontrollable horses rearing in pain.

More important than any technological development of the longbow was the fact that it was under Edward III that the government took action for the first time to ensure an adequate supply of bows and arrows. In the past it had been up to individuals to provide their own equipment; the single sheaf of 24 arrows an archer was likely to bring with him would not last long in battle. In 1338 the king ordered his armourer to supply 1,000 arrows, 4,000 bowstrings and 4,000 sheaves of arrows. Overall, in the years 1338–44, his forces were supplied with 3,705 bows and 5,424 sheaves of arrows. Much larger quantities were acquired later. The accounts for 1344–51, years which include the Crécy campaign and the siege of Calais, show that the armoury at the Tower provided 25,465 bows and over a million arrows. [14] The Black Prince had problems in 1356, when he sent one of his officials to England to obtain 1,000 bows, 200 sheaves of arrows and 400 gross of bowstrings, for 'no arrows can be obtained from England, because the king has caused to be arrested and taken for his use all the arrows that can be found anywhere there'. Despite the Prince's efforts, at Poitiers the archers 'ran out of arrows and picked up stones, and fought with swords and lances, and anything they could find'.[15]

Though the records normally describe the infantry as archers, they had other weapons. In 1338 at Antwerp 644 spears were bought for the Welsh.[16] Bows were of no use in the mêlée, and for close combat the archers would use billhooks, short lances, swords, daggers, knives and anything else suitable. Though the chronicles do not describe their use by English troops, there were considerable numbers of *pavises*, large rectangular shields, in the Tower armoury, which would have been valuable in siege warfare or on ships. Gascon foot-soldiers were armed with pikes and other weapons for hand-to-hand combat, as well as crossbows.

In the field the archers were organized as they had been since Edward I's reign, or even earlier. They were placed in twenties and hundreds, commanded by vintenars and constables. In the case of the Welsh, documents show that there were in addition chaplains, interpreters, doctors and criers (to shout out orders), but curiously there is no such evidence for the English. Many of the archers wore uniforms. The Earl of Arundel's Welsh troops wore red and white, while the Black Prince's men were in green and white. Mid-fourteenth century arrays at Norwich show that the centenars, officers in charge of a hundred men, were well equipped, each with mail shirt, bascinet, breastplate, gauntlets, sword, dagger and spear. The vintenars, in charge of twenty men each, were also well provided with arms and armour. Archers each had a bow, arrows, sword and knife, and were clearly superior to other men who had no more than a staff and a knife.[17]

It was essential that enough men had the right skills for archery, but the evidence of some musters suggests that this might well not have been the case; the record of an array of 1346 in the Suffolk district of Blything listed some 50 men, of whom only two possessed bows.[18] It was certainly a matter of concern. A well-known proclamation in 1363 suggested that 'the art is almost wholly disused', and required all the able-bodied to practise shooting, rather than engaging in 'vain games of no value' such as football.[19] To be a good archer undoubtedly required much training. It is not known how this was organized, or whether it took place in villages or when armies were mustered. There is no evidence for anything like the tedious drill exercises that have occupied so much of the time of army recruits in more recent periods.

Although records provide the names of many archers, historians have not succeeded in working out many biographies of them for the fourteenth century. Robert Fishlake provides a rare example: he served in Brittany in 1378, and on at least six expeditions in the following eleven years. Some served for longer. In 1384 Richard Pupplington, 'one of the oldest archers of the crown', was promised 6*d.* a day for life, a reward for over 40 years' service.[20] No doubt these two were among many who campaigned on a regular basis, but there is no way of determining how many of the archers were regulars who made war their profession.

Nor is it possible to do much more than hypothesize as to where archers fitted in the social hierarchy. The difficulty of tracing them back to their origins is vividly demonstrated by the fact that very few can be identified in the records of the 1379 poll tax. Only one man out of a Northumberland retinue with 40 archers is listed in the tax record for the county. A mounted archer, with his wage of 6*d.* a day, was unlikely to have been recruited from among the poorest villagers. It was only men of some standing who could afford a horse and at least some equipment. The arrays at Norwich show that a few archers even had servants. The professions of the archers listed included tailor, mercer, goldsmith, bowyer and fletcher. These were surely middle-ranking men. Most of the archers in English armies will have been drawn from the countryside, not the towns, but this evidence is nevertheless suggestive.

OTHERS

Armies needed support. Armourers, engineers, masons, smiths, farriers, waggoners and wheelwrights all had vital roles. Clerks were needed to record musters and to calculate wages. Others engaged in war included spies, such as the queen's servant sent to Paris in 1338 'to spy out secretly the doings of Philip of Valois, for forty days', at 18*d.* a day.[21] There is little evidence to show how many non-combatants accompanied armies, but servants and grooms were required to see to the needs of the knights and men-at-arms. Most contracts made no mention of these, for they were not paid by the crown, but it is clear from some private indentures that their numbers were very considerable. It was perhaps exceptional that in

1353 John Sully agreed to serve the Black Prince with one squire and no fewer than eight or nine grooms, but even a squire might have a small entourage of two or three. On a conservative estimate there would have been at least as many grooms and servants in an army as there were cavalry.

Armies contained a good share of criminals. Evil-doers were encouraged to fight by the expectation that they might receive pardons. In the summer and autumn of 1346, Edward III pardoned 1,308 men for a range of offences, on condition that they remained in the army. The great majority of pardons went to ordinary soldiers, but included the earls of Warwick and Suffolk and a few knights. In many cases men received pardons for serious crimes. In 1360 a knight, Robert Darcy, received one for an impressive list of offences, which extended from murders, operating a protection racket and assaulting a royal justice, to the less significant matter of forcing a prior to accept a woman as a nun.

THE NAVY

Naval resources were central to English campaigning. Yet the crown itself possessed few ships, and efforts to build up and maintain a royal navy were very limited. In 1338 there were 13 royal ships, based at the Tower of London. In 1369, 27 were at sea. By 1378, however, there were just five left. Most of the royal vessels were no different from merchant ships in build, with single mast and sail, though they would have featured 'castles', built up platforms on bow and stern, and in some cases fighting platforms at the masthead. The largest, of 240 tons or more, carried big crews: in 1338 the *Cog Thomas* had a constable, a clerk, a carpenter, 116 sailors and 16 ship's boys. Many were of the kind known as cogs, flat-bottomed and high-sided, while others were simply referred to as 'ships', while there were also some hulks (vessels with the hull constructed in reverse clinker) and other types. There were also some oared galleys; in 1336, Edward had *La Philippe* built at King's Lynn at a cost of £666, but there was no attempt to create galley fleets such as the French possessed. In the 1370s, however, some specially built oared vessels, termed barges and balingers, were commissioned. The London barge *Paul* had 80 oars; balingers were smaller. Relatively slender, these were valuable for escort duties and quick crossings to France. The great majority of ships in royal service were merchant vessels, whose recruitment and numbers are discussed in Chapter 9. Some of these were quite as formidable as any royal ship; in 1356 the *Seint Marie* had a crew of 140 men.

There was little distinction between the type of men appointed to command at sea and those who led on land. When the Earl of Arundel was made admiral in 1345, this was because 'no one save he can punish or lead them unless he is a great man'.[22] As a lord summoned to parliament, Robert Morley had sufficient status; he served with distinction as admiral of the northern fleet on several occasions. In the early 1350s the Duke of Lancaster and the earls of Northampton and Warwick were all appointed as admirals. Guy Brian, soldier, administrator and diplomat, rose in the king's household to baronial standing. He served often as admiral of the western fleet. Reginald Cobham also held that position. A knight of the Garter from 1353, Cobham had a distinguished military and diplomatic career. Admirals of this type and calibre were not sailors by training, but no doubt could call on the expertise of their captains. Occasionally, men of lesser status were appointed as admirals. Robert Ledrede was a royal sergeant-at-arms who commanded a fleet sent to Gascony in 1357 to bring wine to England. His writ of appointment suggests that his main duty was seen as the maintenance of discipline 'according to the law of the sea'.[23]

At sea, it was normal to employ equal numbers of archers and men-at-arms. A contract in 1372 with William Nevill, admiral of the north, specified service with 60 men-at-arms and the same number of archers, and in the next year Esmon Rose, esquire, captain of the *Barge* of London, agreed to serve with 20 men-at-arms and 20 archers for four months.[24] The number of soldiers employed on naval expeditions might be considerable. In a disastrous voyage in the winter of 1377–8, Buckingham commanded 4,000 soldiers at sea, in addition to almost the same number of sailors. In 1388 Arundel had almost 3,500 soldiers in a fleet of 53 ships and nine barges, manned by about 2,900 sailors.

***

A common explanation for the successes of English forces in the glory days of Edward III's reign is that they were the product of a military revolution, which provided the archers with a decisive weapon in the form of the longbow. That was just part of the story. It was important that most of the archers were mounted, for this meant they were not left behind on a march. English armies had coherence, demonstrated by the way in which retinues were not composed solely of knights and men-at-arms, but included archers in their numbers. The fact that the English were fighting in France no doubt made for some difficulties, but it also gave them advantages. Desertion had been a problem when campaigning nearer home, in Wales or Scotland, but in France it was much less easy to abandon the army. There were many other reasons for English successes. Morale was important, if hard to analyse. The chronicler Geoffrey le Baker gave an account, in implausibly literary Latin, of the Black Prince's speeches before the Battle of Poitiers. He emphasized, surely rightly, 'honour, love of homeland, and the magnificent spoils of France'.[25]

8

FRENCH FORCES IN THE FOURTEENTH CENTURY

French armies, like the English, looked impressive. Before the Battle of Roosebeke, Philip van Artevelde warned his men that the French lines would 'gleam with gold and silver, with crested helmets'.[1] Nor was it just a matter of appearance. There were good reasons to expect French armies to be successful in the war that began in 1337. The French could recruit far larger armies than the English could muster, and did not have to face the problems involved in fighting overseas. Admittedly, they had suffered a disastrous defeat at the hands of the Flemings at Courtrai in 1302, but in 1328 they had their revenge at Cassel, where they countered a surprise Flemish attack. Though they lost many horses, French mounted forces were triumphant. Against the English, the French were successful in the War of Saint-Sardos in Gascony in 1324. Though Bordeaux remained in English hands, the Agenais and other lands were lost, and the Earl of Kent was forced to surrender La Réole.

RECRUITMENT

The recruitment and organization of French armies has been ably set out by Philippe Contamine.[2] The traditional feudal obligation, whereby those who held land directly from the king had a duty to provide troops at their own expense for a 40-day period, was of limited relevance by the 1330s. However, a general obligation on the nobility to serve when summoned was effective in producing large numbers of paid troops. Also, a much broader obligation, known as the *arrière-ban*, could be invoked in times of urgent necessity, though it was not used after 1356. This extended to all between 18 and 60. The requirements of the *arrière-ban* could be met by paying what amounted to a tax in lieu of physical service. A group of a hundred households might be charged to pay for up to six soldiers. Cities and towns contributed: in 1337, Paris made a grant of 400 cavalry for a six-month period, provided the king led the host in person. If he was not present, service was for four months.

The French crown also used letters of retainer, similar to the contracts employed in England, if not as precise in wording. In 1339 the Count of Foix was retained to serve with 330 men-at-arms and 300 foot-soldiers. Foreign mercenaries, such as the Genoese crossbowmen slaughtered at Crécy, were also recruited by means of contracts. Other foreign troops were provided in significant numbers by rulers allied to the French, such as the King of Bohemia and the Count of Savoy. Money-fiefs might be used to bind such rulers to the French cause; thus the Duke of Brabant did homage to Philip VI in 1332 in return for an annual fee of 2,000 *livres tournois*. By 1339, however, the duke had entered English allegiance, accepting a promised £1,500 a year from Edward III.

The range of recruitment methods may appear unsystematic, but the French crown had no difficulty in raising large numbers of troops. In 1339 a plan envisaged 10,000 men-at-arms and 40,000 foot-soldiers in royal pay, with the forces of the king and his son in addition. That this was no flight of fancy is indicated by accounts which show that on all fronts the French had about 28,000 men-at-arms and 16,700 infantry in pay in September 1340. It is not possible to calculate French numbers at Crécy, but there is no doubt that the English were very significantly outnumbered there.

In addition to paid troops, there was a profusion of servants and camp followers. Merchants, artisans, prostitutes and others provided services which were surely appreciated by the troops, if not by their commanders. They were a hindrance; on the Roosebeke campaign in 1382 the elderly and sick, and all those incapable of bearing arms, were ordered to leave the French camp.

ORGANIZATION

In the field, the army was divided into up to a dozen 'battles'. That led by the Count of Alençon in 1340 totalled over 1,200 men. Within this force, units varied greatly in size. The count's own household provided 73 men-at-arms. There were 23 retinues led by bannerets, varying in size from 60 down to 14. A hundred units led by knights averaged just five. Twenty squires in groups of up to five made up the rest of the contingent.

French forces, despite success in recruiting large numbers, failed disastrously at Crécy. Following that catastrophe, King John issued an ordinance in 1351 in which he attempted to shape the armies more systematically. The main commanders, in charge of their organization, were the Constable, the Marshal and the Master of the Crossbowmen. New wage levels were set. Knights and men-at-arms were to be mustered in units of at least 25, with a maximum of 80. Knights who were in charge of companies of 25 or 30 would be paid as bannerets. Musters were to be held at least twice a month, with written records kept. All the horses were to be valued, and branded with a hot iron for identification. Crossbowmen were to be equipped with bow, sword and knife, and have body defences of steel plates as well as steel skull-cap and gorget (throat protection). Other infantry, termed *pavisiers*, should have plate armour, or a mail hauberk, as well as bacinet, gauntlets, sword, knife and spear. The foot-soldiers were to be in companies of 25 or 30, each with a constable in charge.[3]

This ordinance shows both the similarities, and the differences, between French and English armies. The organization of the cavalry differed relatively little. The pay differentials were much the same, as was the principle of valuing horses so that compensation could be paid for losses in war. The contrast came with the infantry. There was no French equivalent to the English mounted or foot archers. The elite among the foot-soldiers were the well-armoured crossbowmen, while the other infantry were to be far better equipped with armour than was the case with the English archers. They were equipped not with bows, but with a range of weapons such as swords, spears and billhooks. The proportions were very different, for in a French army men-at-arms usually outnumbered infantry.

Fig. 11: A mid-fourteenth-century French knight in full armour

In the 1351 ordinance, there was no attempt to copy the English use of archers. Yet, hardly surprisingly, some efforts were made to employ integrated retinues comprising both men-at-arms and archers, on the English model. In 1351, Jean de Beaumanoir, marshal of Brittany, had a following of four knights, 28 squires and 30 archers. Similarly, in the next year Yvain Charruel, a Breton knight, had a retinue of two knights, 21 squires and 30 archers. A smaller retinue under a squire, Jean de Kergolay, consisted of two knights, five squires and ten archers.[4] This, however, was a short-lived experiment. Later musters show that it was very rare for archers or other infantry troops to feature in retinues.

COMMAND

Command in the field naturally went to the great men, the dukes and counts. At Crécy the King of Bohemia and his son Charles of Luxembourg headed 'battles'. The Duke of Lorraine, the counts of Flanders, of Blois, of Harcourt and of Alençon had similar positions. The Constable and the two Marshals had important roles in command; the latter had responsibility for musters, and disputes within the army were heard in their court. Men of skill and experience, not necessarily of great wealth, were usually appointed to these posts. Moreau de Fiennes, appointed Constable after the disaster of Poitiers, had been brought up in the English court. His military experience went back to 1340, when he campaigned with four knights and 25 squires. He had fought in Artois, Picardy and Normandy in King John's early years on the throne, and remained Constable until his death in 1370. Arnoul d'Audrehem's military career began in 1330s; he was appointed Marshal in 1352, and resigned in 1368, when he accepted the honour of carrying the *Oriflamme*. Boucicaut the elder, who became Marshal in 1357, was another highly experienced soldier, who had first fought in 1337. His successor, Jean, Sire de Blainville, appointed in 1368, was a Norman noble of no great wealth, but with extensive military experience. The most notable appointment came two years later, when the remarkably able soldier Bertrand du Guesclin became Constable, with authority in the field even over dukes who were members of the royal house.

One suggestion is that the appointment of du Guesclin in particular, and a more general shift in French attitudes, was influenced by the doctrines set out in the widely-read late Roman treatise by Vegetius. Charles V was an enthusiast for classical learning, and had his own copy of Vegetius. The treatise stressed the importance of experience and skill in appointing military leaders, and this was reflected in Charles's actions. There is no doubting the popularity of Vegetius; the problem is that it is difficult to determine how far efforts were made to put his theories into practice. Though his authority was greater, du Guesclin's elevation was not so radically different from previous practice in appointing Marshals and Constables. Where Vegetian concepts were perhaps most important was not in the details of military practice, but in the way in which the army was seen as an instrument of the state, acting for the common good. This contrasted strongly with the individualism which found its worst expression in the *routier* leaders.

CHANGE AFTER 1369

Warfare was changing in this period. Skirmishes and sieges, not battles, were the order of the day. Armies were smaller than in the past; most French ones were probably similar in number to the English at around 5,000, though large numbers were recruited for the campaign of 1382 which culminated in the Battle of Roosebeke, and the abortive invasion of England in 1386.

Forces were generally in the field for longer than had been the case in the early years of the war. This brought greater cohesion and professionalism. Command still went, where possible, to members of the upper aristocracy, but, as the career of du Guesclin shows, ability was recognized. As was the case with the English, some captains had lengthy experience. Morice de Trésiguidy, a Breton, was one of the Thirty of 1351. He fought with du Guesclin at Cocherel in 1364 and went with him to Spain. He campaigned regularly in the 1370s, and fought at Roosebeke in 1382. His military career probably ended at Nicopolis in 1396.[5]

There were general summonses issued to the nobility, but the crown largely relied on the service of paid troops recruited by means of letters of retainer. Just as the proportion of bannerets and knights fell in English armies, so it did in the French. Whereas in 1340 there had been one banneret to every 70 men-at-arms, 50 years later the proportion was one to a hundred. That of knights fell similarly, from 15 per cent to 10 per cent. There were significant regional variations; knighthood was less common in the south than in the north. A horse valuation list for a contingent serving with the Duke of Anjou in Gascony in 1369 shows that it was led by a squire and consisted of 87 other squires and ten mounted archers. On the other hand, Olivier de Clisson had two bannerets, 32 knights and 165 squires in his retinue in Brittany in 1380.

In parallel with the decline of knighthood, so the *destrier*, the great warhorse, featured less and less in the records of musters. By the mid-fourteenth century, the elite horse was normally a courser,

Fig. 12: A late fourteenth-century French knight

with others simply termed 'horses'. A muster at Dijon in 1366 revealed three coursers, 19 horses and 12 rounceys. Horses were needed for skirmishing and scouting; in battle, men were expected to fight on foot; at Roosebeke only Charles VI was mounted.

One answer to the power of English archery was to ensure that foot-soldiers were well equipped. Most had crossbows. Armour that could resist arrows was essential. Details of the purchase of infantry armour for 500 men in 1385 show that it consisted of a *côte de fer* (body armour), weighing 25 pounds, a bacinet with visor, weighing 14 pounds, arm pieces and gauntlets, and leg armour, with mail protection to the rear.[6] Such men were not recruited in very large numbers; crossbowmen and other foot-soldiers were usually outnumbered by men-at-arms by about two to one. The contrast was not solely with English armies; in the forces raised in Navarre in the 1360s and 1370s, only about a third consisted of men-at-arms.

There were inevitable problems. Musters were not properly held. Captains might take money for more troops than they took on campaign, and did not always pay them satisfactorily. Men engaged in pillaging and robbery. Goods were seized and not paid for. Some men deserted, or left without leave. A royal ordinance of 1374, which aimed to prevent such abuses, rather than to make radical changes, laid responsibility for discipline on captains, and explained how men-at-arms were to be divided into companies, or *routes*, each of a hundred men. There were to be ten smaller units, known as *chambres*, within the companies.[7] It was hard to maintain the principles of the ordinance; the death of Charles V in 1380 meant the loss of a driving force, and a slipping back into old ways. At the Battle of Roosebeke in 1382 there was a fear that large numbers would desert. Heralds announced severe penalties for any who left the lines, and the horses, on which they might flee, were put out of sight, so that the men 'having lost hope of leaving the fight, might be more aggressive'.[8]

There was no enthusiasm among French commanders in the later fourteenth century for battle. Sieges were a different matter, with all the techniques of blockade, bombardment, mining and escalade in use. Alongside the trebuchets and other stone-throwing machines, guns began to be used on a significant scale to batter walls. Detailed documents show their use at the siege of Saint-Sauveur in Normandy which concluded in 1375. New guns were specially forged for the siege, four of them especially large and capable of firing hundred-pound stones. One such stone crashed into the chamber of the constable, Thomas Catrington, terrifying him. In all, some 30 guns were brought to bear on the castle. The accounts reveal some of the details of manufacture. It took 43 days to make one especially large gun at Caen. To prevent it rusting, it was covered with cowhide, and an iron plate was fitted over the touchhole to keep out the rain. The gun was bound round with ropes, to provide extra strength. It rested in an elaborate wooden framework, which allowed for adjustments to the elevation. For ammunition, it used stones; smaller guns shot lead pellets. In the end, however, it was gold, not stone balls, which brought surrender, with the French buying out the English with 60,000 gold francs.[9] It would be wrong to see the use of siege guns at this time as marking a revolution in military methods, but there was an important evolution taking place, with castles and towns becoming more vulnerable to the new methods of bombardment.

SHIPPING

Naval resources were not as essential for the French as for the English, as their plans to invade England never came to fruition. It was necessary, however, to find ways to counter English strength at sea. At Rouen, there was a naval arsenal, the *clos des galées*, dating from the late thirteenth century. Far more elaborate than anything the English possessed, it was both a shipyard and an arms depot. In the late 1330s the French crown possessed some 50 ships, of various types. Just as in England, the bulk of the fleets were made up of impressed merchant vessels. In 1340 a fleet of 200 ships, none with a crew of fewer than 60, was assembled from northern French ports. Some French ships were very large; one royal ship, known as *La Testiere*, had a crew of 150 men. Galleys might have 200 sailors and crossbowmen. Maintaining the fleet in condition was always a problem. In 1374 Charles V explained that the galleys, ships, barges and other vessels that had been built or bought had deteriorated. The equipment and victuals had been bought too hastily, and at too great a cost. The hope was that by appointing a man with 'great experience and industry in such matters', the situation could be turned round.[10] Rather than rely exclusively on their own naval resources, the French made extensive use of hired galleys, particularly from Genoa and Castile. In 1337 Ayton Doria of Genoa contracted to supply 20 galleys, each with 210 men, in return for 900 gold florins a month. In 1348 the King of Castile promised to provide 200 fully armed ships for a four-month period. Accounts for the distribution of ship's biscuit in 1385 reveal that the fleet consisted of 32 Spanish and 21 French vessels. A dozen of the Spaniards were classed as ships; the remainder were oared barges and balingers.

THE SOLDIER

The chronicles and documents rarely provide much detail about the ordinary soldiers of this period. However, a unique and remarkable record of a muster held in Provence in 1374 gives a rare insight into one small troop, for it provides brief physical descriptions. Most of the men were mercenaries, termed brigands, contracted to serve for two months. Almost a quarter was described as 'young', and nearly all of these were beardless, or had only small beards. Of the others, only four out of 140 were old enough to be white-bearded. Over a quarter of those described had visible scars, perhaps acquired as much through manual labour as from fighting, for the professional hired soldiers were no more scarred than the others. The faces of the men emerge unexpectedly from the record, staring through the centuries:

> Jean Bosquet of Areis, above average height, round face, pale eyes, black beard somewhat whitened, nose rather scarred, also on the right jaw, armed with plates, sword, buckler, knife, iron skull-cap and crossbow.[11]

9

THE LOGISTICS OF WAR

Success in war depended on many things. Leadership and morale were only part of the story. There was a massive organizational task involved in any campaign. It was no use mounting expeditions if the soldiers did not have enough to eat and the horses lacked fodder. A letter from an English official in 1346 explained that 'Since we departed from Caen, we have lived on the country, to the great travail and harm of our people, but, thanks to God, we have no loss. But we are now in such plight that we must in part be refreshed by victuals.' Arms were also important. On the same campaign a letter from the king to the council in England asked 'that you should purvey as many bows, arrows and bowstrings as you can'.[1]

TRANSPORT BY SEA

For campaigning in France, a major problem for the English was the carriage of men, horses and supplies by sea. A few of the ships used were sizeable at 100 tuns burthen (about 150 tons displacement) or more, but many were small: plans in the early 1340s envisaged taking ships of 30 tuns and over into royal service, but the average of those that transported the English forces to Flanders in 1338 was just 28 tuns. In 1353 the king demanded details of all ships from the Thames northwards of over 20 tuns. Some of the ships had to be converted, using gangways and hurdles, to carry horses.[2]

The number of sailors could well far exceed that of the soldiers. For the 1338 expedition, some 400 ships were used, manned by over 13,000 sailors, to transport about 3,000 men, their horses and their equipment to Flanders. In 1342 about 11,000 sailors in about 600 ships took the king's army of almost 4,000 men to Brittany. For the Crécy and Calais campaign of 1346–7, it has been calculated that 853 ships, manned by 23,957 sailors, were used. The capture of Calais in 1347 reduced the problems the government faced, for with the short sea crossing it became possible to use smaller numbers of ships on a ferry system. There remained the problem of transport to Gascony. In 1355, 187 ships and 2,937 sailors were required to take the Black Prince and his army of some 2,600 men there. The size of the crews varied, with the crown often demanding double the normal complement for larger vessels. The *Christopher*, which took the king himself to the Low Countries in 1338, had a crew of 120, while in contrast the little *Godyer* of Newcastle was manned by just 11. Many of the ships had around 30 or 40 sailors.[3]

Various methods were used to acquire ships. The most important was the use of commissioners who were empowered to requisition them for royal service. Thus in 1354 three royal sergeants-at-arms were appointed to arrest ships of over 20 tuns from ports between King's Lynn and London, and send them to Southampton. Similar commissions covered the ports in the south and west. From the mid-1340s, the crown also contracted directly with ship owners. Leaders of retinues might also make their own arrangements. Sailors had to be impressed as well as ships; this was a duty usually laid on captains. The impressment of ships and sailors may have been effective, but it was highly unpopular, for the burden of war fell far more heavily on English ports than on the counties or inland towns. Ports might contribute as much as 40 per cent of their available ships to a major expedition. In 1339 the mayor and leading burgesses of Bodmin were imprisoned in Lostwithiel, because they refused to provide the admiral with four ships. They were released when an inquisition proved that Bodmin was not a seaport. In 1343 it was claimed that Hythe and Romney, two of the Cinque Ports in Kent, had only one ship of war, as 'their shipping is totally destroyed'. In 1349 Roger Larcher and another sergeant were sent to Southampton to arrest ships, when 'William de Froille, assembling a huge multitude of evildoers, assaulted the said Roger and by force prevented him from executing his commission.' In the same year there was trouble with 'certain lords, masters and mariners of ships of Kingston upon Hull and Dartmouth, who contemptuously remained at home and refused to come to the said passage'.[4]

Once shipping was assembled, there might still be problems, particularly with crossings to Gascony. The Earl of Stafford's account for his expedition there in 1352 shows that he had to wait for some time in England, because of a shortage of shipping. When ships did become available, there were not enough to take all the horses, and £686 was spent on buying replacement mounts in Gascony.[5] In 1355 the Black Prince's departure for the duchy was delayed by almost two months because his fleet was not assembled promptly. Wind and weather might add to the problems. In 1355 the king's fleet assembled at Greenwich in early July, and because of contrary winds it reached no further than Portsmouth by the middle of the next month, and never made it to France. Broadly, however, the systems used for acquiring the large numbers of ships essential for the war effort, and for transporting men, horses and equipment to France, worked surprisingly well.

VICTUALLING

Once armies were transported to France, they had to be fed. There were various possible strategies. The crown might organize the provision of supplies on a large scale. Alternatively, soldiers might be expected to make their own arrangements, while armies could live off the land. When Edward III was in the Low Countries in the late 1330s, it made sense for supplies to be sent from England, for supply lines were short. Equally, English-held ports in France, notably Calais, but also ports in Brittany, could be supplied by sea. Convoys might take victuals to Bordeaux. It was far more difficult when it came to raids deep into France. There were limits to how much food an army could take with it. Further, it made strategic sense to pillage and burn. Living off the land was a weapon of war.

Government orders for the collection of foodstuffs show what soldiers were expected to eat. Wheat was the main staple, supplemented by other grains. Meat was pork or bacon, beef and mutton, while preserved fish, particularly stockfish (dried cod) and herrings, was important. Drink might be ale, for which malt was needed, or wine.

Oats were needed particularly for the horses. Estimates tended to be lavish. Those drawn up in 1300 for English garrisons in Scotland suggest that the men were expected to consume some 5,000 calories a day, but the reality, particularly on campaign, was hardly likely to be so high. A calculation of the rations planned by the French for their army in 1327 works out at about 3,250 calories, still a substantial amount. At sea, biscuit was required; a French estimate of 1355 was that 25 tuns were needed for a 200-man galley for a month.[6]

A soldier's pay was normally intended to be sufficient to provide for his costs, including food. It was rare for men to be paid in kind. However, officials were well aware of the need to ensure that troops were properly fed. In England it had been normal from the late thirteenth century for the crown to provide victuals not merely for the forces of the royal household, but for the army as a whole. Huge quantities were collected from English counties and sent to victualling bases, notably Berwick, so that armies could be properly supplied, and English-held castles provided with sufficient stores. To do this the crown used a right known as prise, which gave officials the power of compulsory purchase of foodstuffs. Edward III used this method in his Scottish campaigns of the 1330s; in 1334 he ordered over 12,000 quarters (96,000 bushels) of wheat and 17,000 quarters of oats from 16 counties.

The system was therefore well established when the war with France opened in 1337. Plans put before the royal council provided for the collection of 4,000 quarters (32,000 bushels) of wheat, 6,000 of oats and 1,000 of malt from ten southern counties. Accounts show that between March and August 1338 about 2,000 quarters of wheat, 2,400 of malt, 120 cattle and 650 sheep along with other supplies were acquired from 17 eastern counties. Within the counties, sheriffs were in charge of the task; thus in 1346 the sheriff of Lincolnshire purchased 685 quarters of wheat, 315 quarters of oats and 105 bushels of beans and peas, together with 135 carcases of pork, 213 of mutton, 11 of beef and a dozen weys of cheese. It cost £185 to buy the supplies, with a further £53 spent on sacks, barrels, transport and other items. All this, along with similar supplies from other counties, was needed for the royal expedition to France. Supplies were also needed for the English forces in Gascony: for example, in the summer of 1347 over 10,000 quarters of wheat, with smaller quantities of beans and peas, and rye, were shipped to the duchy.[7]

It was not always easy to know how much was required. An estimate for the northern fleet manned by 4,050, serving for four months, was that it would require 9,100 quarters of wheat, 9,350 of barley, 6,000 of oats, 2,400 of beans and peas, 60 tuns of ale, as well as pork, herrings, stockfish and cheese. The western fleet was smaller, requiring 4,000 quarters of wheat, 6,000 of oats and 1,000 of barley.[8] These figures were well in excess of what was actually needed; a third of these quantities would have more than sufficed. It is probable that when the government requested victuals, more thought was given to how much could reasonably be collected rather than to how much was actually needed. In 1346 more supplies were taken to Normandy than were needed. Some deteriorated in shipment, and in store; some were brought back to England and sold.

Collecting the supplies was complicated. Individuals had to be paid (often in arrears) for the food taken from them. Sheriffs' officials had to organize transport, either in carts or by water, to central collection points, from where the goods would be taken to ports for shipment overseas. Sacks and barrels had to be bought for storage, and warehouses hired. Some grain was milled; in 1351 the grain collected for Calais was ground into flour and put in tuns, so as to reduce the costs of carriage.[9] Accounts had to be kept and receipts given.

The system was all too open to corruption. The early years of the war saw many accusations made. The Abbot of Ramsey allegedly paid over £7 to a royal official in 1339 to leave his abbey's lands alone. There were many cases where grain was seized, but not passed on, and many examples of non-payment. William Fraunk, knight, was alleged to have taken £1,333 from the county community of Lincolnshire in lieu of foodstuffs. It was not surprising that prises were highly unpopular. People resented their food supplies being taken even more than they resented taxation. Opposition to the seizures led to the promulgation of a statute in 1340 which separated purveyance for the king's household from purveyance for the army. Military purveyance should be undertaken by merchants, 'so that the people nor none of them shall not be forced to sell anything against their desire or will'.[10] Yet the sheriffs continued to be responsible for collecting foodstuffs for the major military efforts of 1345–6. In Lincolnshire, 685 quarters of wheat, 365 quarters of oats and 105 quarters of beans and peas were collected by the sheriff, along with

135 bacon pigs, 11 beef carcases, and quantities of cheese. Problems continued. The sheriff of Nottingham and Derby was accused of taking foodstuffs for his own use, while his wife was charged with using false measures, and of moving her foot and putting her hands in as the grain was poured. There was no change in victualling methods in 1351, when on 2 January Edward III set up commissions to collect 7,900 quarters of wheat and similarly large quantities of other victuals from 24 counties, from Northumberland to Kent, largely intended for Calais which was thought to be under threat. There were protests in parliament, with claims that a shortage of corn threatened, and the quantities were reduced, in the case of wheat to 4,190 quarters.[11]

It was far easier to turn to merchants to provide the necessary supplies. Not only were there fewer objections than when royal officials were used, but it was also administratively simpler. The question of how to provision the substantial army assembling for embarkation in 1359 was in part resolved by forbidding merchants in Kent from holding their normal fairs and markets, and compelling them to go to Sandwich. In 1360, three merchants agreed to provide 1,000 quarters of wheat, the same amount of malt and 500 quarters of oats, and of beans and peas, from King's Lynn and the nearby ports for Calais. John Wesenham was both royal official and merchant; by 1361 he had provided Calais with 6,600 quarters of grain.[12]

In addition, commanders took steps to ensure that their men were properly fed. Thus Lancaster had his own ship to bring him supplies during the siege of Calais. In 1356 the Earl of Suffolk was authorized to collect 100 quarters of wheat, 300 quarters of oats, along with quantities of beans and peas, and herring, to be shipped from Ipswich to Gascony. Royal orders made it clear in 1357 that soldiers 'who have taken with them corn and victuals for their maintenance' in Brittany and Normandy were exempt from a prohibition on the export of arms and supplies.[13]

The shift away from the system of prise was marked in formal terms by an important statute in 1362 which went further than that of 1340 had done. It specified 'that the heinous name of purveyor be changed and named buyer'. Such 'buyers' were to make immediate payment for goods they took, and prises were only to be taken so as to supply the households of the king, queen and prince of Wales. Under the terms of the statute, purveyance for entire armies was no longer possible.[14] Nor, as armies were for the most part smaller, was it so necessary by the second half of the fourteenth century, though care had to be taken to ensure that English garrisons in Brittany and elsewhere had adequate supplies.

FRANCE

Developments were similar in France, though they are not so well documented. In 1327 plans were prepared for a possible war. It was envisaged that the army would consist of 5,000 men-at-arms and 20,000 foot-soldiers, serving for five months, and the necessary quantities of wine, wheat, oats, pork, beef, sheep and other supplies were carefully worked out. All were to be taken from wealthy abbeys, so as not to burden the poor. In 1342 the seneschal of Poitou and Saintonge was ordered to 'take and raise' huge quantities of wheat and oats, along with 500 calves, 500 sheep, 200 beef cattle, 500 bacon pigs, 1,000 pipes of wine (500 tuns) and other supplies, for the Duke of Normandy's army.[15] Records show that the right of prise was used extensively to ensure that Calais was adequately victualled in 1346, when siege threatened. Twenty-four measures of grain were, for example, taken from the monastery of Saint-Fuscien at Amiens, and 32 measures from Saint-Valéry. As in England, there were widespread objections to the use of prise, with concessions made by the crown in return for grants of taxation. Promises were made in 1354 that a just price would be paid, but such assurances were worth little.[16] Where the crown provided men with victuals, the cost was deducted from their wages, which no doubt encouraged them to make their own arrangements. Victualling arrangements were not always adequate. Famine threatened the army which triumphed at Roosebeke in 1382, and a detachment of 200 was duly sent off to seek victuals and fodder. Increasingly, as in England, merchants were used. They were encouraged to take their goods to the royal armies; to prevent profiteering, the provost-marshal set fixed prices for their sale. In 1383 Nicholas Boullard, a Paris merchant, provided, so it was claimed, sufficient supplies to feed over 100,000 men for four months. A number of merchants were approached in 1388; just one, Colin Boullard (presumably related to Nicholas), agreed to provide victuals for the ineffective Guelders expedition that year, in return for 100,000 écus.[17]

LIVING OFF THE LAND

Effective as the systems for victualling armies may have been, living off the land was part of the routine of war. It made sense to do so, for it meant that fewer carts carrying supplies were needed. Yuval Harari worked out a theoretical scenario for an army of 10,000 men with 5,000 camp-followers, which showed that had it taken all the supplies needed for a campaign lasting 50 days, over 1,800 carts and more than 7,000 packhorses would have been needed. Large quantities of cattle could have been driven to provide meat. Harari suggested that his figures show that it was possible for a raiding army to carry all the supplies it needed.[18] In practice, such a supply train would have been impractical, and no armies operated in this way. Even on the king's 1355 campaign, which lasted a mere fortnight, the troops did not take enough with them, and 'all the foodstuffs and other supplies were taken into the cities and castles, so that there were no victuals for the English, and therefore they had to return to Calais'.[19]

Although abundant supplies had been brought from England, Edward III's men lived off the land from the outset of his campaign in 1346. A letter reported with evident pleasure the discovery of foodstuffs at Valognes, and of 1,000 tuns of wine at St-Lô. After the capture of Caen, the army stayed there two or three days to resupply with victuals that were there in plenty.[20] As the army was forced to advance further and further inland, up the Seine, foraging became increasingly important. Among other sources of food, the rivers provided welcome fresh fish.

When the Black Prince led his two great raids of 1355 and 1356 from Gascony, supplies sent from England were very limited. Instead, he was paid £6,666 to buy victuals locally. Descriptions of his raids emphasized the scale of destruction as town after town, village after village was sacked. 'Those who wished to do so went out and took provisions and forage, burning enemy territory, and they did everything that would bring back peace to the country.' Some days were difficult. One march was particularly hard on the horses, especially since there was no water for them, so they had to drink wine. It was perhaps less of a hardship for the men that their food had to be cooked in wine, but this was plainly not to their taste.[21]

Even with a lengthy baggage train, it would have been very difficult to take adequate supplies for Edward III's lengthy campaign in 1359–60. At the start, food, and particularly fodder for the horses, was hard to come by, as Artois had suffered acutely from the war. Matters improved when the Abbey of Fémy proved to have ample stocks of victuals. At Reims it was difficult to find sufficient supplies, for instructions had been given to the city authorities: 'You are to guard our said town, and all the grain and other victuals from all the land should be taken there; and if you cannot do this, destroy all that cannot be taken, so that our enemies cannot be helped in any way.'[22] Later in the campaign the discovery of ample supplies of wine at Tonnerre was extremely welcome. One story suggests that grinding the grain taken by foragers was a problem for the English, even though handmills had been brought from England. A group of five squires from the Black Prince's division seized a mill. As they were grinding corn, 50 men attacked, but they were driven off, with 11 slain. Near the close of the campaign, monasteries in the Beauce were seized, 'and through this the whole army was amply resupplied with food'. Lack of supplies for the horses was a major problem, compelling the troops on one occasion to make a long march in search of fodder. Thomas Gray explained in his *Scalacronica* that on this campaign Lancaster's men had 'lived all the time on the land, sometimes well, sometimes just as they found it, in lands already destroyed and raided by the English before their arrival'.[23]

Foraging was not easy, as was very evident on John of Gaunt's ambitious *chevauchée* across France in 1373. As it lasted almost five months, it would have been impossible to transport sufficient supplies for the men and horses, so living off the land was essential. Gaunt was unfortunate that there had been severe flooding, leading to the destruction of much stored produce. On occasion his men had to go without bread for five or six days. According to a French account, he had started out with over 30,000 horses, and reached Bordeaux with just 6,000, while a third of his men failed to complete the journey. Only a third of the carts got through. With so little transport, knights were forced to go on foot, having thrown away their armour when they could no longer carry it. However, lack of food only became an acute problem when Gaunt reached English-held Gascony, for he gave instructions that no one was to take foodstuffs without immediate payment. Living off the land was no longer possible.

Garrisons in towns and castles looked to the surrounding countryside for supplies. In 1352 Walter Bentley condemned the extortionate behaviour of the English garrison forces in Brittany, which he blamed on their lack of wages. In the early fifteenth century the rebuilding of the castle of Camarsac, near Bordeaux, was criticized because the garrison would inevitably descend on the locals and 'take their grain, wine, kids, calves and hay, and beat those who would not let them'.[24] However, it was not always easy to exploit the surrounding countryside. Villagers might succeed in hiding what food they had, and pillagers were in danger of attack. The English wintering in Vannes in 1381 sent out foragers, who found nothing save empty barns in the countryside, while the threat from French garrisons meant they could not ride far in search of food. It was supplies brought in by sea that saved the situation.

It made less sense for French armies to live off the land than it did for the English, for they were not operating in enemy territory as the English generally were. Even in Gascony, they were fighting in what they regarded as French lands. Yet often there cannot have been any option other than to seize food on the march. In 1373 Bertrand du Guesclin and Olivier de Clisson 'ransomed all the land around for victuals, and found much to pillage and to profit around the fine river Marne'.[25] The *routiers*, irrespective of who they were fighting for, had no compunction whatever. The chronicler Jean de Venette described the activities of the Archpriest's men: 'As long as war lasted his men had plundered the land extensively under colour of provisioning themselves for the conduct of war.' In 1365, 'as they passed through the county of Champagne, they rapidly despoiled its merchants and other inhabitants of horses, money, goods, furnishings, and food, wherever opportunity offered'.[26]

ARMS AND EQUIPMENT

Arms were needed as well as food. Knights and men-at-arms provided their own horses and equipment; the crown's stock of armour in the Tower of London was intended for members of the royal household, not the army as a whole. Archers, too, were supposed to come on campaign with all the equipment they needed. When the Black Prince ordered the recruitment of 300 Cheshire archers in 1359, they were 'to be well armed with bows and arrows and all the necessary equipment'. In practice, this was not enough, and in subsequent instructions the Prince's officials were ordered to provide green and white cloth for the men's uniforms, as well as bows and arrows.[27] The crown's efforts to ensure that archers had sufficient bows, bowstrings and arrows have been discussed above, in Chapter 7. Typically, in 1359 a royal writ announced that 'the king must have a great number of bows and arrows speedily for the furtherance of his war with France', and 115,000 sheaves of arrows were requested.[28] All this made work for bowyers and fletchers, who seemed to have little difficulty in meeting the crown's demands.

Other equipment was also required. Standards, banners and pennons were needed in profusion. To reduce the discomfort of campaigning, great men needed tents and pavilions. An account for 1346 reveals that for the expedition to Normandy the king had a 'cloister' of blue cloth, eight round tents, blue outside and green inside, two chapels, four green tents for hunting, three stables and a 'palace' of blue canvas. A 'great hall' called Bermondsey had six posts to hold it up. One tent was embroidered with crowns, and the cloth for the hall called Westminster featured roses. There was even a tent to be erected on the king's ship, the *George*.[29]

Froissart's description of the 1359 expedition as it left Calais brings out the sheer scale of the logistical operation: 'The carts, taking up two leagues in length, followed the king's battalion. There were over 6,000 carts, carrying all the army's provisions. There were items not previously brought with men-at-arms, such as hand-mills, cooking ovens, and other necessaries.' Five hundred workmen with spades and pick-axes were needed to level the roads and cut down trees so that the carts could pass. There were even light leather boats, so as to ensure a supply of fresh fish.[30]

***

The administrative and organizational effort put into campaigning was impressive. Surprisingly, however, this was not an area where the state, English or French, developed increasingly sophisticated and effective methods as the war proceeded. Rather, it was in the early stages of the war that governments put the most effort into organizing the supply of food and equipment. Increasingly, responsibility was laid on military commanders to make their own arrangements, while it became simpler to rely on merchants to provide victuals rather than making royal officials responsible.

10

AGINCOURT

Charles VI came to the French throne in 1380, at the age of 11. As early as 1382, according to Froissart, he was enthusiastic at the prospect of war, declaring that 'I do not want anything other than to arm myself. I have never been armed, and if I want to reign with honour and glory, I need to learn the art of arms.'[1] His personal rule began in 1388. He seemed to be all that was required of a king. Good-looking, he was of above average height though not too tall, and 'his nose was neither too long nor too short'.[2] He was a fine horseman and had considerable skill in the use of weapons; he was a good archer and could throw a javelin. An affable man, he entered into conversation with ease.

Yet Charles had major problems. On a hot day in 1392 he was riding near Le Mans with his companions. Startled when a page dropped his lance, in a frenzy Charles drew his sword, and attacked his brother, the Duke of Orléans. Eventually the king was subdued. His eyes rolled, he could not speak, nor could he recognize his companions. This was the first attack of a long series of illnesses in which the king lost his mind. He was unable to recognize anyone, claiming his name was George; there was no possible treatment for his many delusions. For five months he refused to change his clothes or to take baths, with the result that he was covered in lice, which burrowed deep into his flesh. The most plausible diagnosis is that Charles suffered from paranoid schizophrenia. For France, the king's condition was a disaster, leading as it did to bitter infighting

Fig. 13: Charles VI and his queen, Isabeau of Bavaria

between the dukes of Orléans and Burgundy. The feud would leave France divided for over 40 years. It provided the English under their new Lancastrian dynasty with fresh opportunities for intervention. English ambitions in France, however, were but one element in a highly complex situation.

BURGUNDY AND ORLÉANS

The rivalry between the houses of Burgundy and Orléans was disastrous for France. Philip, duke of Burgundy, was Charles VI's uncle. Through marriage to the daughter of the Count of Flanders, he acquired lands on a huge scale when his father-in-law died in 1384. He gained not only Flanders, but also Brabant and Artois in the Low Countries, and the Franche-Comté of Burgundy (held of the Empire). On Philip's death in 1404 he was succeeded by his son,

John the Fearless, so called for his bravery at the Battle of Nicopolis in 1396. For the Burgundian rulers, the commercial links of the Low Countries across the North Sea meant that peace with England made far more sense than war.

Louis, Charles VI's younger brother, became Duke of Orléans in 1392. Marriage to a daughter of Gian Galeazzo Visconti of Milan brought him wealth. His estates were dispersed across all of France, not concentrated so as to provide a single power-base. He did much to increase his landholdings, and his acquisition of rights over the duchy of Luxembourg in 1402 was a direct challenge to Burgundian power in the Low Countries. Eloquent, cultivated and pious, Louis was at the same time a gambler and something of a libertine.

There was no easy resolution of the rivalry between the dukes of Orléans and Burgundy. Assassination offered a horrific solution, and in 1407 Orléans was murdered in Paris, an act for which the Duke of Burgundy accepted responsibility. Two years later he was pardoned by the king, and with the support of the queen, Isabeau of Bavaria, he seized power in France. His rivals were a powerful group, headed by the new Duke of Orléans, which included the dukes of Berry and Bourbon, the counts of Armagnac and Alençon, and Charles d'Albret. Orléans was married to a daughter of the Count of Armagnac; the faction was soon termed the Armagnacs. There was real hatred between Armagnacs and Burgundians. Seeking support, the Armagnacs turned to England under Henry IV, and a formal alliance was agreed at Bourges in 1412. The Burgundians led Charles VI to the siege of Bourges, which featured two great bombards, called *Griete* and *Griele*. The siege ended with negotiations; the keys were handed over to the king. Peace, of a sort, was re-established, and the Armagnac treaty with England was renounced. Yet the civil war soon reopened. In 1414 Soissons was taken by the Armagnacs, and sacked with full brutality. 'It was said that the Saracens had never done worse than what those in the army did as result of the evil counsel of those around the king.'[3]

WAR UNDER HENRY IV

Given the heated political atmosphere in Paris, it is hardly surprising that the war with the English was not pursued with great vigour when it reopened following the fall of Richard II in 1399 and the advent of the new Lancastrian monarchy. Most of the action took place in the south-west. The English hold on Gascony was much reduced from what it had been under Edward III, amounting to the cities of Bordeaux and Bayonne, their hinterlands and a strip of land linking the two. Beyond that, there were fortresses held by *routier* captains with a loose allegiance to the English. Yet for many Gascons, English rule seemed preferable to French. This puzzled the scholar Jean de Montreuil, who considered that the Gascons 'through ignorance, thought things were otherwise than they were, and were guided by error and false information to the opposite of the truth'.[4] In 1405 the English suffered major losses. Bordeaux itself came under siege, and a large number of English-held fortresses fell. By 1406 the English position in Gascony was on the verge of total collapse. The Duke of Orléans led a substantial Armagnac army to besiege Bourg and Blaye; if they fell there was little hope for Bordeaux. However, the siege of Bourg proved difficult. It had been unwise to attempt the operation in winter. A fleet bringing supplies to the army failed to force its way through. The besiegers suffered badly from the cold, disease and lack of supplies, and in January 1407 the siege was abandoned. Henry IV had provided little by way of assistance to the Gascons, yet the duchy had survived.[5] Meanwhile, in the north, the Duke of Burgundy's attempt to lay siege to Calais was abandoned. Truces followed; France was in no state to conduct an effective war.

There were small-scale attempts by the French and their Castilian allies on the English coast in these years, but these did not create the level of panic that those of the 1370s had done. In 1404 a French fleet reached Falmouth, and prepared to fire the town. The local peasantry rallied; the French crossbowmen drove them back, but only one man was killed. He had charged on horseback, and had his head chopped off by a Spanish fighter. Then, 'his horse carried him, headless, 120 paces, before his trunk fell to the ground'.[6] In the following year, Castilian galleys had no more success. A skirmish with the locals took place at Portland, and there was an inconclusive engagement at Poole, after which 'the arrows lay so thick upon the ground that no man could walk without treading on arrows in such numbers that they picked them up in handfuls'. Under the impression that they had reached London, when in fact they were outside Southampton, the Castilians turned their galleys towards the Norman coast and safety.[7]

Henry IV displayed military ambition very early in his reign, though a two-week-long invasion of Scotland in 1400 achieved little. While the king and his son were dealing with Owain Glyndŵr's rebellion in Wales, in 1402 Henry Percy, known as Hotspur, crushed a Scottish invasion of Northumberland at Humbleton Hill, near Wooler. In a further disaster for the Scots, shortly before his father Robert III died in 1406, the young heir to the Scottish throne, James, was captured at sea, on his way to safety in France. He remained in English hands until 1424, and this ended the prospect of direct conflict between England and Scotland. Many Scots, however, went to France to fight the English, particularly after 1415.

It was not until 1411 that the English once again sent an expedition to northern France. The earls of Arundel and Warwick led a small army from Calais in support of the Duke of Burgundy. The English archers proved their worth in fighting around Paris, but the expedition as a whole achieved little. That autumn saw English policies reversed. The Prince of Wales had been dominant since early in 1410, and it had been he who favoured the Burgundian cause in France. Now, late in 1411, the king reasserted himself. In the following year, Armagnac ambassadors offered to restore all of Aquitaine to the English. The Prince of Wales was bitterly opposed to abandoning support for Burgundy, and therefore command of a new expedition, in support of the Armagnacs, was given to his younger brother, Thomas duke of Clarence. He led a *chevauchée* from Saint-Vaast-la-Hogue to the Loire valley in 1412. No fighting took place, but Clarence demanded an impressive 150,000 écus as a condition for leading his troops back to England.

HARFLEUR

Henry V came to the throne in 1413. He had military experience, for he had fought the Percies at Shrewsbury in 1403, and had led forces to put down the Glyndŵr rebellion in Wales. An arrow in the face at Shrewsbury, removed with a special surgical instrument, left him with the scar of a veteran soldier. Like many heirs to the throne, he had been at loggerheads with his father. A cultured man, his deeply-felt piety was thoroughly orthodox. He encouraged the use of the English language in government, an indication of the importance of his nationality to him. Records show that he took an active interest in the details of administration, checking accounts and responding to complaints put before him. He did not transform government, but he did his best to ensure that it operated in the best interests of his subjects.

Diplomatic efforts to achieve a lasting peace between England and France came to nothing. Henry V envisaged marrying Charles VI's daughter Catherine, and obtaining a territorial settlement which would see him hold Aquitaine, Normandy, Maine, Anjou, Touraine, Poitou and Ponthieu, and more besides, in full sovereignty. He would abandon his claim to the French throne, and the French would pay what was still due from King John's ransom. Unsurprisingly, the negotiations broke down. Discussions with the Burgundians were no more successful, for early in 1415 the Burgundians and Armagnacs came to terms. As diplomacy was not yielding the results Henry looked for, he turned to war. He faced a new leader in France, for in April, Louis the Dauphin, aged 18, took control of the government of a country which was still bitterly divided.

Indentures made with leading captains left the destination of the 1415 expedition open; the king would either campaign 'in our duchy of Guyenne, or in our kingdom of France'.[8] In the event, Henry took his army of some 10,000 men to Normandy, to besiege Harfleur. The port was important, for it commanded the Seine estuary, the route towards Rouen and onwards upstream to Paris. A letter from the chancellor of Gascony, written at Harfleur, explained that rather than entering the town after its capture, the king 'intends to go to Montivilliers, and thence to Dieppe, afterwards to Rouen, and then to Paris'.[9]

The English lacked recent experience in siege warfare; the last town they had captured was Limoges in 1370, and the last large-scale successful siege that of Calais in 1346–7. Harfleur was well defended. However, the English had formidable siege weapons; the Monk of St Denis explained that 'among them were some of extraordinary size, which cast enormous stones in the midst of thick smoke, with a horrible noise such that you would have thought they came from hell's fury'.[10] In all, about 7,500 gunstones were fired.

The outworks were gradually weakened by the bombardment, and much damage was done to the houses within the town. It proved impractical to mine the walls, or to use movable wooden towers to make an assault, but after five weeks a final attack on the barbican persuaded the garrison that further resistance was futile. The French had made no attempt to save the town, perhaps persuaded that the English army was far larger than was the case. A captured Frenchman was released by the English on condition that he told Jean Fusoris, canon of Notre Dame in Paris (a notable maker of clocks and other instruments), 'that the king of England had landed in France, and had taken land in front of Harfleur, which he was besieging accompanied by 50,000 men'.[11] He was also to say that they had 4,000 tons of flour and 4,000 tons of wine, and a dozen great siege guns.

In fact, the government had made surprisingly few efforts to ensure that the army was properly supplied with victuals. Bakers and brewers in Hampshire had prepared for the arrival of the troops ready for embarkation at Portsmouth, but responsibility for taking foodstuffs to France was laid firmly on the men themselves, who were instructed to have sufficient supplies for three months. Keeping a large army immobile for weeks at Harfleur was asking for trouble, particularly given the inevitable insanitary conditions of an encampment. Dysentery swept through the lines, affecting nobles and common soldiers alike. The records show that, because of the epidemic, 1,330 men were allowed to leave for England. Whether this was a true total is open to question; many were said to have 'stealthily slipped away to England' out of 'sheer cowardice'.[12]

The siege ended with a negotiated surrender, followed by a magnificent ceremony. The king sat on his throne, decked with cloth of gold. His helmet, bearing his crown, was on his right, mounted on a staff. The French commander handed over the keys to the town. A feast followed, at which the hostages surrendered by the townspeople were entertained. A further formality followed, when Henry issued a challenge to the Dauphin, offering to settle the issue between their two countries by personal combat, and demanding a response within eight days. Arguments in the royal council followed. According to the account by Henry's chaplain, the king proposed a march to Calais, but most of the councillors argued that this was far too dangerous. The French might 'enclose them on every side like sheep in folds'.[13]

AGINCOURT

Henry's purpose in marching to Calais is not clear. He was taking an extraordinary risk. It is all too easy to assume that the eventual outcome was what was originally intended, but for Anne Curry, 'The idea that the march northwards was the result of his desire for battle is not credible.' Clifford Rogers has argued the opposite case, suggesting that Henry 'hoped for a general engagement'.[14] The French, however, had not attempted battle during the siege of Harfleur, and it must have seemed unlikely that they would do so. Yet, as events were to show, the English army was prepared for battle. Further, the king was imbued with a strong religious sense of mission; as his chaplain put it, he was 'relying entirely on divine help and the justice of his own cause'.[15] There was, however, no rush to battle on Henry's part, nor did he try to negotiate with the French as to where and when to fight.

The French intended to fight. Remarkably, a plan showing how the troops would be drawn up in order of battle survives. The veteran Marshal Boucicaut was primarily responsible for it; he had battle experience from Roosebeke in 1382 and Nicopolis in 1396. He had good information about the English army, noting that Henry might form his men into one single division. The plan set out the way in which a cavalry force 'would attack the archers and break their power'.[16] Another division would attack the English baggage train. In practice, the narrow terrain at Agincourt meant that the plan was not fully carried through. In particular, the French crossbowmen and archers were not placed in front of the two flanking wings of troops. However, the plan shows that the French were well prepared for the coming battle.

Henry did not have a large army. His chaplain estimated it at 900 men-at-arms and 5,000 archers. Anne Curry, using the records, has calculated that it totalled 8,680 men; Rogers prefers an estimate of about 6,000. Contemporaries would not have had access to the muster rolls available to the modern historian, but there are difficulties in working out the numbers. Records show that the Earl of Arundel's retinue lost 87 men out of 400 through sickness, yet his accounts suggest that it was only six men-at-arms below strength on the campaign.[17] Whether the army numbered around 6,000 or 8,500 is a nice point for historians to debate; what is important is that it was much smaller than the French host.

French numbers are even more difficult to calculate. Contemporary estimates varied wildly, as do those by historians. Curry has argued that the army totalled about 12,000 men. Given that plans at the end of August were to raise a host of 6,000 men-at-arms and 3,000 archers, this seems reasonable. Rogers, however, considers that the conventional estimate of around 24,000 men is acceptable. One problem is whether those termed *gros varlets* were combatants, or just support staff. [18] The contemporary view was that the French substantially outnumbered the English, four to one being a common estimate. All that can be safely concluded is that the English were at a considerable numerical disadvantage. Not only was there a clear disparity in overall numbers between the two armies, but there was also an even greater difference in the count of men-at-arms, for the French had a much higher proportion of such men in their ranks than did the English.

The English march from Harfleur was difficult. Orders had been given that the men were to take supplies for eight days. This was totally inadequate, for all the bridges over the Somme were broken, and the army was forced upstream. It took a week and a half to reach a crossing point. The troops were hungry, and rumours were rife that the French were about to attack. The French then challenged Henry to battle, though without specifying when or where. Campaigns were frequently punctuated by such challenges; how genuinely they were intended is a difficult question. The army continued its march; the French were then spotted, in battle array, higher up a valley. They withdrew after a time, and the English spent the night waiting in silence. On the next day, 25 October, the French drew up their forces blocking the road to Calais, close to Agincourt. The vanguard was on foot, flanked by cavalry. The main body of men-at-arms was dismounted, while the rearguard was mounted. In contrast to the Battle of Crécy, on this occasion it was the French who chose the battle site.

The English knights and men-at-arms were in three side-by-side divisions. There has been much inconclusive argument over the way the archers were disposed. Were there formations of archers between the divisions, or were they all on the flanks? The chaplain's account states that Henry interposed wedges of archers in each line. One French account has it that Henry told his troops that 'our 12,000 archers will range themselves in a circle around us'. Another suggests that the archers were behind the main English formation, and yet another that they were on both flanks of the men-at-arms.[19] Any answer to the problem needs to take into account the fact that the archers greatly outnumbered the men-at-arms; most diagrams of the battle suggest the opposite. The evidence is contradictory, but it seems likely that there were large formations of archers on each flank of the English army, and that there were also archers around, and intermingled among, the men-at-arms. There was one innovation in the archers' equipment. They were provided with lead mallets, used to hammer in stakes to be cut on campaign. There was a possible precedent for this, as stakes for protection were used by the Turks in 1396 at Nicopolis when they defeated a crusading army, though whether the English commanders would have been aware of this is open to question.

The two armies stood still for some time, neither prepared to move. Some of the French 'had gone off to get warm, others to walk and feed their horses, not believing that the English would be so bold as to attack them'.[20] They were quite mistaken, for the English eventually took the initiative. On Henry's orders Thomas Erpingham, steward of the king's household, threw his baton in the air, signalling that the archers should advance. There has been argument over how far they moved forward. It was surely very risky for the archers to lift their stakes, march through thick mud, and then replant the stakes. This would have left them open to attack from the French. One tempting answer is that the English advanced just a short distance. The implication of most of the sources, however, is that the English moved forward a considerable way, with much shouting. When the French cavalry charged towards them, many riders were driven back by the hail of arrows, their horses maddened and uncontrollable.

The French men-at-arms advanced on foot in three columns. By the time they reached the English lines they were exhausted from struggling through the mud. In the mêlée the English archers, unencumbered by armour, used their mallets and stakes to savage the French. The front was too narrow for French numbers to be of any advantage. Rather, their forces, crammed together, became an unmanageable crowd. When those in front were halted by the English, their comrades pushed forward from behind. This was not the behaviour of an army, but of a mob, crushing in on itself. Soon, great heaps of dead and dying men built up. It was horrific. It was not only the French who died in this mass; no less a man than the Duke of York was killed in the press of desperate men. It seems that about 90 of his following were either slain, or died later of their wounds.

The battle seemed won, but there was panic when it seemed that the French rearguard was about to attack. Henry gave orders that the prisoners who had been taken should be killed. Many were slain, and the French withdrew from the field of battle. Henry's action has been much criticized, but contemporaries did not accuse him of acting contrary to the laws or conventions of war. Burgundian chroniclers provided a very different justification for the killing. It was the fault of 'the wretched company of the French' who had regrouped, threatening a renewal of the battle.[21] Nor was Henry's command wholly exceptional; the Battle of Aljubarrota was another where prisoners were slain.

Why were the English victorious? Contemporary explanations were, for the most part, simple. God had given the English victory: 25 October was the day of two obscure saints, Crispin and Crispinianus, and it may be that as the claimant to the French throne, Henry considered it sensible to attribute the victory to the intercession of French saints. He also acknowledged St John of Beverley, for 25 October was the day of his translation. For the English, the victory was a divine sentence on Henry's claim to the French throne. For the French, it was a verdict on the evils that affected society. Sex was part of the explanation; as Henry had 'not consented to burning, ravaging, violating nor raping girls and women', the English troops had showed themselves to be more virtuous than the French, whose forces had shown no restraint prior to the battle.[22] Arthur de Richemont, later Constable of France, provided a straightforward military explanation. Richemont himself was captured in the battle, and his biographer preserved his views. The battlefield was too narrow for so many to fight; the cavalry that should have attacked the wings of the English army were driven back by archery, and in retreating broke up the French lines, which could barely be reassembled before the English were on them.

The command structure of the English army was clear, that of the French was not. Henry V appointed the Duke of York to lead the vanguard. Henry himself led the central division, and Thomas, Lord Camoys, the rearguard. The choice of the latter is one of the mysteries of the campaign, for Camoys was elderly and had relatively little military experience. As for the French, neither the king nor the Dauphin were present; the young Duke of Orléans, the most senior noble at the battle, only arrived shortly before hostilities began. D'Albret and Boucicaut, as Constable and Marshal, had an important role in command, while there were many nobles, such as the Duke of Bourbon and the Duke of Alençon, in leading positions. 'All the lords wanted to be in the first battle, so that each would have as much honour as another, as they could not agree to do anything else.'[23] Debate and discussion characterized the French leadership, as compared to the English army, in which one man provided determined direction.

The terrain was important in determining the outcome of the battle. The site of the battle was chosen by the French, presumably because the woods on either side made it simpler to block the English route to Calais. However, it also nullified the French advantage in numbers, for they were forced to fight on a relatively narrow front, probably of not much more than 750 yards. With rain-soaked fields newly ploughed, mud was a major problem. It made it impossible to use cavalry effectively, and it was exhausting for heavily armoured men-at-arms to struggle though.

Most explanations of the battle emphasize the importance of English archery. The French were better protected by armour from the hail of arrows than they had been in the days of Crécy, but English archery was highly effective in the early stages of the battle, particularly against the horses. If there were about 6,000 English archers, they would have had some 150,000 arrows to shoot. While arrows may not have killed many soldiers, they could cause disabling wounds. Letting fly a barrage was not the only importance of the archers. Men-at-arms were vulnerable to the nimble English archers in the appalling mêlée. Joints in the carapaces of armour were vulnerable to knives and daggers, while steel plate could not withstand crushing blows from the leaden mallets.

Questions about morale, courage and cowardice are not easy to answer. The English should have been despondent. They were exhausted and hungry after the march from Harfleur; the French had cleared the land before them, so that there were no food supplies to plunder. They were well aware that they were heavily outnumbered. Prior to the battle, Henry did his best to encourage them, riding along the lines on a small horse, making speeches as he went. One account has it that he told his men that 'the French had boasted that if any English archers were captured they would cut off the three fingers of their right hand', which can hardly have improved their mood.[24] There must have been a determination born of desperation in the English lines. The troops were also well disciplined, for this was an issue that Henry took very seriously. There was nothing particularly novel about the ordinances he issued at the start of the campaign, but the king was a strict disciplinarian, and he took their enforcement with a rare resolve.

Some of the senior French commanders, notably Boucicaut and d'Albret, were dubious about fighting. The general mood among the French, however, was enthusiastic, with much eagerness to be in the front line. That was where honour was to be won with great feats of arms. Individual acts of chivalrous bravery ended in disaster; one knight broke free from the rest of the cavalry. Riding ahead, he was promptly killed. The Duke of Brabant hastened into the battle, short of men and equipment. The moment he dismounted to fight, he was slain. Overconfidence among the French was quickly reversed. Many will not have fought at all, leaving the grim battlefield in fear for their lives. In his *Livre des quatres dames*, written soon after the defeat, the poet Alain Chartier condemned the coward at Agincourt 'who was so led on by his own selfishness to flee from that place and to harm others, who made his bascinet shine and put on armour only to flee'.[25] For Ghillebert de Lannoy, taken prisoner at Agincourt, 'If I was in a battle I would prefer to be found among the dead than listed with those who fled.'[26]

THE PRISONERS

Not all the prisoners taken at Agincourt were killed on the battlefield. Those of political and financial value, among them the dukes of

Orléans and Bourbon, the counts of Richemont and Vendôme and Marshal Boucicaut, were taken back to England. They were paraded through London in Henry's triumphal procession. Whereas Boucicaut had been ransomed fairly quickly after his capture by Sultan Bayezid at Nicopolis, this time he was held in reasonably comfortable captivity until his death in 1421. Richemont agreed to support the English, and returned to Brittany in 1420. Bourbon remained a prisoner until his death in 1434. Vendôme was held prisoner until 1424, and Charles of Orléans was not freed until 1440. Holding the prisoners provided Henry with some political leverage, but it was hardly chivalric.

The treatment of some lesser prisoners showed Henry's vindictiveness. One group was kept in the Fleet prison, 'living from alms waiting for the grace and pity of God and the king', until they were finally released after the king's death.[27] Others were more

Fig. 14: An imaginative engraving showing Henry V and his standard-bearer, with a prisoner kneeling before him

fortunate. Wounded in the knee and the head, Ghillebert de Lannoy was taken to a house with some others taken in the battle. When the order came to kill the prisoners, so as to save the trouble of cutting their throats one by one, the English set fire to the house. Ghillebert managed to crawl to safety. When the English returned, his captors sold him to John Cornewall. He was taken to England, and in 1416 was ransomed for 1,200 gold écus and a horse. Cornewall even gave him 20 nobles to buy the equipment he needed.[28]

***

Like most battles, Agincourt was not decisive. It did not provide Henry with what he wanted in France, nor did it help to resolve the continuing rivalry of Burgundians and Armagnacs. Far from concluding the war, it led to its continuation. Henry supposed that his victory was a divine verdict on the justice of his cause, but it fell far short of delivering his aims in full. The next phase was the conquest of Normandy.

11

THE CONQUEST OF NORMANDY

The character of the war changed in the fifteenth century. Though there were significant battles after Agincourt, notably at Verneuil, Patay, Formigny and Castillon, siege warfare dominated what was increasingly a war of attrition. The age of the *chevauchée* was over. In part this was because the defence of Normandy, conquered by Henry V, created a new situation, and in part it was because the balance between attack and defence of towns and castles shifted with the development of gunpowder artillery. Further, English archers were no longer as invincible as they had been in the fourteenth century. Nor was the war often punctuated by chivalric incidents and interludes.

THE INVASION OF 1417

In 1416, diplomacy had achieved little, despite the efforts of the emperor Sigismund to broker a peace. Military activity was centred on Harfleur. In April 1416 the Earl of Dorset, captain of the town, wrote in some desperation to the king's council. His men could not 'long endure without provision of supplies and other things', above all meat, grain and malt. Commissions had in fact been issued before the earl's letter was received, for the collection of 1,000 quarters of wheat, the same amount of oats, 2,000 quarters of malt and 1,000 quarters of beans and peas had been ordered, along with 200 bacon pigs and 200 oxen.[1] In August an important naval battle took place, which saved Harfleur. An English fleet, of perhaps 200–300 ships, commanded by Bedford, engaged a smaller Franco-Genoese force in the Seine estuary. Fierce hand-to-hand fighting lasted for several hours. Two of the royal ships, the *Holy Ghost* and the *Trinity Royal*, suffered damage to rigging and sails. The English captured three large ships, and one was sunk.

In 1417 Henry sailed for Normandy with an army some 10,000 strong. His aim now was conquest. The strategy was entirely different from that of the *chevauchées* of the past, which had aimed to put pressure on the French and bring them to battle provided the conditions were right. Now, the aim was not to burn and destroy. Henry intended a war in which towns and castles would be captured and held by the English, and an entire province taken over and occupied.

Caen fell after just two weeks, stormed and brutally sacked by Henry's troops. Many other places surrendered. The castle at Falaise held out against the English for over two months, until February 1418. Cherbourg fell in the following September after a five-month siege. The castle at Domfront, with its old Norman keep, held out for four months. Elsewhere, English commanders oversaw capitulations on a startling scale. The major operation, which began in August, was the siege of Rouen. A ditch and bank was constructed round the city, and the English prevented access from the river Seine. Food began to run out: the citizens 'had no bread, or ale or wine, only water and vinegar to drink. And they had no meat or fish; they ate horses, dogs, mice, rats and cats.'[2] The city authorities turned the elderly and infirm out of the gates, so as to preserve supplies for a few more weeks. Henry's attitude was merciless. He would not let them through the English lines, nor would he provide food for them. Only for Christmas Day did he relent. Finally, in January, Rouen surrendered. Hostages were handed over, and along with other terms, payment of a substantial fine was agreed.

The conquest of Normandy demonstrated Henry V's mastery of the art of siege warfare. This was much more important in the long term than the dramatic victory at Agincourt. Armies faced major problems when confronted with stone walls. Castles and walled towns acted as 'force multipliers', enabling a small number of men to resist far larger forces. Henry may not have been responsible for any striking advances in the art of siege-craft, but efficient organization and carefully considered strategy brought the results he needed. As always, intelligence was important. For example, the captain of Calais was asked to send reliable men to the borders of Picardy and elsewhere 'to spy and observe the intentions of our adversary and those of his party, especially what they intend to do and to proceed against us'.[3]

GUNS AND LOGISTICS

Henry fully appreciated the potential of gunpowder artillery. Royal letters show that he took an active personal interest in ensuring that artillery was available where it was required. He noted with some irritation that 'We have understood that out great guns at Caen may not be brought down to the waterside to be shipped in the vessel we sent there for this', and asked that the ship should instead be loaded with 'as many gunstones of the greatest sort that lie on the wharf there'.[4] An official, the clerk of ordnance, ensured effective provision of guns, powder and ammunition, with depots established at Caen and Rouen. At Falaise, the town surrendered through 'terror of the guns', and a bombardment ruined the castle.[5] In addition, Henry and his commanders used a wide range of siege equipment and methods. Stone-throwing machines, such as trebuchets, were widely employed. Mining was often attempted, though with limited success. Wooden siege towers might be deployed. Where weapons failed, blockade succeeded.

Great efforts were made to ensure that there was a sufficient supply of bows and arrows. In a remarkable order of 1417, the sheriffs were ordered to take six wing-feathers from every goose in the land, while the use of ash for clogs was forbidden, as the wood was needed for arrows. By 1420 the crown was demanding the purchase of 400,000 arrows in England, while further supplies were being manufactured in Normandy.

Though the crown no longer took steps to collect foodstuffs as it had in the first half of the fourteenth century, measures were put in place to ensure that troops were properly supplied. English merchants were encouraged to take victuals to Normandy. In 1417 anyone shipping goods to Caen was excused payment of customs duties. In the following year the king asked the Londoners to organize shipping to go to Harfleur, laden with food and especially drink, and from there up the Seine to Rouen, the main distribution centre. As the conquest proceeded, careful arrangements were made to ensure that the English-held castles were properly supplied.

THE NAVY

Henry himself fought no naval battles, but he appreciated that the security of the sea was essential if he was to succeed in France. To transport his troops, he largely relied on the tested methods of arresting merchant ships and taking them into royal service. In addition, he built up a small fleet of royal ships. The maximum number of such vessels under Henry IV had been six, but when Henry V came to the throne, there were only two capable of going to sea. Six ships were swiftly acquired in 1413, soon followed by others. These were all bought, but a building programme also began in that year, with work on the *Trinity Royal*. Nine royal ships were in the fleet that sailed for Harfleur in 1415; Henry himself sailed on the *Trinity Royal*. By 1417 the royal ships numbered 32, including some that had been captured.

Henry's ambitions for his fleet went beyond what was technologically possible. He clearly considered that, at least when it came to ships, size mattered. The *Grace Dieu* was laid down in 1416, and at 1,400 tons was probably the largest ship built in England before the seventeenth century. She was double the displacement of Henry VIII's *Mary Rose*. Launched in 1418, she never left the Hamble estuary. Her simple two-masted rig was not sufficient for a ship of such size, and her clinker construction, with overlapping planks, was not ideal. Yet more ambitious was the ship that was begun at Bayonne, measuring 186 feet from bow to stern, with a beam of 46 feet. However, a letter about the progress of the build remarked of the keel that 'he is rotted, and must be changed'.[6] Had this ship been completed, she would not have been exceeded in size by any British naval vessel until the launch of HMS *Britannia* in 1682.

SETTLEMENT, DIPLOMACY AND WAR

Conquest involved settlement. Henry V granted six Norman counties to his chief commanders in 1418–19, and many lesser soldiers were rewarded with grants of land in the duchy. The need to provide for the defence of Normandy explains why Henry made grants of land conditional upon the provision of military service. Feudal service was long outmoded both in England and France, but it made sense to ensure that those who received lands should contribute to the efforts that would be needed to defend them. English merchants were encouraged to settle in Harfleur and Caen. Some English clerics received canonries in Normandy. All this helped to create a vested interest in the English retention of Normandy.

Henry benefited from French collapse and disunity. The Dauphin had died in December 1415. The next of the king's sons in line to the throne was Jean, whose marriage to a daughter of the Count of Hainault put him in the Burgundian camp, though the government remained in Armagnac hands. Jean, however, died in 1417; the next Dauphin was the future Charles VII. French government finances were at a very low ebb; one calculation is that receipts in 1418 were the equivalent of 17 tonnes of silver, in contrast to 88 tonnes around 1390. The currency was also heavily debased.[7] In politics, the breach with Burgundy was disastrous. In 1418 Paris came under Burgundian control amid scenes of horrendous violence. The Count of Armagnac was brutally slain by the mob. The Dauphin, however, was saved, and in the following year it seemed that John, duke of Burgundy would be reconciled with him. With reluctance, the duke agreed to a meeting in September, on the bridge at Montereau. There he knelt before the future king. As he rose up, he was attacked by one of the Dauphin's men with a sword. Another struck him with an axe. Whether his assassination was premeditated cannot be conclusively proven, but a good deal of evidence points to a plot in which the Dauphin himself was complicit. The murder of the Duke of Orléans in 1407 was avenged, but at an appalling cost to France.

The murder of the Duke of Burgundy led his successor, Philip, to support the English cause. An Anglo-Burgundian alliance was sealed in December 1419. Peace between England and France was agreed in the Treaty of Troyes in May 1420. Henry was to marry the French king's daughter, Catherine. The Dauphin was to be disinherited, and Henry would act as regent in France. On Charles VI's death, the French crown would pass to Henry or his heir. This put the English position in France on a new footing. No longer was it a matter of the claim to the throne through descent from Philip IV; the English accepted Charles VI as king of France, and the French accepted Henry V's position as his heir. There was, of course, a problem. The Armagnacs did not accept the treaty. For them, the Dauphin remained the rightful heir. France south of the Loire, apart from English-held Gascony, largely supported his cause. He ruled what became known as the kingdom of Bourges. Even in England there was concern about the treaty, with worries expressed in parliament that 'neither his said kingdom of England nor the people of the same, of whatever status or condition they might be, should at any time in the future be placed in subjection to or obedience to him, his heirs and successors, as king of France'.[8]

With the Treaty of Troyes, English interests expanded far beyond Normandy. A new stage of conquest began, with attacks on places held by troops loyal to the Dauphin. Melun, south-east of Paris, was a major obstacle. The siege began in July 1420. Bombards and trebuchets failed to reduce the place. A mine was met by a countermine; Henry V and the Duke of Burgundy themselves fought underground. Disease struck the besieging army; many of the Burgundians left. Eventually, in November, the defenders surrendered, hungry and exhausted. Many were taken off to imprisonment in Paris; Henry was not a man to be merciful.

Paris itself was in a dreadful state. The Armagnacs, by one account, were all around the city, 'pillaging, robbing, setting fires, killing, and raping women, girls and nuns'.[9] Food prices hit exorbitant levels. In December Henry V entered the city with his queen, along with Charles VI and Queen Isabeau, and the Duke of Burgundy. A court was held, in which the Dauphin was held guilty for the murder at Montereau and declared unfit to rule. When Henry left Paris, he appointed his brother Clarence to the captaincy of the city. The English occupation began.

A major setback for the English came in 1421, when Henry V's brother, the Duke of Clarence, led a raid into territory held by the Dauphin's supporters. At Baugé, not far from Angers, he was killed when he engaged a Franco-Scottish force, which included the earls of Buchan and Wigtown. The earls of Huntingdon and Somerset headed the list of notable prisoners; Huntingdon was released in 1426, for a ransom of about £13,000. Somerset was less fortunate, and was not freed until 1438, at a cost of £24,000. Yet catastrophic as it seemed at the time, Baugé was no more than a single reverse. The Dauphin marched towards Paris, only to be forced back when Henry V returned from a visit to England. The king then led a campaign which succeeded in capturing Dreux and a number of other places. He was as savage as ever: a group of 50 or 60 French skirmishers who had taken refuge in a castle were all drowned in revenge for the death of a single Englishman. The final siege was that of Meaux, which began in October 1421. The defenders held out for seven months, giving up the fight just as the English were about to deploy a huge wooden tower, floating on two large ships. Executions followed the surrender; Henry V was unmerciful. He was, however, fully entitled under the law of arms to act as he did, though one later comment on the death of the French commander (a man renowned for vicious cruelty) was that 'it was not an honourable deed for such a valiant king as the king of England to have put to death such a brave man-at-arms and nobleman just because he had so loyally served his sovereign lord'.[10] It is likely that it was at Meaux that Henry contracted the illness that would kill him; he died in August 1422.

HENRY V'S ACHIEVEMENT

Henry's many successes testify to his abilities as a military leader. He was inspirational, and not just at Agincourt where he encouraged his men in the long night of worry before the battle. Keeping his forces together in the lengthy sieges of Rouen and of Meaux cannot have been easy, but he had the right qualities for leadership. Henry's personal charisma must have been significant, but affection and admiration for the king were not the only elements. Discipline was an important key. Henry had no qualms about enforcing his will through executions. An austere man, his faith provided him with confidence in his intentions. He had a strategic grasp, displayed better in his later campaigns than on the Agincourt expedition. He was, of course, fortunate. Agincourt was a victory won against the odds, and one which saw the French desolated and discouraged.

The assassination on the bridge at Montereau meant that rather than the neutrality which had been the most the English could expect from Burgundy, Henry had full Burgundian support in his final campaigns.

The Treaty of Troyes meant that the English claim to the French throne was radically transformed, with the recognition of Charles VI as king for his lifetime, and the French acknowledgement of Henry V as his heir. Paris itself was in English hands, and the Bastille had an English garrison, though the city officials were mostly Burgundian, and its defence largely the responsibility of the citizens. Nor did the English find the Parisians always welcoming. One night in 1424 two of them shouted at Jeanette Bardin, described as 'an amorous woman', who was asleep in her house. Not knowing them, and suspicious of their intentions, she blocked their entry. They tried to force their way in, but she retaliated by throwing stones at them, and hit one on the head. He died some days later.[11]

CRAVANT AND VERNEUIL

Henry V's death was shortly followed by that of Charles VI. Under the terms of the Treaty of Troyes, he was to be succeeded by the English king's heir, the infant Henry VI. The Dauphin, Charles VII, was a far more plausible candidate for the throne. His decision in 1422 to establish a strong currency, after frequent debasements in the previous five years, was indicative of a new approach. There was, however, no sudden collapse of the English position. They had a very capable leader in Henry V's brother, John duke of Bedford. In 1423 the Anglo-Burgundian forces triumphed at Cravant in Burgundy over a Franco-Scottish army. Careful arrangements were made in advance to ensure that the allies took an equal part and did not quarrel. These provide exceptional evidence of the advance planning that took place. There was to be a forward party of 60 English and 60 Burgundians. The men-at-arms were ordered to dismount; their pages were to take the horses well to the rear. As at Agincourt, the archers would have stakes for their protection. Once the army was drawn up for battle, no one was to leave their position under pain of death. Prisoners were not to be taken until the battle was won. The English, under the Earl of Salisbury, forced a crossing

Fig. 15: John, duke of Bedford

of the river Yonne with the aid of their archers. A barrage from 30 or more Burgundian guns, *veuglaires* brought from Auxerre, slew many, as did the English arrows. A sortie by the besieged garrison caught the French from the rear. The Anglo-Burgundian army won the day; the Scots, cursing in bad French, suffered particularly badly from the defeat.

The next year saw the English win a far greater victory at Verneuil, in Normandy. The English, who had a large force themselves, estimated that the French numbered 14,000. This may have included as many as 6,500 Scots. The initial trigger was the siege of the castle at Ivry. Agreement had been reached for its surrender, provided it was not relieved by 15 August. The French were too late, and responded by capturing nearby Verneuil-sur-Avre by trickery. Bedford then marched to confront the French army. Both sides sought battle, though by one account there was a dispute among the French commanders, with the younger nobles and the Scots eager to fight. The English spent the night in prayer;

the chronicler Waurin commented sardonically that 'by nature they are very devout, especially before drinking'.[12]

The Battle of Verneuil is hard to reconstruct; as so often, the sources do not tell a consistent story. The armies were drawn up in familiar fashion. The English divisions of dismounted men-at-arms were flanked by formations of archers, equipped with stakes. Some archers stood in front of the men-at-arms. The carts and horses were held in the rear. Some 2,000 archers protected this baggage train. The main French force was dismounted, but it was supported by cavalry units, one French, one Italian. The latter were particularly formidable, with horses as well as men fully armoured, and so far less vulnerable to English arrows than the cavalry troops of the past. One account suggests that the cavalry were positioned in front of the men on foot; others that they were on the flanks. Both armies advanced towards each other, the English with deliberation, the French and Scots too quickly, losing their breath. The cavalry charges were devastating, as the armoured horses forced their way right through the English formation. The baggage train came under attack, but the archers managed to drive the cavalry off. The French almost triumphed when part of the English line broke, many fleeing. Pardons issued later described how 'varlets, pages and others of lax courage left the battle' and spread rumours that the English had lost.[13] The English then regrouped into a single body. The fight against the Scots was especially bitter. The mêlée continued, punctuated by the shouts for St George. Bedford was in the thick of it, swinging a great two-handed battleaxe. Eventually, the French began to flee. Bedford reported an impressive list of the dead, headed by the Earl of Douglas, his son, the Earl of Buchan, and five French counts. He noted that 'there remained very few Scots who were not dead'.[14] Much later, the chronicler Thomas Basin would consider that the defeat brought one clear advantage to the French, in that the country was rid of the Scots, with their intolerably contemptuous attitude towards their allies.[15]

The defeat at Verneuil transformed attitudes in the uncrowned Charles VII's court. Those who had been bitterly opposed to Burgundy were removed, and replaced by men committed to coming to terms. Relations between England and Burgundy deteriorated. Humphrey duke of Gloucester, one of the king's uncles, had married Jacqueline of Hainault, whose previous marriage to the unwordly

Duke of Brabant had been annulled. Humphrey's intervention in Hainault on behalf of his wife in 1424 was a clear threat to Burgundian ambitions in the Low Countries. Bedford intervened to halt his brother, but the damage was done, and a truce was established between Burgundy and France.

English success did not end with the Battle of Verneuil. In 1425 Le Mans fell. By 1428, Maine was fully under English control. The English had never before held so much of France, but their ambitions were not satisfied. Contrary to Bedford's advice, the Earl of Salisbury began the siege of Orléans. This was overambitious. There were not enough troops to blockade the town effectively. Salisbury himself was killed soon after his arrival at Orléans, by a gun: 'The shot from this canon struck him on the head, so that it took away half his jaw and removed one of his eyes.'[16] Nevertheless, the siege continued. The English had one success, in February 1429, when a French attempt under the Bastard of Orléans to seize a large baggage convoy, largely containing salted herrings, was thwarted by John Fastolf, who drew up the wagons in a strong defensive circle, much as the Hussites did in their wars in Bohemia. Chaotic French cavalry attacks were met with a hail of arrows, and were broken on the English defences in what became known as the Battle of the Herrings.

***

The conquest of Normandy and the establishment of Anglo-Burgundian rule in Paris were remarkable achievements, which owed a great deal to the determination and drive of Henry V and his brother Bedford. It is conceivable that had he lived, Henry V might have made a success of the concept of a dual monarchy, in which England and France would be separate, under a single ruler. Without him, despite all Bedford's efforts, it was never likely to work. However, the English successes were made possible only by the faction-fighting in the French court. Henry V did not have to face really formidable opposition. His achievements left the English vastly overextended in France. At Orléans they would soon receive an unexpected and unlikely setback.

12

THE MAID AND THE ENGLISH COLLAPSE

In 1429 Orléans was relieved by a force that marched from Blois. The most remarkable thing about this army was not its size, which was considerable, but the fact that at its head was a young woman, who called herself *La Pucelle*, or the Maid. She had a banner showing Christ crucified, and a number of priests accompanied her; armed soldiers followed on behind.

Far more pages have been written about the Maid than about anyone else in this period. There is a wealth of evidence from her trial in 1431, and from hearings in the 1450s for her rehabilitation. However, in all these proceedings there was far more concern over the question of whether she was a heretic than over her military role and abilities. Climbing a scaling ladder while carrying a banner was not as questionable as was wearing male clothing or seeing visions.

It was an extraordinary decision on the part of Charles VII and those around him at Chinon to accept a strange young woman, given to having visions, as part of the military effort. She claimed to be divinely inspired, with a mission to assist Charles in the crisis engulfing France. She had a visceral hatred of the Burgundians; when questioned later about her home village of Domrémy in Lorraine, she explained that 'She only knew one Burgundian there, whose head she would have wished to have been cut off, that is, if this had pleased God.'[1] As for the English, she wanted to boot them out of France. It is a measure of the desperation at court that the Maid was not simply dismissed out of hand. As it was, Charles and his advisers cannot have intended that she should be anything more than a figurehead, but everything possible was done to train and equip her. Her first action was to join the troops sent to relieve Orléans.

ORLÉANS, PATAY AND PARIS

Orléans should not have been under siege. Under the accepted conventions, it should have been exempt from attack, as the Duke of Orléans was in captivity in England. Yet the laws of war were overridden. The town was too large for the English to enclose completely with siege works, and they were unable to prevent supplies and weapons from being brought in. They had established various strong-points so as to control the city, but these could be assaulted one by one. The Maid was determined to attack, but there were many arguments between her and the experienced French commanders. Nonetheless, the assaults were successful. In the attack on one earthwork, the Boulevard des Augustins, Joan was wounded in the attack, struck by an arrow below her neck, but she was undaunted. The English, unwilling to risk a full-scale battle, withdrew from the siege.

Charles VII was faced with various options after the relief of Orléans. The Maid was keen that he should go to Reims to be crowned. Other advice was to move on Normandy, or to capture the English-held positions on the Loire. The latter strategy was adopted. A month after Orléans was relieved, the siege of Jargeau began. A battering by the French guns led the English to offer surrender within a fortnight if they were not relieved. However, the French successfully assaulted Jargeau, with the Maid to the fore. Near the village of Patay they overwhelmed the English, commanded by John Fastolf. The English had carefully positioned 500 of their best archers behind hedges, ready to ambush the French. However, a stag leaped out, and the archers 'raised a great shout, not realizing that their enemies were so close'.[2] They were attacked, and the English vanguard fled, followed by the remaining troops. Fastolf managed to escape; John Talbot and other English commanders were taken prisoner. Well-laid plans had been thwarted by the accidental entrance of the stag. The problem of communication with the troops was acute; it proved impossible to inform the vanguard properly as to what was happening. Confusion led inexorably to defeat. The Maid appears to have taken no part in the fight, probably because the troops she was with reached the battlefield too late, but her reputation rose to unparalleled levels. Patay showed that the English were no longer invincible in battle.

After Patay, the way was open for Charles VII's triumphant march to Reims and his coronation there. Paris was the next target for the Maid and the Duke of Alençon, who was devoted to her cause. On the way there, the town of Troyes, faced with the threat of assault, had capitulated, but Burgundian Paris did not surrender. The author of the *Journal d'un bourgeois de Paris* was venomous about 'the creature in the form of a woman' as he termed the Maid. He reported the derision that greeted her threat that if Paris did not surrender, the inhabitants would be slain without mercy. He also noted, with some pleasure, the wound she received from a crossbow bolt which went through her leg. When the assault on the city failed, the Maid's troops were, he claimed, bitter, as she had promised them 'that they would all be made rich from the city's goods, and that all those who resisted would be put to the sword or burned in their houses'.[3]

With the failure of the attack on Paris, the wheels began to come off the Maid's bandwagon. By now, her powerful anti-Burgundian sentiments did not suit Charles VII, who realized the need for an understanding with the duke. The Maid laid siege to La Charité-sur-Loire, but this failed. In May 1430 she was captured by Burgundian troops at Compiègne. She was tried for heresy at Rouen, in English-held Normandy; the court was headed by Pierre Cauchon, Bishop of Beauvais. If she was proved to be a heretic, and even a sorceress, it would be clear that her victories had not been God-given. Also, if she was a heretic, there could be no question of treating her with any chivalric courtesy. The outcome was predictable. Joan was burned as a heretic in 1431.

THE MAID'S ACHIEVEMENT

The brief stellar career of the Maid presents a great many puzzles. Not least is that of how an uneducated peasant girl could achieve such startling military successes. War in the early fifteenth century was a professional business, requiring training and experience. Joan had expert assistance, for she was accompanied by experienced men, such as the young Duke of Alençon, recently released after his capture at Verneuil, and Étienne de Vignolles, known as La Hire. Yet much was due to her own force of character. She may not have performed individual feats of arms, but she led her troops both by example and instruction. One of the witnesses in the rehabilitation proceedings, Margaret la Touroulde, stated that 'She was simple and ignorant, and scarcely knew anything, save about deeds of warfare.'[4] The Duke of Alençon was full of praise, noting her ability with a lance, her skill with artillery and her abilities in organizing troops, as well as her beautiful breasts. She acted 'as if she had been a captain with twenty or thirty years' military experience'.[5] Such memories, recorded some 25 years later, were no doubt exaggerated in the telling. There was one striking contrast between Joan's approach and that of the professional soldiers. She was constantly impatient and eager to attack. There was no careful assessment of the strength of opposing forces; her faith and her self-confidence drove her to take risks that others would have found unacceptable. The tactics of frontal assault, on occasion with scaling ladders, may not have been new, but fighting in this way was not the accepted wisdom. She claimed divine inspiration, though her visions did not give her all the guidance she wanted. At Orléans, 'My voices tell me I should attack the English, but I do not know whether I should go against their bastions, or against Fastolf, who will try to re-victual them.'[6]

The Maid's most important contribution to the war was the way she transformed morale. When she was mounted, 'the soldiers are all affected by her spirit, while on the opposite side, her adversaries are filled with fear and act as if they had lost their strength'.[7] The force of her personality was such that she inspired an extraordinary devotion. Some of her attitudes were not best calculated to please the troops. The ravaging of the countryside was not acceptable to her. She could not abide swearing, and she hated the prostitutes and other women who followed the army, driving them off with the flat of her sword. Yet she was adored and revered. The reverse of the coin was that she was regarded with awe by the English and Burgundians. One witness in the rehabilitation proceedings explained that he had heard from an English knight that 'the English feared her more than a hundred armed men'.[8]

The Maid's success needs to be qualified. The English had overextended themselves, particularly with the attack on Orléans, and even without her intervention the balance of the war was surely likely to have shifted in favour of Charles VII. Nor was the Maid's death a disaster for the French, for had she lived, and maintained her hostility to Burgundy, this would have been a major problem for the French king.

TOWARDS THE CONGRESS OF ARRAS

In 1431 an apparent English triumph took place, for Henry VI was crowned king of France in Paris. The ten-year-old king made a ceremonial entry to the city, and was greeted by a succession of magnificent pageants, as the guilds tried to outdo each other. Mermaids swam in one fountain, and near another a miniature stag hunt took place. The ceremony itself was followed by a great feast. Much of the food had been cooked days before, to the disapproval of the French, who even then had no opinion of English cuisine. A sour chronicler noted that the newly crowned king 'departed without doing any of the good things that were expected of him', such as pardoning prisoners or cancelling taxes.[9]

The splendid, if superficial, symbolism of the coronation meant little in practice, as the war became more difficult for the English. Nor did the weather help: in 1432 the Seine froze in January, and in the spring severe frosts and strong winds put paid to that year's fruit harvest. In July there were 'fully twenty-four days of solid rain', and in August unaccustomed heat ruined the vintage.[10] In 1433 there was a serious mutiny at Calais, where members of the garrison refused to allow Bedford's lieutenant to enter the town. The soldiers still trusted Bedford, until he sat in judgement and exiled 80 of their number. Further, 'a great part of them were put out of wages, and lost all that was owing to them'.[11] In 1435, a year of severe cold and heavy snowfalls, there was a peasant rebellion: 'The said commons of Caux made a marvellous great rising, and took our towns, castles and fortresses, and slew our captains and soldiers, at such a time as we had but few men of war lying in that country.'[12]

Diplomacy failed to resolve the issues between England and France. Negotiations at Auxerre in 1432 came to nothing; the English and French were unwilling to recognize each other's use of the title of king of France. In 1435 the papacy attempted to mediate in a huge peace conference, the Congress of Arras. The French demanded that Henry VI renounce his claim to the French throne, hand over territory and acknowledge French suzerainty in the south-west. They showed flexibility, even indicating a readiness to exchange Normandy for the imprisoned Charles of Orléans. The English, however, were intransigent, and their ambassadors departed before the congress ended. The disaster for them was that, as they clearly feared, the French came to terms with the Duke of Burgundy.

English relations with Burgundy had never been straightforward; this had been an awkward alliance at best. A personal link was severed in 1432, when the Duke of Bedford's wife Anne, the Duke of Burgundy's sister, died. Failure to pay Duke Philip all of the subsidies he was promised was one of a number of difficulties. Measures taken by the English to protect their exports of wool and cloth, and to force foreign buyers to pay a third of the price in bullion, hit the towns of the Burgundian Low Countries hard. The new Franco-Burgundian alliance seriously weakened the English position in France. Further, the English cause was hit hard in 1435 by the death of the Earl of Arundel, shot in the leg, and far more seriously by that of the able Duke of Bedford. He had been absolutely committed to the Lancastrian cause in France, and though he may not have had the charisma of his brother Henry V, he was a brave soldier and an able politician, who had governed in France with skill and understanding.

POLITICS IN FRANCE AND ENGLAND

Despite the success of the Maid in transforming morale, Charles VII faced severe political problems. In 1433 financial charges were brought against the Chamberlain, the unsavoury Georges de La Trémoille. Previously he had been pardoned for a range of offences including the blocking of the collection of royal taxes and impositions on his lands, because of 'the great, notable, profitable and pleasing services he has performed carefully and with great diligence in our business'.[13] His fall from grace opened a route to power for the Constable, Arthur de Richemont, but in 1440 political stability was threatened by a brief noble rising known as the *Praguerie*. This was led by the dukes of Bourbon and Alençon, who offered reforms and aimed to replace Charles with his son. Another menace was the activity of brigands known as *écorcheurs*, mostly former soldiers. They ravaged Burgundy initially, but their activities quickly spread much more widely. They were joined by a Spanish adventurer, Rodrigo de Villandrando. The *Journal d'un bourgeois de Paris* reported that in 1444 no one dare leave the city, for fear of being robbed and left stark naked by bands of 'thieves and murderers, firebrands, and rapists'.[14] Yet there was a growing unity and strength of government in the 1440s. Charles treated the leaders of the *Praguerie* with commendable moderation, and the *écorcheurs* were brought under control. Negotiations with local assemblies were increasingly successful in obtaining subsidies. No longer did the crown rely on debasement of the currency.

While Charles VII's position was strengthening in the 1440s, the situation in England was very different. Although Henry VI began to exercise his authority in 1435, attending councils even though he was only 13, he proved to have no capacity for rule. Pious and peace-loving, his generosity weakened royal finances. Nor was he capable of arbitrating between ambitious and quarrelsome nobles. Disputes between the king's uncle, Humphrey, duke of Gloucester, and the wealthy Cardinal Beaufort destabilized the realm. William de la Pole, duke of Suffolk, emerged as dominant by the mid-1440s. Suffolk adopted a peace policy which, though it was all the country could afford, proved disastrous. In 1450 he was impeached, and when he attempted to flee, he was captured at sea and beheaded by rebellious sailors. Popular rebellion followed. Up to 1453, the year the war with France came to an end, power lay with the Duke of Somerset. That year saw the king's complete mental collapse, possibly a condition inherited from his maternal grandfather, Charles VI of France. With the Duke of York threatening the fragile regime, the scene was set for the outbreak of civil war.

ENGLISH STRATEGY

The English thought hard about the military strategy they should adopt. In 1435 John Fastolf directed a remarkable memorandum to the English council in France. He explained that there should be no question of Henry VI abandoning his title of king of France; if he did so, it would mean that 'all the wars and conquests had been but usurpation and tyranny'. Were that so, God would not have given the English their victories. Fastolf advised that there should be no more sieges, for 'no king may conquer a great realm by continual sieges'. Rather, there should be two forces, each of 750 lances, which should go as far as Champagne and Burgundy, 'burning and destroying all the land as they pass, both houses, corn, vines and all the trees that bear fruit for man's subsistence'. Cattle were to be killed, or driven back to Normandy. Another force should protect the Norman frontier, and take the war into Anjou, Maine and the Beauce. There should be no question of taking ransoms or protection money; as the French were rebelling against rightful authority, this was to be 'a more sharp and more cruel war' than one against a natural enemy. If battle took place (and Fastolf did not advise that it should), it ought to be on foot, as in the past. However, when it came to drawing up 'advertisements and instructions concerning the war' for the Duke of York in 1440, the council, which included Fastolf, did not give any strategic advice. York's financial terms were set out, as were his requirements for six 'great guns' and a dozen 'great fowlers' along with spear shafts, bows, arrows, *pavises* (shields) and sufficient carts. When Fastolf advised the Duke of Somerset in 1448, he recommended the appointment of captains 'discrete and cunning in the war, not covetous oppressors or extortioners', who would not (unlike Fastolf himself) enrich themselves. He was concerned that castles should be properly equipped and garrisoned.[15]

ENGLISH DEFEATS

The impact of the Burgundian change of sides in 1435 was clear in the next year, when the Duke of Burgundy besieged Calais. However, a barrage lasting two weeks from 15 bombards and many smaller guns failed to break the defences. One of the duke's councillors was clear about the reason for the failure of the siege, telling him that 'You must have appreciated during the siege of Calais what harm was done by the lack of finance.'[16] Though Calais was held by the English in 1436, Paris, 'which is the heart and principal place of the kingdom', as the Duke of Burgundy put it, was lost.[17] A blockade threatened the city with famine, and the populace had no reason to support the English. A relief force was defeated; the English and their supporters took refuge in the Bastille, but had no option other than to surrender. The English positions in the Ile-de-France soon fell to the French. Late in August 1437, Montereau, south-east of Paris, came under siege. Jean Bureau, expert in artillery, directed the construction of elaborate siege-works. Charles VII himself took a leading role in the assault on the town, 'mounting a scaling ladder during the assault, his sword in his fist'.[18] The castle, with its small English garrison, held out longer, but surrendered in late October.

In 1439, Meaux was lost to forces led by Arthur de Richemont. Pontoise, which had been taken by the English in 1437, by means of a surprise assault in the depths of winter, was besieged in 1441. Once again, Bureau's artillery proved very effective, softening up the defences before an assault. The prisoners were badly treated. Taken to Paris, they were paraded almost naked through the streets, treated, as one observer saw it, 'without mercy, worse than dogs'.[19] Many were publicly drowned. As they had not negotiated terms of surrender, the laws of war entitled the victors to do as they chose, but the incident displayed a new bitterness in the conflict. Chivalry had no place.

THE DEFENCE OF NORMANDY

The English were not to be defeated swiftly everywhere. Their occupation of Normandy lasted until 1450. The war was a matter of sieges, assaults, raids and skirmishes rather than set-piece battles. There were some successes. When Richemont laid siege to Avranches in Normandy in 1339, his troops, many of them *routiers*, were routed in a surprise attack. In 1440 John Talbot took Harfleur by conventional means, after a long siege. However, by 1441 the situation was deteriorating. The English council at Rouen wrote in dramatic terms that Normandy was 'abandoned like the ship tossed about in the sea by many waves, without captain, without steersman, without rudder, without sail, tossed, staggering and driving among the stormy waves'.[20] The Duke of York lacked the ability to be an effective successor to Bedford. In 1443, in a reversion to the strategy of the past, John Beaufort, duke of Somerset, led a *chevauchée* which he hoped would force Charles VII into battle. In the event, Charles was not to be tempted, and the raid was a disaster. Somerset had not recruited troops in sufficient number or quality. The English war effort came to a halt.

In 1444 the Truce of Tours was agreed, and Henry VI was betrothed to Margaret, daughter of the Duke of Anjou. The marriage took place in the following year. Peace proved impossible, however, as the English remained intransigent over the question of sovereignty over Normandy and Aquitaine. As for Somerset, he died in 1444, perhaps committing suicide. In 1445 it was agreed that Maine should be handed over to the French. The ambitious new Duke of Somerset (brother of the previous duke) had been appointed governor there in 1438, and was bitterly opposed to the proposal, demanding substantial financial compensation. As governor of Normandy from 1447 he had a weak hand to play, and played it badly. Instructions given to a French herald going to England in 1448 reveal the depths of French frustration, particularly at Somerset's attitude. The French would not receive letters from him, 'because they were in a style derogatory to the honour of the king, and different from what had been used in past time by the duke of York'. They were 'framed either by too great arrogance or ignorance'.[21] The problem was familiar: Somerset had not addressed Charles VII as king. Awkward as the diplomatic issues were, there were more serious difficulties facing the English than this.

English garrisons in Normandy exploited their localities in ways which hardly endeared them to the people. Complaints reached the English government about the 'pillaging, robberies, enormous ransoms, beatings and other great violence and injuries' for which the troops were responsible.[22] Victualling, both of field armies and garrisons, was often difficult, and caused much resentment. Villages were forced to pay *appatis*, or protection money. Accounts show that labourers, sailors, merchants and other non-combatants were seized by garrison men anxious to maximize their profits from the war. Goods and beasts might be seized. An account for 1430 recorded that 'On 7 January next, 24 horses, both stallions and mares, were taken to Pontoise by several members of the garrison there. They were sold one by one by William Heron, man-at-arms in the garrison, total 43 *livres tournois*.'[23]

The occupation was made all the more difficult by economic circumstances. The late 1430s saw poor harvests. The weather was bad in 1436, and prices rose startlingly in the next year. One chronicler explained that in 1438 'there was great mortality and incredible famine throughout France, and the Normans fled from Normandy ... the rich went by sea to Brittany, and the poor by foot to Picardy'.[24] An improvement in conditions in the 1440s was not sufficient to transform the financial position of the occupying English.

One of the effects of the hard times in Normandy was the threat from bands described by the English as brigands, but who some French historians have preferred to characterize as patriotic freedom fighters. Whether these 'brigands' were in fact loyal subjects of the French king is difficult to determine. The evidence shows a widespread breakdown of law and order, with parts of Normandy subjected to terror inflicted by outlaw bands. Many stories in the records reveal the horrors people faced in a society that was collapsing. In 1424 one unfortunate woman, Thomasse Raoul, was buried alive for having 'counselled and comforted the brigands and enemies of the king'.[25] Colin Decharpy, a married man with nine children, lived near Falaise. He claimed that brigands forced him to provide them with money, horses and goods. He was imprisoned by the English, but escaped through a tunnel. Recaptured, he obtained a pardon, but he was again arrested and imprisoned. After escaping, he took refuge in sanctuary for a time. He then tried to flee from Falaise using a rope to shin down the walls, but the rope was too short, and he fell, injuring himself badly. He managed to return home, but was once again seized and returned to prison in Falaise. Finally, he received a pardon.[26]

Records also reveal incidents that show how in some cases the English fitted, or failed to fit, into Norman society. Like soldiers of almost any period, drink and sex were the main preoccupations of the garrison troops. There was some integration with the Norman populace. Some soldiers took French wives. A murder case at Pontaudemer revealed that the victim, a local prostitute, was 'chambermaid and concubine of an Englishman called William Ross'.[27] Though life in Norman towns may have had its attractions, for the garrison of over a hundred men on the tiny rocky outcrop of Tombelaine, close to Mont-Saint-Michel, there can have been few comforts beyond the ten pipes of wine and twenty of cider delivered to them in 1425. As for the Normans, they had to be careful about expressing their view of the English; one unfortunate found himself locked up in irons for declaring, when extremely drunk, that he preferred the Armagnacs to the English, and 'loved the king of France, Charles, more than King Henry of England'.[28]

Any hopes that Norman revenues would be sufficient to provide for the defence of the duchy were vastly overoptimistic. Grants from the Norman estates yielded declining revenues. The average of receipts for 1442–5 was little more than half that for 1435–40. Much of the burden therefore fell on England. However, the financial position there had deteriorated disastrously. High expenditure at home was combined with a fall in the revenue from the customs, and unwillingness on the part of the Commons to make new grants. Cardinal Henry Beaufort, a man of great influence but of questionable statesmanship, had provided the crown with loans since 1417. In just over two years from April 1437 he advanced almost £26,000 to help cover the costs of war. He lent an impressive £20,000 to fund Somerset's 1443 expedition, but some ventures, such as Salisbury's expedition to Orléans in 1428, did not have his support. After Beaufort's death in 1447, no one emerged to take his place. Debts vastly exceeded the available revenue, and the government was unable to pay York the arrears due on his salary, or the wages of the garrisons in Normandy. Parliament increased its grant of a half-subsidy to a whole in 1449, but this came nowhere close to meeting the needs of war. As 'we be not as yet purveyed of money' to pay for an army to defend Normandy, the king pledged an impressive quantity of jewels and plate, including 'a tablet of gold with an image of St George, garnished with a ruby and eight diamonds', but this was hardly sufficient.[29]

THE FINAL FRENCH SUCCESS

The Truce of Tours was due to expire in April 1450. Before that, there were many infractions on both sides, but the most important came when an Aragonese captain in English service, François de Surienne, stormed Fougères in Brittany in 1449. The action had been planned for some time; Somerset and the Earl of Suffolk were behind it. Its purpose was to obtain the release from prison of Gilles de Bretagne. He was a younger brother of the Francophile Breton duke, and had been arrested in 1446. The scheme was unbelievably unwise. A later French account produced a bizarre story of how the English attempted to trick the French, by listing the duke as their ally in a document handed over in a castle ditch at midnight, when it was impossible to read it. Somerset and his associates were not as devious as that; it was, however, an extraordinary miscalculation to use Surienne as they did.

The Duke of Brittany appealed to Charles VII following the capture of Fougères, and this led to the reopening of the war in July 1449. Charles had used the period of truce wisely, reorganizing his forces. French artillery made quick work of the English house of cards in Normandy. Jean Chartier, writing a life of the king, explained that no Christian ruler had ever brought together so many guns, well equipped with powder, protective mantlets and carts for transport. Jean Bureau and Gaspard his brother had charge of the artillery. It was not just a matter of bringing guns to bear on castles and fortifications. Complex siege works, with 'bastions, embankments, trenches, ditches, and mines' were also needed, as well as negotiating skills to secure surrender.[30] The French task was made much easier when it was clear that favourable surrender terms were available; the Bishop of Lisieux, Thomas Basin, negotiated the submission of his city skilfully, setting a valuable precedent. There was just one battle, at Formigny. The English expeditionary army, perhaps 6,000 strong, under the experienced veterans Thomas Kyriell and Matthew Gough, had ample time to prepare for the engagement. An advance by the archers succeeded in capturing two French guns that had done some damage to the English position. It seemed that the English were gaining the upper hand. Fresh forces appeared on the crest of a hill after two or three hours; English hopes that they were reinforcements under Somerset were dashed when they proved to be led by the French Constable, Richemont. 'I believe that it was God who brought us the constable' was one comment after the battle. Slaughter followed the battle; local peasants killed those who managed to flee. Whether or not the precise figure given by one chronicler for English casualties of 3,774, along with that of five or six for the French, is believed, this was a disastrous defeat which contributed to the swift collapse of English Normandy.[31] Morale had fallen disastrously, and treachery aided the French. Richard Merbury, captain of Gisors, surrendered his charge, offering no defence. His son John provided valuable services to the French, which the king 'did not wish in any way to be declared'.[32] In the end, Somerset had little choice other than to surrender. The English occupation of Normandy came to an ignominious end.

There remained Gascony. The English had maintained their position in the duchy until the late 1430s. In 1339 negotiations failed, and an expedition commanded by the Earl of Huntingdon achieved some success. However, he was soon withdrawn, and in 1442 Charles VII invaded the duchy. Bordeaux had hardly been affected by the war until this time, but now a desperate letter sent to Henry VI from the city declared that 'We have not the wherewithal to help ourselves, which causes great heaviness, desolation and sorrow among all your people here.' Help had been promised, but 'in all this time no comfort comes, not such so much as one balinger to revive their hearts'.[33] The balance of warfare was changing, as French artillery was proving increasingly effective. Dax fell after being bombarded by French guns for three weeks, and then La Réole was captured. Yet the campaign was not carried through, and Dax was eventually retaken. However, when the truce collapsed in 1449, there was little resistance. In 1451 at Blaye, the besiegers' guns brought down part of the walls, leaving the town open to the final assault. Bourg fell in less than a week, even before the French guns had been brought to bear on the fortifications. Place after place fell to the French. At Bordeaux, the citizens and the English, 'considering the grand chivalry and noble company ready to put them under siege', surrendered on generous terms.[34]

However, appeals were made to the English government for help, and in October 1452 Talbot arrived with a small expeditionary force. Initial English success was remarkable. A plot saw the English enter Bordeaux. Early one Sunday morning a gate was

Fig. 16: The French victory in the battle of Castillon, 1453

opened, and Talbot launched a surprise attack. There followed a remarkable series of successes, as town after town submitted to him. Reinforcements brought his forces up to about 7,300 in the following year.[35] Yet the French triumphed, as three separate armies advancing on Bordeaux. At Castillon the commander of one of these forces, the master of artillery Jean Bureau, established a defensive earthwork enclosure outside the town. Talbot's men took an abbey occupied by the French. He was told, mistakenly, that the French were fleeing, and ordered his men to attack. With shouts of 'Talbot, Talbot, St George', they advanced on the enclosure, only to be cut down by murderous fire from bombards, *coulovrines*, *veuglaires* and other guns. A mêlée followed. Talbot himself fought heroically but was killed by a dagger to his throat. Along with him it was estimated that some 4,000 died. The next day Talbot's herald was taken to see his master's corpse. It was only when he felt Talbot's teeth that he was sure of the identification, so savagely had he been mutilated in the fighting. After that there was no hope for the English. Bordeaux held out for some time, but a French blockade led to its surrender. Gascony was in French hands. The only English possession left in France was Calais. There the English government had taken care to buy 24 new iron guns, and to build two bastions, and the defences were not seriously challenged.

The Battle of Castillon marks what is normally seen as the conclusion of the Hundred Years War. It did not, however, bring Anglo-French hostilities to a complete end. Edward IV invaded France in 1475 with what was probably the largest army the English took overseas in the fifteenth century. The outcome, however, was an advantageous treaty rather than battle. In 1513 Henry VIII won a victory over the French in the Battle of the Spurs, and succeeded, where Edward III had failed, in a siege of Tournai. There is even a case for arguing that the Hundred Years War did not end until the French capture of Calais in 1558. However, for this book, the war came to its end with Talbot's death and the loss of Bordeaux.

NATIONAL SENTIMENT

These years saw national feelings enhanced and emphasized by the war. It was not, however, a straightforward matter. There were a number of treatises written in France, which stressed the wickedness of the English and held that France was for the French. These, however, were primarily intended for the use of diplomats, rather than for general propaganda purposes.[36] For the English, Agincourt had demonstrated both divine approval for their cause, and their superiority over the French. The author of the *Gesta Henrici Quinti* had hoped that following the victory the French might 'repudiate their acts of injustice and abandon those most wicked ways by which, lured and confused, they are being led astray'.[37] Yet it made little sense to denigrate the French when Paris, much of the surrounding lands and Normandy, as well as Gascony, were in English hands. For the French, it was easy enough to write of the 'malice, damnable schemes and intentions of the English, ancient enemies of my lord the king'.[38] Yet France was not a united country. The scholar Jean de Montreuil, writing in the early fifteenth century, was puzzled by the attitude of the Gascons, with their allegiance to the English. They were, in his view, misguided by false information, and were ignorant of reality.[39] For the Maid, the Burgundians were far worse than the English. Breton and Norman particularism ran counter to the concept of a united France. However, the expulsion of the English from Normandy and Gascony was a major step in the realization of that ideal.

***

What is surprising is not that that the English were driven out of France, but rather that they succeeded in holding Normandy and Gascony for as long as they did. There were many reasons for their eventual failure. England under Henry VI was not in a position to provide the financial support that was needed. Nor were there sufficient local resources in Normandy or Gascony to provide for the defence of towns and castles. There were extremely able English commanders, notably Bedford and Talbot, but as Somerset's *chevauchée* of 1443 showed, not all were of high calibre. Somerset's brother and successor had distinguished himself in Normandy, as when he commanded the recapture of Harfleur in 1440. Yet he failed disastrously in the final act.

13

ARMIES IN THE FIFTEENTH CENTURY

The English faced new issues in the fifteenth century. Not only did they have to recruit expeditionary forces, but they also needed to find ways of providing effective defences for their possessions in France. Despite the pressures, there were no attempts to transform English armies. The methods that had served well in the past continued to be employed, against a background of financial difficulties and a lack of enthusiasm for an increasingly unsuccessful war. One major change came with Henry V's death, for after that, with an underage king, the royal household ceased to play its central part in providing troops and organizing the military effort. In contrast to their rivals, the French made considerable efforts in the 1440s to reform their armies, with major ordinances setting out the principles on which well-organized and properly integrated armies should operate.

The largest force that Henry V led to Normandy was that of 1417, some 10,000 strong. However, expeditionary forces were subsequently much smaller, generally numbering under 2,000. There were exceptions: the Earl of Gloucester commanded about 7,500 men in 1436 when Calais was threatened. Beaufort led 4,500 in 1443, the largest force in the final decade of the war. In some cases, as with the Earl of Salisbury's expedition of 1428, when he had about 2,700 men, the crown entered into a single indenture with the leader of an expedition, who would then make his own agreements with smaller companies. In others, separate indentures were made by the crown with the leaders of such companies; in 1430 there were 114 such contracts. This made no difference to the forces in the field, which were organized as ever into retinues of varying size. Regular musters took place, ensuring that the men were properly equipped, and that the terms of contracts were properly fulfilled.

Large numbers of men were employed on garrison service in Calais and in Normandy; it has been calculated that in 1436 there were almost 6,000. Recruitment followed the same pattern as for expeditionary forces. Contracts were made with individual captains, who then provided retinues. Evidence suggests that career soldiers might serve under a number of captains, in different retinues.[1] Though there was no true standing army, garrisons provided an element of permanence. Men could be detached from garrison service so as to reinforce field armies. In addition, there were troops raised locally in Normandy. There, feudal summonses could in theory have raised 1,400 men, while general summonses of 'all the nobles and other people who are accustomed to war' were backed by threats that anyone who did not respond would be reputed to be 'rebels and disobedient to the king our lord'.[2]

SUPPORT FOR THE WAR

There was a powerful tradition that the greatest men in the land would take a leading role in war. In 1436, eight dukes and earls, and 17 barons, served on the campaign to defend Calais. Thereafter the story was very different. In 1443 Somerset complained of the 'lack of barons, bannerets and knights' on his expedition.[3] There was no aristocratic involvement at Formigny in 1450, and John Talbot, earl of Shrewsbury since 1442, had no earls or barons with him when he was defeated at Castillon in 1453, save his son, Viscount Lisle. The level of overall support for the war from the nobility was far from what it had been earlier.

Knightly involvement in the war also fell. An enquiry in Yorkshire in 1420, seeking the names of those prepared to serve Henry V in Normandy for wages, revealed a striking lack of enthusiasm for the war. Some were too old. Poverty was the most common excuse for refusing to take up arms, with illness, often unspecified, the second explanation most often used. Other reasons were also given. William Thornlynson denied that he was a gentleman. Another said that he was a lawyer. One man said that 'he will do any service that he can within this realm of England, but he will not pass it.' In all, 70 'gentlemen' said they could not serve. One man was volunteered: the local community of Holderness was anxious to get rid of John Routh, 'a right able man for your wars and one busy at home to vex your poor people as it is plainly said'. Negotiations with the Norfolk gentry were even less successful, and the commissioners sadly concluded that 'We cannot see that the king may be served of any men here in this country as it is desired, the which is to us great heaviness and disease.'[4]

This meant that the proportion of knights in the armies fell dramatically. Beaufort's army of 1443 contained just seven knights, 0.15 per cent of the total force. In contrast, 10 per cent of John of Gaunt's force in 1370 had been knights. One reason was that there was a decline in the number of knights in the country; it seems likely that there were no more than about 200 in the 1430s. This fall needs to be qualified by the fact that esquires were coming to take the place in society that had been held by knights. In war they served as men-at-arms, just as knights did. Even so, the numbers available for recruitment were limited: 'In Warwickshire in 1436 there were eighteen knights, fifty-nine esquires and something in the region of fifty-five gentlemen.'[5] The latter regarded themselves as entitled to bear coats of arms, but their expectation was that they would serve in local politics and administration, looking to law not war. The war, particularly in its final phases, did not see society become increasingly militarized; rather, the reverse was the case.

ARCHERS AND OTHERS

As noble and knightly involvement in the war declined, the proportion of archers in English armies rose. Whereas it had been normal in the late fourteenth century for there to be equal numbers of archers and men-at-arms, as when the Earl of Warwick agreed to serve in 1373 with 200 men-at-arms and 200 archers, by Henry V's reign a ratio of one man-at-arms to three archers was usual. In 1425 the Earl of Suffolk was contracted to have a force of 100 men-at-arms and 300 mounted archers for the siege of Mont-Saint-Michel. The proportion in expeditionary forces rose higher still, from one to five in 1428 to one to nine by 1449.

In contrast to the knights and men-at-arms, there was no great difficulty in recruiting archers. Pay, at *6d.* a day, for a mounted archer was higher than what a skilled craftsman might expect to earn, and there was always the hope of gaining plunder. The social origins of the archers are not easy to discern, but some were men of substance, of at least yeoman status. There were veterans with extensive experience among them. Hegyn Tomson served at Harfleur for almost 30 years, on and off, and Richard Bullock served in the garrison of Saint-Lô for at least 19 years, and overall for 22.

The conventional view is that the English archers were superb soldiers, 'some of the finest, most highly trained and militarily efficient troops that any nation ever put into the field of battle'.[6] Such hyperbole is difficult to justify. The victory of Agincourt certainly owed much to the archers; the case is harder to argue for Verneuil. Archers were valuable in some minor engagements, such as the Battle of the Herrings, but they did not serve the English well at Patay. The performance of English armies by the 1440s suggests that the low proportion of men-at-arms was a disadvantage. In the final stages of the war the archers did not provide the English with the battle-winning capability they had displayed earlier.

There were some specialist troops needed. Gunners were increasingly important. In readiness for the siege of Harfleur, Henry V recruited 29 master gunners and 59 others, mostly from the Low Counties. A typical ordnance company was that established later at Rouen, consisting of a master gunner, a forger (or foundryman), his assistant, a master carpenter and his helper (to make the gun carriages and protective shields), a master mason (to prepare ammunition) and a carter. A man-at-arms and up to 18 archers provided an escort. When Meulan was besieged in 1436, this company was reinforced by eight additional gunners. Crossbowmen were valuable in siege warfare, both in attack and defence. The crossbow was slow to load, but in these circumstances that was no great disadvantage. Few were recruited in England; Gascony and Normandy provided men with this particular expertise. A number of professions made their contribution to the war effort. Armourers and fletchers were needed, and victuallers were needed in castle garrisons. Miners, mostly from the Forest of Dean, were required for siege warfare.

DISCIPLINE

The chronicler Jean de Waurin, commenting on the ill-disciplined troops from Brabant, remarked that 'a thousand men of war of good stuff were worth more than 10,000 of such shit'.[7] To judge by the ordinances that were issued, English armies should have been well disciplined. Henry V's ordinances show that for him, obedience to orders was vital. Sacrilegious actions were forcibly forbidden, and women in childbirth were given special protection. Foraging was regulated, and there was to be no pillage in conquered territory. There were detailed regulations for the taking of prisoners. There was to be no taunting on grounds of national origin, be it English, Irish, Welsh or French. Prostitutes were allowed no nearer than a league away from the army.[8]

Not surprisingly, the disciplinary ordinances were not easy to enforce. The Duke of Bedford wrote in 1423 that he understood that churches were being broken into, women raped, goods seized, men imprisoned and unjust tolls levied. There were 'certain vagabond English who wander from place to place robbing and inciting the soldiers to desert'.[9] In the following year some newly arrived from England left their retinues and offered their services to whichever captain paid the best, an act of 'fraud and deceit'. Others promptly deserted.[10]

FRENCH FORCES

In France there was an acknowledgement of the need for reform which was not matched in England. French forces were markedly larger than those the English could muster; Charles VII had up to 20,000 men in pay for the Normandy campaign of 1449–50. There were, however, similarities. The numbers of knights in French armies fell startlingly at the start of the fifteenth century. Only 1.7 per cent of the men-at-arms retained by the Armagnac government in 1414 were bannerets or knights. Remarkably, Pierre de Rochefort, created Marshal of France in 1417, though a banneret, was a squire, not a knight. Social changes provide part of the explanation for this decline in knighthood, but there was surely also a reluctance to take up arms in support of an unsuccessful cause. In France, unlike England or Burgundy, there was an acknowledgement that the distinction between knights and other men-at-arms had little warrant in military terms, for from the late 1430s all were paid at the same rate. The title of banneret fell out of use; command of companies went to captains. At the start of the fifteenth century the proportion of men-at-arms to *gens de trait* (archers and crossbowmen) stood at two to one, or even less. In agreements made in 1414, the Count of Vendôme was to serve with 2,000 men-at-arms and 1,000 *gens de trait*, and Arthur de Richemont with 500 men-at-arms and 100 *gens de trait*. By the 1430s the ratio had shifted to one man-at-arms to two archers.

Foreign mercenaries from Scotland, Spain and Italy provided an important element in French armies, particularly in the 1420s, when they formed up to half of Charles VII's forces. In 1424, 2,500 Scottish men-at-arms and 4,000 archers mustered at Bourges. At Verneuil the English faced Lombard cavalry as well as the Scots. The battle was a disaster for the foreigners in French service, and marked the end of their recruitment on such a large scale. Nevertheless, during the siege of Orléans, foreign soldiers received about a third of the garrison's limited food supplies, while there were 60 Scottish men-at-arms, with 300 archers, in the relief force. By 1445 there were just two companies of Scots, one of Italians and one of Spaniards in the French armies.

By the 1430s, despite the successes inspired by the Maid, French forces were in chaos. Attempts to revive the *arrière-ban* had failed. Proper systems of pay and review had collapsed. Undisciplined *routiers* and *écorcheurs*, completely out of royal control, ravaged the countryside, demanding goods and money. Aiming to deal with these problems, in 1439 a royal ordinance set out plans for reform. The fundamental principle was that commanders should be responsible to the king. Captains were to be appointed by the crown. Anyone who led a company without royal approval was guilty of *lèse-majesté*. Companies were not to seize crops or cattle. Frontier garrisons should not leave their positions, and were not to live off the land. Garrisons that were oppressing the people should

Fig. 17: A mid-fifteenth-century mounted knight

be disbanded, and defence left to local lords.[11] The ordinance was understandably unpopular with the nobility; it contributed to the Duke of Bourbon's brief rebellion in 1440. However, it marked the beginning of a crucially important process which saw the transformation of the French army.

In 1445 there were fresh demands for reform, and a new military ordinance, for which Arthur de Richemont was largely responsible. It aimed to deal with the problem of the undisciplined *routiers* and *écorcheurs* who plagued France, rather than to achieve the expulsion of the English. Unfortunately the text has not survived, but its chief contents are clear. It set out the organization of the army into companies, known as *compagnies d'ordonnance*. The lance, composed of six men, was the basic unit for the men-at-arms. One man would be fully armed and equipped, with full armour, a second more lightly armed, with the third acting as a page. In addition there were to be two mounted archers, with their page. This provided the basis for effective, integrated forces, much as the incorporation of mounted archers into retinues had done for English armies in the fourteenth century. The victuals required by a lance were carefully worked out; each month the six men would need two sheep and half a cow. Each man was allocated a substantial two pipes of wine (252 gallons) a year. The worthless hangers-on who accompanied armies, who did no more than pillage the countryside, were to be sent home. Richemont's biographer commented that 'Thus the pillage of the people that had lasted so long was ended, for which my lord was joyful, for it was one of the things he most desired, and which he had always failed to achieve, but the king would not listen to him until now.'[12] In 1448 there was a further important reform, when the *franc-archers* were established. These militia-men provided the crown with a new kind of national infantry force, intended to deal with local disorder. They were to be mustered regularly. Each man was to have a light helmet, a padded jacket or a brigandine (made of cloth heavily reinforced with plates), sword, dagger and bow. To see the reforms as amounting to the creation of a standing army is to go too far; but they did create the potential for such an army. The reforms, probably influenced by ideas drawn from Vegetius, set new standards, and it was armies created in this new spirit that achieved the French reconquest of Normandy and of English Gascony.

ARMOUR AND WEAPONRY

The chronicler Jean Chartier emphasized that the French troops who reconquered Normandy were well armoured. He described the men-at-arms 'all armed with good cuirasses, leg armour, swords, *salades* [rounded helmets], of which most were garnished with silver, and with lances carried by their pages'.[13] Other troops included mounted archers, equipped with brigandines, leg armour and *salades*. A driving force in the development of armour was the need to provide effective protection for men fighting on foot,

Fig. 18: A fifteenth-century French crossbowman

as had become the normal practice for both English and French armies. A knight in up-to-date armour of this period looked very different from his fourteenth-century predecessor. He would no longer have a fabric surcoat or jupon; rather, he would display the bright steel plates of his armour. A breastplate in one piece replaced the 'pair of plates', and the armour was carefully jointed, with internal leather straps. The mail aventail, that had provided neck protection, was abandoned in favour of plate; with the great bacinet this became part of the helmet. English fashion in the early fifteenth century, as shown on memorial brasses, was for large circular *besagnes* to protect the shoulder joints.[14] Well-made armour was little hindrance to mobility. Boucicaut was said to be able to jump into the saddle, fully armoured, without using the stirrup. He was an athlete of very considerable ability, and it was said that, after taking his helmet off, he could even perform a complete somersault wearing full armour. Nevertheless, despite the ease of movement that was possible, it still took a great deal of energy to move about in armour.

The hand weapons used changed little. Lances, swords, daggers, battleaxes, bill-hooks and gisarmes all featured. Crossbows were improved with the use of steel bows and winches for reloading; longbows required no development. Nor was there significant progress in the design of stone-throwing siege engines; trebuchets in particular, powered by heavy counterweights, continued in use. Traditional types of siege equipment, such as movable towers, or belfries, were also employed, while mining remained an important part of the means available to besieging forces.

GUNS

The major technological change during the Hundred Years War was the development of guns. An important shift had begun in the final quarter of the fourteenth century, when besieging forces began to employ them to good effect. The evolution speeded up in the fifteenth century. Great bombards were used extensively in siege warfare, as at Harfleur. There were various types of gun, and several methods of manufacture. The largest were normally fabricated using long staves of iron, bound together with hoops, while others were cast using bronze or iron. Most were breech-loading, with separate powder chambers: such guns would have had a faster rate of fire than muzzle-loaders. Bombards were the largest. They had a wide bore, and used stone ammunition, shot in a relatively flat trajectory. It took two years and 35 tons of iron for the *donderbusmeester* Pasquier den Kick to make one ordered by the Duke of Brabant in 1409. The largest bombards were capable of firing a stone of almost half a ton. *Veuglaires* were smaller: in 1445 a dozen Burgundian *veuglaires* had two chambers each, holding three pounds of powder. They could fire ammunition weighing 12

Fig. 19: *Dulle Griet*, a fifteenth-century bombard now in Ghent

lbs. *Crapaudaux* were similar, but shorter and lighter. The smallest guns were *coulovrines*, handguns shooting lead bullets, used against troops, not stone walls. Guns were made more effective by improvements to gunpowder in the early fifteenth century, particularly by 'corning', forming it into dense grains. Furthermore, by about 1430 gunpowder came down in price, as it began to be manufactured on an increasingly large scale.

There were many problems. The transport of huge siege guns was difficult. In 1409 a Burgundian bombard, weighing 7,700 lbs, required 25 men, 32 oxen and 31 horses to move it at a pace of a league a day. It took 48 horses in 1436 to pull the cart carrying the 22-inch calibre barrel of a gun called *Bourgogne*, while 36 horses hauled another cart with the powder chamber. In addition, an 'engine' to hoist the bombard into place was hauled by five horses. The convoy was too much for the bridges over the Marne, and boats had to be used instead.

Despite the difficulties, guns were available in considerable quantities. For his expedition to France in 1428 the Earl of

Fig. 20: A nineteenth-century reconstruction drawing of a bombard

Salisbury had seven bombards and 64 smaller guns, 16 of them hand-held weapons. In 1436 the Duke of Burgundy assembled an astonishing arsenal for his unsuccessful siege of Calais. By one count there were ten bombards, 60 *veuglaires*, 55 *crapaudaux* and 450 *coulouvrines*. The noise and smoke from a bombardment by such a battery was a weapon in itself. Guns were not always successful; a day's bombardment in 1431 saw 412 stones fired into Lagny-sur-Marne, but the only casualty was a single chicken. Yet bombards were capable of breaching stone walls, as in 1441 when Charles VII brought 'several bombards and other artillery against the town of Pontoise, and they fired incessantly against the walls, until it was broken in various places'.[15] By the late 1440s, under the Bureau brothers, French artillery was formidable indeed, with place after place surrendering at the threat of bombardment.

In a classic study, J. R. Hale argued that it was not until the second half of the fifteenth century, with the development in Italy of a new and more scientific approach, that defences were constructed in a novel style so as to deal with powerful artillery. Bastions offering flanking fire were a crucial element in complex interconnecting systems of defence. However, earlier in the fifteenth century in France a new style of defence against gunpowder artillery had been introduced, with earthen ramparts known as *boulevards* constructed around existing fortifications. With their palisades and timber reinforcements, *boulevards* were able to absorb the shock of gunfire, as well as providing platforms on which artillery could be mounted. Existing defences were reinforced with earth, but it was not until around 1450 that massive purpose-built artillery towers appeared.[16]

AN ORDINARY SOLDIER

The records provide a few glimpses of the men who served at this time. Gilet de Lointren, a poor man of good descent, aged about 30, became a man-at-arms through poverty and 'went to the land of Normandy to seek adventure, as men-at-arms do'. He served first with the lord of Ivry for a couple of years. Then he moved from one garrison and one lord to another, until he was captured and held in prison for seven months, as he could not afford the ransom demanded of him. He made four écus, his share from ransoming an Englishman, Robin Maine. Captured again by the English, he was bought by a consortium of four, with his ransom set at 81 écus. He was held in prison for six months, and eventually agreed to serve the English, as he could not afford the sum demanded. Further captures, imprisonments and ransom demands followed, until finally he was condemned to death. The tale has an extraordinary happy ending, for a girl of about 15, a 'maiden of good renown', accompanied by her parents and friends, went to Lord Scales, the English commander at Alençon, and offered to marry Gilet. The sentence was deferred, and in 1424 Gilet finally received a pardon.[17]

14

PROFIT AND LOSS

For one fifteenth-century Spanish writer campaigning was grim, for it offered knights 'the shelter of a tent or branches, a bad bed, poor sleep with their armour still on their backs, burdened with iron, the enemy an arrow-shot off'.[1] Yet war had its attractions, for it offered fortune as well as fame. Thomas Gray, in his *Scalacronica*, explained how some Englishmen 'lived off the war' in the late 1350s, taking tribute in Normandy, and acquiring castles in Poitou, Anjou and Maine. 'They achieved so much, that all Christian people marvelled. And yet they were nothing but a gathering of commoners, young men, who until this time had been of little account, who came to have great standing and expertise from this war.'[2] The chronicler Jean de Venette recorded the delight in Paris at the news of the peace agreed at Brétigny in 1360, but added a perceptive note of caution: 'All men rejoiced, and rightly, save perchance those who in time of war make great gains from the deeds of war through which other men suffer loss.'[3] Before the Battle of Auray in 1364, a group of English knights and squires told John Chandos that they were alarmed at the possibility of peace. They had spent all they had, they said, and battle offered them a chance to recover.[4] In explaining why war was endemic from 1337, the fact that many participants saw it as a way of making money was important. A French view of the English in the fifteenth century was that they 'make war on all nations of the land by sea and land. They send back everything they gain in foreign lands, and send it back to their realm and because of this it is rich.'[5]

REWARDS AND RANSOMS

Pay was not sufficient to enable men to become rich; it did little more than cover some of the expenses of campaigning. Additional elements such as compensation for horses lost in war, and the bonus payment known as the regard, welcome as they no doubt were, would not transform a man's estate. However, there was the prospect of receiving grants, of money and land, in return for notable service. In 1347 John de Coupland was granted £500 a year for life as a result of his 'stout bearing' when he captured the king of Scots at Neville's Cross. In the same year the Earl of Huntingdon was promised the curiously specific sum of £823 12*s*. 4*d*. 'for good service in the war', and the Gascon Amanieu de Mote was promised 500 *livres tournois* a year as reward for capturing a castle. The gallant James Audley, who was almost killed at Poitiers in 1356, was granted £400 a year for life by the Black Prince.[6]

There were enough examples of huge rewards from the ransoming of prisoners to persuade men that there were large profits to be made, even if those cases were exceptional. At the outset of the war, Walter Mauny's capture of Guy of Flanders in 1337 demonstrated the potential profits available, when Edward III bought Guy for £8,000. When Caen was taken in 1346, Thomas Holland captured the Count of Eu, and later sold him to the king for £12,000. After the Battle of Poitiers, Edward III entered into agreements to purchase prisoners for some £65,000. Nor was it just the English who profited in this way, as the capture of the earls of Salisbury and Suffolk in 1340 showed. The later stages of the war offered increasing opportunities for the French. The Earl of Somerset, captured at Beaugé in 1421, claimed that his release cost him £24,000. There were, however, disappointments. John Talbot, later earl of Shrewsbury, was taken at Patay in 1429. His captor demanded an 'unreasonable and importable ransom', but Charles VII paid him about £2,100 for Talbot, before the Englishman was released in a prisoner exchange.[7] Some *routiers* did well. Perrinet Gressart was one who knew how to make money out of war. Late in 1426 he captured Georges de La Trémoille, the French royal councillor. Perrinet demanded a ransom of 14,000 gold écus, and in addition Trémoille promised to make lavish gifts of 'of gold coinage, of plate, and of silk cloth and jewels' to Perrinet's wife and members of his household, so as to hasten his release. In the end, in 1432 the Duke of Burgundy promised to pay the ransom.[8]

Making money from ransoms was not, however, a simple matter. There might be a prohibition on the taking of prisoners, as at the Battle of Crécy. There, Edward III's German allies protested to him, pointing out that if he had not allowed so much noble blood to be spilled, 'you would have achieved much in your war, and had a very great ransom'.[9] If a prisoner was captured, there might well be arguments over who had taken him, and difficulties about arranging custody. Nor was it always easy to know at what level a ransom should be set. An important part of the interrogation of a French soldier captured in Scotland in 1384 was to get him to identify the wealthy knights and squires in the French force and to say 'what ransom they could suffer and pay if they were captured'.[10]

It was common for men to be unable to pay their ransoms in full, and as the levels of ransom demands became increasingly inflated, so the difficulties increased. In 1366 John Chandos wrote to Charles V, saying that he was owed 20,000 francs for Bertrand du Guesclin's ransom, of which he had only received 12,500. He asked for the balance, and requested that 1,000 francs out of it be paid for the ransom of Nicholas Dagworth. Thomas Felton wrote in desperation to Richard II in 1379. He had sold some of his land, his plate and his jewels, had borrowed from the Count of Foix, and had raised money in England, in an attempt to raise the 30,000 francs of his ransom. He offered to put all his lands into the king's hands in return for £6,000.[11] It might take many years to settle a ransom claim. The Earl of Huntingdon was captured at Baugé in 1421, but 7,500 marks of his ransom of 20,000 marks were still unpaid in 1455. Somerset, also taken at Baugé, was not released until 1438, after complex negotiations for a prisoner exchange.

Nor, when a ransom was paid, did it all go to the man who took a prisoner. There were various claims to be met. Complex rules meant that the captor was obliged to hand over part of his gains to his captain, the proportion in England varying from a half in the early stages of the war to a third from about 1370. In turn the captain was due to pay part, usually a third, of his winnings to the king. In 1369 regulations for the French fleet laid down that half of any gains, whether at sea or on land, were to be paid to the king.

PROTECTION PAYMENTS

The practice of levying what amounted to protection money, *appatis*, on villages offered unscrupulous soldiers easy gains. When the English raided as far as Toulouse in 1386, many towns and villages agreed to pay *appatis*. They were then faced with having to make payments to the French crown, in order to obtain pardons. Further sums were extracted by *routiers*.[12] A whole district might agree to pay: in 1438 that of Gévaudan in southern France agreed to hand over 2,000 *moutons d'or* to the Spanish *routier* Rodrigo de Villandrando. When Villandrando and the Bastard of Bourbon, nominally acting for the French, encamped near Toulouse in the following year, 'they took and ransomed men and women, and did innumerable wickednesses, such that no victuals or merchandise could enter our said town or others in the land'.[13] Nor was it just the English and the *routiers* who extorted all they could; rather than offering protection, castles provided oppression, as French garrisons also often took all they could from the surrounding countryside.

LOOTING

Looting was an institutionalized element of war, approved and organized. The scale of the brutal way in which in the French countryside was exploited is hard to imagine. For ordinary soldiers, this was the chief way in which they could profit from the war. In 1352 Walter Bentley complained about the way in which English garrisons in Brittany were profiting from pillaging, but there was no way to prevent this, for this was their main source of income. Money, livestock and crops were taken. Attempts were made to limit looting, as when Edward III in 1346 tried to protect churches, women and children, or when Henry V forbade his men from taking anything save food on the march from Harfleur, but such orders were hard to enforce. After the 1346–7 campaign, 'there were few women who did not have something from Caen, Calais and other overseas towns; furs, bedcovers, cutlery. Tablecloths and necklaces, mazers and silver bowls, and linen sheets were to be seen in every English house.'[14] An inventory of goods forfeited by Robert Knollys in 1354 (when he was temporarily out of favour) is suggestive. As well as a couple of

Fig. 21: The execution of the notorious *routier* Mérigot Marchès in 1391

new pairs of boots, it lists a substantial quantity of silver, starting with a basin and ewer weighing over seven pounds.[15] A newsletter described Lancaster's *chevauchée* in Normandy in 1356: 'Every day they took various fortresses, and a great quantity of prisoners and pillage, and on their return they brought with them 2,000 of the enemy's horses.'[16] Three years later, Knollys plundered Orléans and Auxerre with typical brutality. In his force 'there was no Englishman so poor but that with gold, and silver, and jewels, and other precious things he was made a wealthy man'.[17] Over ten years in the late fourteenth century the notorious Mérigot Marchès was said to have made 100,000 gold francs from his brigandage. Froissart reported him as saying:

> There is no pleasure nor glory in this world like what men at arms, such as ourselves, enjoyed. How happy were we, when riding out in search of adventures, we met a rich abbot, a merchant, or a string of mules, well laden with draperies, furs or spices, from Monpellier, Béziers, or other

> places. All was our own, or at least ransomed according to our will. Every day we gained money [...] and when we went abroad, the country trembled: every thing was ours.[18]

Ordinary people could only hope for miracles to rescue them from an appalling situation. A few found their prayers answered. A record was made of the 73 miracles attributed to St Martial at Limoges between 1378 and 1389. His shrine was decorated with the chains of prisoners freed by the saint's intervention. He even restored two babies, seized by English troops, to their parents, quite naked. The difficulty of paying ransoms looms large among the saint's achievements, while among the other effects of war were abductions, destruction of villages and refusal to honour safe-conducts.[19]

PROFITS

There are many examples of men who made fortunes during the war. Robert Knollys, 'a page who in time became a great knight and powerful lord, the captain of many castles, towns, fortresses and places in France', was a case in point.[20] He acquired estates in Brittany, through capture and purchase, but his fortune was largely made from ransoms and plunder. It was not all easy for him; he was forced to return some of the booty he took from Auxerre in 1358, while the failure of his *chevauchée* in 1370 resulted in the temporary confiscation of his English properties. Nevertheless, the proceeds of war enabled this man of obscure origins to build up a property empire. In his later years, investment in trade brought further profits, and by the 1380s he was in a position to lend money to the crown.

It was not even necessary to fight in order to make money from the war. William de la Pole, merchant and financier, made a fortune by advancing money (much of it raised from others) to the crown. He profited from the failure in the 1340s of the great Italian companies, the Bardi and the Peruzzi, and with his questionable business practices skilfully avoided the bankruptcies that plagued a series of consortiums of English wool merchants. Even his trial in 1341, and his subsequent imprisonment until the following year, failed to halt him. He died in 1366; his family rose in rank, his son becoming Earl of Suffolk.

John Fastolf provides the best example of an English commander who did well financially in the later stages of the war. He rose from the ranks of the squirearchy, with an inheritance valued at a mere £46, to become a major landholder worth over £1,000 a year. His profits were sufficient to enable him to build a castle at Caister in Norfolk. Grants of conquered lands in Normandy were a major source of his wealth; he was able to add to these by purchasing further estates. He was fortunate in that he was never captured, while he made a wise move in returning to England in 1439, to take no further part in the war. He claimed that he made £20,000 from the victory at Verneuil, where he captured the Duke of Alençon, but there were other claimants to the duke's ransom, and Fastolf was due only 5,000 marks from it, of which he received no more than 1,000 marks. It was through his business acumen rather than his military success that Fastolf thrived, but without the war he could not have built his fortune.

Nor was it just the English who made money. Olivier de Clisson acquired a fortune by various means. He had a good start with the estates bequeathed by his mother, widow of Walter Bentley, and his two marriages brought him further lands. In Brittany he accumulated, by grants and by purchase, almost a quarter of the duchy. He also acquired estates in Normandy, and had custody of the castle of Montlhéry near Paris. If the fees and wages due to him from the crown did not materialize, he obtained land in lieu. He built a splendid castle at Josselin in Brittany, and had a magnificent town house in Paris. His wealth was such that he was able to lend on a large scale to the Pope, the Duke of Berry, the Duke of Orléans, the Queen of Sicily and others. No doubt ransoms and other profits of war contributed to his fortune; he was lucky in never being captured. In 1374 Charles V allowed Clisson to keep all of the ransoms and other payments that he and his men might take from English-held lands, over and above the wages to which he was entitled. In 1382 he was promised all of the English possessions in Flanders. Ten years later it was claimed that his wealth in cash and movable goods amounted to a staggering 1,700,000 francs. Hardly surprisingly, his enemies then turned on him, accusing him of embezzlement. However, he escaped conviction. How much of Clisson's wealth was directly derived from war, and how much from his inheritance, his marriages, his lack of generosity and his skilled

Fig. 22: The tomb effigy of Olivier de Clisson, in the basilica at Saint-Denis

management of his vast estates is impossible to determine; all was intertwined in an astonishing story of success.

Of course, such success stories were exceptional. For some, the war spelled financial disaster. Ingergier d'Amboise was taken prisoner in 1350 and charged with a ransom of 32,000 florins. Capture at Poitiers saw him burdened with a further ransom of 10,000 écus. Unable to pay, he died in prison. Many French families never recovered from such financial disasters. English sufferers included John Bourchier, captured in 1372, who spent at least seven years in prison, partly because there were disputes between his captor's heirs. He wrote sadly to his wife, who had to find ways of raising his ransom of about £2,000. Rights to it were bought by Olivier de Clisson, always out for a profit, and it was finally paid off in 1380. Bourchier still had to repay those who had made him loans. His capture, however, did not lead him to the conclusion that campaigning was unwise; he returned to the war as soon as he could, perhaps in the vain expectation that he might now make a profit. John Knyvett, knighted in 1415, was captured twice, and had to sell two manors to cover the costs of his freedom. Cases such as that of John More, who petitioned the king 'showing that for eighteen years and more he continued in the wars in France and Normandy at his own risk and costs' and was taken prisoner seven times, 'detained in great duress' with heavy ransoms demanded, as a result of which he had to sell and mortgage all his lands, should have deterred others from taking up arms.[21] Yet for many the risks remained worth taking.

There was a difficult balance to be struck between the hope of gains from the war, and the fear of losses. The Bascot de Mauléon, whom Froissart met in 1388, put it philosophically: 'Sometimes I have been so thoroughly down that I hadn't even a horse to ride, and at other times fairly rich, as luck came and went.'[22] The balance changed in the course of the war, favouring the English in the years up to 1360, and the French in its final years. For individuals, there was always a risk in going to war, but the hope of a rich ransom was one of the elements that meant that many considered it one worth taking.

ECONOMIC IMPACT

The economic impact of the war was debated in the 1960s, when K. B. McFarlane challenged orthodoxy by arguing that England gained rather than lost from the conflict. His views were then dismissed by M. M. Postan. A valuable French perspective on the debate was later provided by Philippe Contamine.[23] The arguments concentrated on the scale of manpower devoted to the war, the effects of war taxation, the proceeds of ransoms and other yields from the war, and the destruction caused by campaigning.

War was not continual; there were many years when calls on manpower were very limited. Though it is possible to provide reasonable estimates for the numbers of active combatants, it is far harder to give an approximation of how many were involved in providing support services. Also, even had there been no war, many would have been employed on what can be classed as military activities, for nobles would still have built castles, and men-at-arms would still have bought armour. There is no evidence from record sources that suggests that a loss of manpower when men were called to the army caused significant problems in the long term. The recruitment of sailors and the requisitioning of ships were probably more significant, for the proportion of England's sailors who took part in the war was undoubtedly high. As much as 40 per cent of a port's shipping might be involved in the war in a single year. Yet while trade was hit when ships were taken into royal service, there was a positive aspect for the ports. The crown's requirements encouraged shipbuilding, and there were profits to be made from transporting troops, horses and supplies.

The impact of taxation is difficult to assess. In broad terms, taxes took money from the less well-off sectors of society and redistributed it to the wealthy. Some will no doubt have trickled back down from the nobles and military captains to the artisans and peasants, but how much cannot be calculated. In France, one of the ways the crown raised funds, through heavy debasement, had different implications, for the real value of the currency was reduced. The French writer Alain Chartier, writing in 1422 when tax receipts were at a very low level, considered that wealth had flowed from the wealthy to the peasantry, for 'the coffers of the nobles and the clergy are reduced by the length of the war, for the feebleness of money has reduced the value of dues and rents they are owed'.[24]

Taxation also affected trade. McFarlane estimated that English tax receipts over the whole period of the war amounted to some £8 million. He argued that as almost £5 million of this came from the customs, much of this burden was, in effect, borne by foreign consumers who had to pay higher prices for wool, rather than English producers. Customs duties certainly had considerable implications for the English economy. The impact of the heavy taxes on the export of raw wool, introduced at the outset of the war, increased costs for Flemish weavers who relied on English wool, and gave an incentive to English cloth producers. These customs duties, combined with the policy of channelling all wool exports through a single 'staple', fixed at Calais from 1363, led to an inevitable decline. In the first decade of the fourteenth century exports had reached over 40,000 sacks of wool a year; in the 1440s they did not rise above 10,000 a year. The other side of the coin was a growth in cloth exports, for duties were low on these.

It was not only exports in wool and cloth that were affected by the war. The trade in wine between Gascony and England suffered badly, as vineyards and shipping were hit hard. In the early fourteenth century over 20,000 tuns of wine were imported annually from Gascony. The immediate impact of war in the late 1330s was to reduce that level by three quarters. By the 1360s, wine exports from Bordeaux were little more than a third of their early fourteenth-century level. The reopening of the war in 1369 saw a further immediate fall take place. In the fifteenth century, imports ranged from as little as 5,400 tuns in 1437–8 to an average of 12,000 tuns from 1444 to 1449.

How much was actually paid in ransoms cannot be calculated. The English clearly gained far more than the French in the fourteenth century, and McFarlane was probably right to argue that in the fifteenth the English did not lose as much from their defeats as they gained from Agincourt and Verneuil. Yet while the ransoms won in battle were important for individuals, the sums involved were not so great that they had significant economic effects. The exception is the huge payments made for the French king John, which amounted to as much as a tonne of gold. In two years from September 1360 the London mint produced almost £340,000 in gold coins. The total value of the currency at this time was probably no more than around £1 million.

The war undoubtedly contributed to economic change in England, but its impact was far more serious in France, though there was very considerable regional variation. The extent of destruction caused by English *chevauchées* and the actions of the *routiers*, together with the depredations committed by castle garrisons and others, was serious. Yet large-scale invasions were intermittent, with many years of relative inactivity. Nor did the fifteenth century see ravaging by English armies on the scale of the 1350s. It was also the case that the countryside was affected more than the towns, for villages provided none of the protection offered by town walls. However, local warfare and the actions of garrisons meant that destruction extended far beyond the routes taken by invading armies. In the 1440s the *écorcheurs* did a great deal of damage by 'living off the land as men-at-arms are accustomed to do', while Normandy was hard hit by brigands as well as by military action.[25] Yet despite the extensive evidence documenting destruction, the resilience of the medieval economy should not be underestimated. Arable land, for example, could be brought back into cultivation relatively quickly, in contrast to vineyards and orchards. There is a little that can be put on the positive side of the balance. Those involved in the armaments industry no doubt benefited from demand for their products, but much equipment was imported from Italy and Germany. Masons and other workmen will have benefited from the scale of castle-building and of the construction of new town walls.

The coinage provides a test for the ideas put forward by McFarlane and Postan. If the former was correct in seeing England gain, this should have led to an increase in the country's bullion supply relative to France. However, the evidence points to a more complex situation. Mint accounts show that the output of silver coinage in England and France was roughly parallel in the fourteenth century; production of a large quantity of coin in one country was swiftly followed by a similar rise in the other. From the 1360s, the output of silver from English mints was at a very low level, with the exception of that at Calais in the 1420s and 1430s. There is little to indicate that war was a significant driving force in shifting silver from France to England. The low levels of silver in circulation on both sides of the Channel in the early fifteenth century were the result of a European-wide silver famine, not of the Anglo-French war. The story is different when it comes to gold. Output of gold coins from English mints peaked in the early 1360s, surely a consequence of the French king's ransom. From 1411 to 1424 the English mints were exceptionally active, with £138,826 of gold coin produced in 1412–13. From 1435, mint outputs were once again low. It is tempting to link this with success and failure in the war, but the reality was otherwise. There was a recoinage in England in 1411–12, and gold was overvalued there as against silver. It is these factors, rather than ransoms paid by the French, that explain the high level of mint activity up to the mid-1420s. The author of the *Libelle of Englyshe Polycye*, writing in the late 1430s, considered that gold coin was in short supply, largely because of Italian merchants:

Who bear the gold out of this land,
And suck the thrift away out of our hand
As the wasp sucks honey from the bee.[26]

In practice, the problem at that time was that the Duke of Burgundy's debasement of his gold coinage attracted bullion to his mints in the Low Countries.

The author of the *Journal d'un bourgeois de Paris* painted a dark picture of the second quarter of the fifteenth century. Three factors stand out from his pages: the savagery of conflict, the appalling weather, and the many deaths from plague. War, climate change and disease all affected the economies of England, France and the Low Countries during the Hundred Years War, and it is not easy to determine their relative importance. With the loss of half the population, the Black Death of 1348 transformed the labour market. Subsequent outbreaks prevented the population from recovering. Lower temperatures from the start of the fourteenth century, and unexpected fluctuations in the weather, were difficult to cope with. War presented further problems, and for some, opportunities. The widespread destruction and the efforts made to find men, horses and equipment were only part of the story; a transformation of trade was another. While the demands of the military for armour, weapons and other necessities of war stimulated some sectors of the economy, this did not lead to more general economic growth. For a few, there were profits to be made from the war; for the majority it added to the many difficulties they faced. Alain Chartier described a peasant victim of war, who supported soldiers by his labour, and suffered as a result: 'Armies are mustered, and standards are raised against the enemy, but the actions are against me, destroying my poor livelihood and my miserable life.'[27]

15

CHIVALRY AND WAR

Material motives may have been important, but for Geoffroi de Charny, in his tract on chivalry, it was very wrong to see fighting as a means of acquiring wealth. 'In this profession one should set one's heart and mind on honour, which lasts for ever, not on profit and booty which can be lost in a single hour.'[1] Honour was central to chivalric culture; prowess, best displayed in fighting, was another essential quality. Other notable chivalric virtues were courtliness, generosity and piety. The cultural expectations bound up in chivalry, broadly defined, were a driving force in aristocratic and knightly society, though it is not always easy to tell whether the ideals and the rhetoric mitigated or aggravated the harsh realities of war.

A great deal was written in France about chivalry. It was expounded, analysed and criticized in treatises such as Geoffroi de Charny's *Book of Chivalry* and Honorat Bovet's *Tree of Battles*. Lives of heroes of the war, such as those of the Duke of Bourbon and of Boucicaut, glorified chivalric deeds. Yet there was remarkably little along these lines produced in England, nor were the French treatises known and circulated on any scale there until the 1440s. On the other hand, romantic chivalric literature, notably but not exclusively expounding tales of King Arthur, was widely read in England as well as in France. The importance of honour and the value of prowess were very clear in such works, though in contrast to the treatises on chivalry, they mirrored rather than dictated contemporary attitudes. Their relevance to the reality of war is questionable; it is implausible that hardened soldiers would have listened to romances in order to decide how to conduct campaigns. Admittedly, Boucicaut enjoyed hearing tales from Roman history, as well as saints' lives (though not romances), but it was practical considerations which determined his actions, not lessons from a distant past.

HONOUR AND PROWESS

Honour was crucial. Ghillebert de Lannoy, who narrowly escaped death at Agincourt when he was taken prisoner, advised his son, 'I would prefer you to die gloriously in an honourable battle, with banner unfurled, than to return cravenly from it.'[2] The increase of honour was one of the fundamental purposes of King John's Company of the Star. Any knight of the Star who left the field of battle shamefully would have his membership suspended. His shield would be turned to face the wall, until he was restored to his position. A deed of 1373 written by Thomas Percy, when imprisoned in Paris, stressed that if he went against the terms of an agreement for his release he would lose all honour and be 'reputed to be a false knight, a traitor and perjurer, and would incur all the blame, villainy and reproach in all places as a false knight, traitor and perjurer'.[3] For John Fastolf, the defeat at Patay resulted in the loss for a time of his position as a knight of the Garter, and there always remained a question mark over him.

Prowess was another important chivalric quality. The statutes of the French Company of the Star proclaimed that the knights 'eager for honour and glory in the exercise of arms, shall bear themselves with such concord and valiance, that the flower of chivalry [...] shall blossom in our realm'.[4] Skill in the use of arms required lengthy training and a high level of fitness to excel. The life of Boucicaut described how he gained endurance through running, and strength through such exercises as climbing the reverse side of a ladder, using only his arms, wearing a steel breastplate. Yet important as such skills were, the chivalric ideals did not fit perfectly with the realities of war. Training was individual, not collective. Chivalry exalted individual skill and personal courage, rather than the spirit that might unite and inspire a body of men. It also exalted mounted warfare, even though tactical developments favoured fighting on foot. The author of the life of the Spaniard Don Pero Niño considered, somewhat implausibly, that 'A brave man, mounted on a good horse, may do more in an hour of fighting than ten, or mayhap a hundred could have done afoot. For this reason do men rightly call him knight.'[5]

Some of the chivalric virtues had no more than a minor place in war. Generosity and courtliness were on occasion displayed to respected foes, as when Edward III honoured Eustace de Ribemont after fighting him at Calais in 1350. In a flush of chivalric enthusiasm, he gave Ribemont his own chaplet of pearls, and freed him without any ransom, in recognition of his bravery. Piety was naturally extolled; it was displayed by Henry of Lancaster in the fourteenth century by writing a lengthy religious tract, and by Arthur de Richemont in the fifteenth by burning more heretics than anyone else.

While chivalric ideals may have done much to inspire men who fought in the Anglo-French wars, it is also the case that such ideals were capable of diverting them to fight elsewhere, above all by crusading both in the Mediterranean or the Baltic lands. John de la Ryvere, a Gloucestershire knight, went on crusade in 1346 to expiate the sins committed on campaign in France. He fought heroically against the Turks, served as a spy in Syria and Egypt, and was fulsomely praised by the Pope.[6] Thomas Clifford, an experienced jouster, and some other Englishmen were picked out for the way in which they 'bore themselves royally' on the Duke of Bourbon's crusade in 1390 to North Africa.[7] Clifford returned to England, but soon set out on a crusading expedition to the Baltic. He would die on the way to Jerusalem. These are just two examples among very many; it was through crusading expeditions, not wars in France, that men could best prove their chivalric credentials.

There were, however, many incidents that show how men sought to demonstrate their qualities of chivalry in the Hundred Years War. On the Crécy campaign a French knight challenged his English opponent, Thomas Colville, to three jousting bouts 'for the love of his lady'. The third bout was abandoned as the French knight's shield was broken, and the two men swore 'to be friends in perpetuity'.[8] The single-handed charge by William Felton, campaigning in Spain in 1367, which ended with his death, was probably an attempt to redeem his honour after he had failed in a lawsuit against Bertrand du Guesclin before the *parlement* of Paris. At Agincourt one French knight, Guillaume de Saveuses, charged to his death with an escort of two men. Such incidents had little effect on the outcome of campaigns. Chivalric considerations rarely outweighed the practical realities of warfare.

TOURNAMENTS

Jousts and tournaments were key elements in the rituals of chivalry. Edward III was a great patron of tournaments, in which he himself was often an eager participant. No doubt this was in considerable measure a reflection of his personal enthusiasm, for the king himself participated keenly, often taking part incognito. There was a play-acting element, as when Edward and some of knights dressed as the Pope and cardinals at a tournament held at Smithfield in 1343. Such events are unlikely to have provided much training for war, but they were a means of encouraging and channelling the martial spirit of nobles and knights. Equally, in France Charles VI demonstrated his passion for the tournament and its associated festivities. In May 1389 the young sons of Louis, duke of Anjou and king of Naples, were knighted by the king, tournaments took place and a grand funeral service was held for du Guesclin (who had died in 1380). The king adopted colours of green and red, and had a flying stag as his symbol. There was jousting and feasting on a lavish scale, enjoyed by the ladies of the court as well as the knights. This was not all, for three months later, after the coronation of his queen, Isabeau, Charles VI enjoyed three days of jousting. He took part himself, and naturally was declared the victor. All this helped to encourage the ambitions of a militarized aristocracy. This time was the heyday of jousting. In 1390 one of the most famous events took place, at Saint-Inglevert, not far from Calais. There, Boucicaut and two companions challenged all-comers over a month. They triumphed despite suffering inevitable injuries. Such an event offered a way of proving prowess in times of truce. In contrast, patronage of tournaments was not essential for success in war. The specialist skills needed in the joust were very different from those needed for the mêlée of battle. Henry V in particular had no time for what he probably regarded as frivolous activities; he did not even bother to attend the tournament laid on to celebrate his wedding.

The chivalric world is sometimes seen as one of a refined masculinity. Geoffroi de Charny considered that women should stay at home and 'pay more attention to their physical appearance and be more splendidly adorned with jewels, rich ornaments and apparel than would be suitable for men'. Yet women had their part to play, and Charny also acknowledged the role of 'these noble ladies and others whom I hold to be ladies who inspire men to great achievement'.[9] Women gave those they admired tokens to wear in battle, and encouraged them to take vows to perform valorous deeds. In a possibly satirical poem, Henry of Lancaster's daughter placed two fingers over one of the Earl of Salisbury's eyes. He swore not to open it until he had fought the French. Eustace d'Auberchicourt was encouraged by his lady-love when she gave him a fine white horse. The girls of the Channel Isles, when French invasion threatened, made chaplets of violets and other flowers, which they gave to the men, encouraging them to put up a stout defence.[10]

CHIVALRY AND BRUTALITY

It was exceptional that at the sack of Caen in 1346 Thomas Holland and his companions did their best to 'preserve women and girls from rape and villainy'.[11] The practicalities of war were far removed from the ideals of courtliness, generosity and mercy. If men held back from delivering a fatal blow in a battle's mêlée, it was in the hope of gaining a rich ransom, not for reasons of chivalry. The destructive methods of the *chevauchée*, the savage sacking of towns, the brutal treatment of villagers: such common features of war are hard to equate with the dictates of chivalry. Horrific incidents punctuated warfare. At the siege of Derval in 1373 Robert Knollys' refusal to surrender was countered by the Duke of Anjou's action in executing four hostages. Knollys, with a touch of the psychopath, then had four of the prisoners he held beheaded, and flung into a ditch, heads on one side, bodies on the other.[12] There was little that was chivalric about the warfare conducted by Olivier de Clisson, whose slaughter of English prisoners led him to be known as 'the Butcher'. Neither did Henry V's treatment of prisoners fit easily into a chivalric mould. John Talbot was responsible for various outrages, notably by setting fire to the church at Lihons in 1440, where 'there were piteously burned to death a good three hundred or more people, men, women and children, and very few escaped of those who were in the church'.[13]

There are possible explanations. John Fastolf argued that the laws of war meant that 'burning and destroying all the land' was justifiable because 'traitors and rebels must needs have another manner of war, and more sharp and cruel war than a natural and ancient enemy'.[14] For him, the French were rebels against their rightful king, Henry VI. More broadly, the laws of war permitted savage treatment in cases where towns or castles failed to surrender. Another explanation is that the common people were outside the magic circle of chivalry: honour and courtliness was for nobles and knights, not peasants. When Boucicaut set up a knightly order, its aim was to protect ladies 'of noble lineage' from oppression, not all women.[15] Nor did the literature of chivalry necessarily exclude the brutality of the *chevauchée*. In one work, Arthur's troops invaded Normandy and 'as soon as they had come from the ships, they ran through the land and took men and women and booty and wasted the country most harshly, and you may be sure that never before had a land been so dolorous'.[16] In one tale, King Arthur himself, when out hunting, met a beautiful maiden and despite her cries 'did what he wanted anyway'.[17]

In the later stages of the war, the star of chivalry did not shine as brightly as it had done in the past. In France there were many critics of knightly attitudes. Honorat Bovet in his *Tree of Battles*, written in the late 1380s, was unsympathetic towards those who fought for 'vainglory, and valour and personal prowess'. In his lengthy treatise he explained that the poor, who had no idea of how to 'put on a coat of mail, close a pair of *Crapaudaux* or a bacinet' should not be killed or imprisoned.[18] A common view, expressed by the poet Eustace Deschamps among others, was that knights had become soft, even effeminate. There were similar views put forward in England, though the chorus was not as loud. At the end of the fourteenth century in his *Vox Clamantis*, John Gower assaulted the knights with his pen, accusing them of being soft and empty of honour. John Clanvowe, himself a knight, condemned those who 'spend outrageously on meat, drink, clothing and building, and in living in ease, sloth and many other sins'.[19] Chaucer, surely pointedly, did not make his knight take part in the war in France.

To some extent, such criticisms reflected the changes of the time. By the fifteenth century the war was not punctuated as frequently as in the past by individual acts of bravery (or folly), or by notable feats of arms. Chivalrous offers might be refused. When an English commander in Gascony, probably the Earl of Huntingdon, encountered the Spanish adventurer Rodrigo de Villandrando, he suggested that the two should share bread and a bottle of wine, before the outcome was determined 'by the pleasure of God and the help of St George'. Rodrigo would have none of it, and in the end, no battle took place.[20] The character of the war, particularly with the many sieges involved in the English defence of Normandy, was very different from that of the days of Edward III and Philip VI. A decline in knightly involvement in war and an increase in the proportion of archers and other common soldiers in both English and French armies provide a part of the explanation.

Yet courtly chivalric culture was far from forgotten, particularly by the dukes of Burgundy. Philip the Good instituted the Order of the Golden Fleece in 1430, and patronized elaborate jousts and tournaments. The Feast of the Pheasant, held in 1454, featured extraordinary pageantry and display. 'My lord the duke was served at table by a two-headed horse ridden by two men sitting back to back, each holding a trumpet and sounding it as loud as he could.'[21] Such lavish chivalric display was, however, increasingly divorced from the hard reality of campaigning.

GUILT AND GENEROSITY

It might be expected that the contrast between the ideals of chivalry and the brutal character of war would have created a sense of guilt. No doubt this was sometimes the case. There will have been others like John de la Ryvere who went on crusade to redeem themselves. However, the devotional treatise written by one crusading knight, John Clanvowe, suggests broader penitential motives. In most cases motives cannot be established; there could, for example, be a number of reasons to explain why Edward III's warlike keeper of the privy seal, William Kilsby, went on pilgrimage to the Holy

Land and Egypt in 1342, though guilt for taking up arms seems a likely one.

Yet in many cases guilt is not easy to demonstrate. Henry, duke of Lancaster made many gifts to the church, notably transforming the hospital at Leicester into a college for a hundred poor people, providing it with a substantial endowment. However, rather than this being related to his military career, the statutes for the foundation make it clear that its purpose was for the clergy there to pray for the royal family, the duke's parents and for the duke himself after his death. In his will, made in 1402, the Breton soldier Morice de Trésiguidi detailed a host of bequests to his family and the poor, including the prisoners in the Châtelet, and to churches, but there is no hint that his generosity was linked to any regrets over his long fighting career. Indeed, nothing in his will even reveals that he had been a soldier.[22] John Chandos died unmarried, but his property went to his sisters, not the Church. During his whole long career, he made just one small donation to the Church. Olivier de Clisson could have afforded to make lavish grants, but even in his final days showed a characteristic lack of generosity. The one large gift he made to the Church was of an unpaid debt, which would have been almost impossible to collect.

***

The contrast between the savagery of campaigning and the idealism of chivalry may have troubled some writers, and puzzled some historians, but it was of little concern to most of those who fought. They were not aware of the contradictions. Chivalry was important in encouraging nobles, knights and men-at-arms to fight. It provided a finely polished veneer, which covered over the brutality of war. Chivalry did little to protect non-combatants, or to prevent the destruction of towns and villages. It did not soften sharp swords. Rather, with its myths and rituals it served to make war acceptable.

Conclusion

Writing in the mid-twentieth century, the historian Edouard Perroy saw dramatic change in France and England as a result of the Hundred Years War. 'Out of their wounds, out of their blood, the modern monarchies were born, and the transition from a feudal society to a State bureaucracy was hastened.'[1] It is difficult to sustain such a grand conclusion if the France and England of 1300 are compared with the same states in the mid-fifteenth century. In the case of England, government bureaucracy was no more complex, or more efficient, by 1450 than it had been a century and a half earlier. Royal finances were markedly weaker, and the authority of great nobles was far more threatening. The military might of the crown, as demonstrated by the great castles in Wales built by Edward I, and the huge armies he mustered, had been far greater in 1300 than it would be in 1450. In France the monarchy in the early fourteenth century under Philip IV was powerful, with an effective bureaucracy. By the 1420s, threatened both by the English and by civil war, the country was close to collapse, though within 30 years there was a considerable recovery, with a striking increase in fiscal and administrative strength. Rather than the many years of conflict seeing the state exercising increased control over the organization of war, the reverse was the case, particularly in England, as the role of royal officials in matters such as recruitment and victualling was reduced. Though for some men war became a way of life, armies became smaller over the course of the war. By the fifteenth century, knightly involvement was far more limited than it had been in the early stages of the conflict.

Historians first identified a military revolution as taking place in the sixteenth and seventeenth centuries; medievalists have been eager to see similar changes in their own period. The main elements of the early modern military revolution have been identified as tactical changes, leading to the development of standing armies; a major increase in the size of armies; ambitious strategies involving the co-ordination of several forces; and a substantial impact of war on society, due both to the cost of maintaining armies and to the destruction they wrought. Technological change, with developments in artillery and fortification, was a further factor. Two military revolutions have been identified for the Hundred Years War: the first the way in which infantry came to dominate the battlefield in the fourteenth century, and the second the manner in which gunpowder weapons transformed siege warfare in the fifteenth.

Some elements of the classic military revolution were clearly absent from the Hundred Years War. There was no increase in the size of armies; rather, the reverse was the case. It was in the early years of the war that large forces were deployed, with Edward's force for the invasion of Normandy in 1346 numbering up to 14,000 men, while other English forces were engaged in Gascony and Flanders in the same year. Numbers in the fifteenth century, with the exception of Henry V's army in 1415, were very considerably reduced. Nor were true standing armies developed, though many men did serve on a regular basis, in campaign after campaign.

There was surprisingly little technological development, with the exception of gunpowder weaponry. The great bombards of the fifteenth century provided besiegers with much more potent weapons than trebuchets and springalds, but eventually they proved to be an evolutionary dead-end. The longbow was remarkably effective, but was not an innovation. Rather, change took place in the scale of its use, and the efforts made to ensure that archers had sufficient supplies of arrows. The main changes in armour came in the early fourteenth century; as the war proceeded, there were improvements as well as changes in fashion, but no revolutionary transformation took place.

There can be no doubting that strategy was carefully considered throughout the Hundred Years War, even though it did not inspire treatises and proposals on the same scale as the Crusades. There was no lack of ambition, particularly in the English strategies, from the grand alliance of the late 1330s onwards. The co-ordination of several armies was notable, above all in 1346. Later in the fourteenth century French defensive strategies under the guidance of Bertrand du Guesclin and Olivier de Clisson worked superbly, though the English concept of the 'barbicans' was an overambitious failure.

Given that battles were rare, and were only one element in a complex conflict, tactics have perhaps received undue attention from historians. The major change took place in the first half of the fourteenth century, when fighting on foot became the norm. Flemish infantry routed French cavalry at Courtrai in 1302, and the Scots on foot routed the English at Bannockburn in 1314. In the Scottish wars of the 1330s, English knights and men-at-arms dismounted, fighting with archers in support. The pattern was consolidated in the Hundred Years War. There were changes, as for example the French developing ways of dealing with English archery in the later fourteenth century, but these did not amount to a tactical revolution.

The overall impact of war brought major change, but it is no easy matter to isolate war from other factors, notably the Black Death and subsequent plagues, which led to the abandonment of villages and contraction of cultivation, and to significant social shifts. Nor without the war would all military expenditure have been diverted to more productive enterprises. Nonetheless, the war was a crucial element in the transformation of the late medieval world. The pressures of war were not uniform. Campaigning was intermittent, with the war interrupted by truces, though for many there was little relief from the burdens. France suffered the direct impact of armies, castle garrisons, *routiers* and *écorcheurs* in a way that England did not. Yet even within France there were major differences, with the borders of English-held Gascony, Brittany and Normandy particularly hard-hit.

In constitutional terms the war had very different effects in England and France. The many demands for taxation put to the English parliament were influential in developing the authority of that assembly, particularly of the commons, who acquired considerable political leverage. In France, however, the estates-general did not acquire the kind of control that the English parliament established. The financial crisis caused by the need to pay King John's immense

This story shall the good man teach his son;
And Crispin Crispian shall n'er go by,
From this day to the ending of the world,
But we in it shall be remembered –
We few, we happy few, we band of brothers.

Fig. 23: Sir Kenneth Branagh rallies the troops in *Henry V* (1989)

ransom led to the levy of taxes without the consent of the estates. Further, regional assemblies retained a degree of authority that was absent in England. The need to finance war therefore contributed to the development in England of a monarchy limited by parliamentary power, and in France to that of an absolute monarchy.

There was no inevitability about the shape of France that emerged by the mid-fifteenth century; linguistically and culturally distinct, the south, and particularly the south-west, might well not have come under the rule of the Valois monarchy. However, the conquest of Gascony and the regaining of Normandy marked the end of English control of lands in France. Subsequent English ambitions would be directed towards maritime expansion and the New World. National sentiment was enhanced. Memories of the war affected Anglo-French attitudes for centuries. The brief and astonishing career of Joan of Arc provided France with a national heroine. Nor could the French forget the defeats at Crécy, Poitiers and above all Agincourt. Equally, there was English pride in those victories, reinforced on stage and in film by Shakespeare's Henry V.

It seems right not to end this book with chivalric glories, but rather with those who fought and suffered. War was tough. A blow to the face saw Hugh Hastings lose several teeth; he suffered pain in his shoulder and elbow joints, and probably died from illness contracted at the siege of Calais in 1347. One soldier wrote from France in 1419, 'I pray you to pray for us, that we come out of this unlusty soldiers life into the life of England.' Thomas Hostelle lost an eye at Harfleur in 1415, and was also wounded at Agincourt, and at sea. He was 'sore feeble and bruised', and claimed that his service had never been recompensed or rewarded. William Crawford served at Harfleur in 1415, and then 'having often been taken prisoner and mutilated hand and foot, was grievously wounded in the head so that his recovery was improbable'. Royal charity at least ensured that he ended his days at Windsor in some comfort.[2]

Further Reading

GENERAL

Pride of place among histories of the Hundred Years War must go to Jonathan Sumption's magisterial multi-volume history *The Hundred Years War I: Trial by Battle* (London, 1990); *Trial by Fire: The Hundred Years War II* (London, 1999); *Divided Houses: The Hundred Years War III* (London, 2009); *Cursed Kings: The Hundred Years War IV* (London, 2015). These provide a narrative of unparalleled richness. Short histories of the war include E. Perroy, *The Hundred Years War* (London, 1951); P. Contamine, *La Guerre de Cent Ans* (Paris, 1972); Anne Curry, *The Hundred Years War* (Basingstoke, 1993); Christopher Allmand, *The Hundred Years War: England and France at War* c. *1300–*c. *1450* (Cambridge, 1988). David Green, *The Hundred Years War: A People's History* (London, 2014), provides a valuable discussion of a number of themes. A. H. Burne, *The Crecy War* (London, 1955) and *The Agincourt War* (London, 1956) are still useful. For general discussions of medieval warfare, see P. Contamine, *War in the Middle Ages*, trans. M. Jones (Oxford, 1984), and J. F. Verbruggen, *The Art of Warfare in Western Europe during the Middle Ages: From the Eighth Century to 1340 (*Woodbridge,1997). Valerie Tourelle et al., *Guerre et Société 1270–1480* (Neuilly, 2013), provides valuable summaries of a large number of themes.

There are many collections of essays which contain important papers. They include Anne Curry and Michael Hughes (eds), *Arms, Armies and Fortifications in the Hundred Years War* (Woodbridge, 1994), and L. J. Andrew Villalon and D. J. Kagay (eds), *The Hundred Years War: A Wider Focus* (Leiden, 2005); *The Hundred Years War (Part II), Different Vistas* (Leiden, 2008), and *The Hundred Years War (Part III), Further Considerations* (Leiden, 2013). P. Contamine, C. Giry-Deloison and M. H. Keen (eds), *Guerre et societé en France et en Bourgogne XIVe–XV siècle* (Villeneuve d'Ascq, 1991) contains valuable papers in both English and French.

This period is covered by two volumes in the New Oxford History of England: Michael Prestwich, *Plantagenet England* 1225–1360 (Oxford,

2005), and Gerald Harriss, *Shaping the Nation: England 1360–1461* (Oxford, 2005). G. Small, *Late Medieval France* (Basingstoke, 2009), provides a brief general history.

The Yale series on English Monarchs contains the following, all highly relevant: W. M. Ormrod, *Edward III* (London, 2011); Nigel Saul, *Richard II* (London, 1997); Chris Given-Wilson, *Henry IV* (London, 2016); C. T. Allmand, *Henry V* (London, 1992); Bertram Wolffe, *Henry VI* (London, 2001). For the French monarchy, there are R. Cazelles, *Société politique, nobles et couronne sous Jean le Bon et Charles V* (Geneva and Paris, 1982), Françoise Autrand's studies, *Charles V le Sage* (Paris, 1994) and *Charles VI: La folie du Roy* (Paris, 1986), and Malcolm Vale, *Charles VII* (London, 1974).

SOURCES

Rather than list all the sources used for this book, I list here solely some readily available in English translation. Many others are detailed in the endnotes. There are various translations of Froissart's work; *Froissart Chronicles*, ed. and trans. G. Brereton (Harmondsworth, 1968), provides convenient extracts. Other chronicles available in English include *The Chronicle of Jean de Venette*, ed. R. A. Newhall (New York, 1953); *Sir Thomas Gray Scalacronica, 1272–1363*, ed. Andy King (Surtees Society, 2005); *Knighton's Chronicle 1337–1396*, ed. G. H. Martin (Oxford, 1995); *Gesta Henrici Quinti*, ed. Frank Taylor and John S. Roskell (Oxford, 1975). There is also *The Chivalric Biography of Boucicaut, Jean II le Meingre*, ed. and trans. Craig Taylor and Jane H. M. Taylor (Woodbridge, 2016).

Collections of a range of sources include *The Wars of Edward III: Sources and Interpretations*, ed. Clifford J. Rogers (Woodbridge, 1999); *The Battle of Crécy: A Casebook*, ed. Michael Livingston and Kelly DeVries (Liverpool, 2015); *The Life and Campaigns of the Black Prince*, ed. Richard Barber (London, 1979); *The Battle of Agincourt: Sources and Interpretations*, ed. Anne Curry (Woodbridge, 2000); *Joan of Arc: La Pucelle*, ed. Craig Taylor (Manchester, 2006); *Society at War: The Experience of England and France during the Hundred Years War*, ed. C. T. Allmand (Edinburgh, 1973).

CHAPTER 1: THE CAUSES OF THE WAR

Malcolm Vale, *The Origins of the Hundred Years War* (Oxford, 1990), concentrates on the issue of Gascony, while H. S. Lucas, *The Low Countries and the Hundred Years' War, 1326–1347* (Ann Arbor, MI,1929), examines a different region. For the failure of crusade plans, see C. J. Tyerman, 'Philip VI and the Recovery of the Holy Land', *English Historical Review* 100 (1985). Dana L. Sample, 'Philip VI's mortal enemy: Robert of Artois and the beginning of the Hundred Years War', in L. J. A. Villalon and D. J. Kagay (eds), *The Hundred Years War (Part II), Different Vistas* (Leiden,

2008), pp. 261–84, looks at another element in the crisis. Craig Taylor discussed 'Edward III and the Plantagenet Claim to the French Throne', in J. S. Bothwell (ed.), *The Age of Edward III* (Woodbridge, 2001), pp. 155–69. For the Scottish dimension, see James Campbell, 'England, Scotland and the Hundred Years War', reprinted in Clifford Rogers (ed.), *The Wars of Edward III: Sources and Interpretations*, and for a recent discussion, see Michael Penman, *David II, 1329–71* (East Linton, 2004).

CHAPTER 2: THE FIRST PHASE, 1337–45
CHAPTER 3: CRÉCY AND CALAIS

Edward III's campaigns were the subject of Clifford J. Rogers' *War Cruel and Sharp* (Woodbridge, 2000), in which he transformed discussion by arguing that English strategy was battle-seeking. Individual battles are examined in Kelly DeVries' *Infantry Warfare in the Early Fourteenth Century* (Woodbridge, 1996). For the Battle of Sluys, see G. Cushway, *Edward III and the War at Sea: The English Navy, 1327–1377* (Woodbridge, 2011), and for the siege of Tournai, Kelly DeVries, 'Contemporary Views of Edward III's Failure at the Siege of Tournai, 1340', *Nottingham Medieval Studies* 39 (1995), pp. 70–105. Lancaster's campaigns in Gascony and elsewhere are detailed by Kenneth Fowler, *The King's Lieutenant: Henry of Grosmont, First Duke of Lancaster* (London, 1969). The Battle of Crécy has received much attention. Andrew Ayton and Philip Preston, *The Battle of Crécy, 1346* (Woodbridge, 2005), is essential; a different interpretation was offered by Richard Barber in his *Edward III and the Triumph of England* (London, 2013), and by Livingston and DeVries in *The Battle of Crécy: A Casebook*. For the siege of Calais, see Craig Lambert, 'Edward III's siege of Calais: A reappraisal', *Journal of Medieval History* 37 (2011), pp. 245–56, and for the difficulties the capture caused, see S. J. Burley, 'The Victualling of Calais', *Bulletin of the Institute of Historical Research* 31 (1958), pp. 49–57. David Rollason and Michael Prestwich (eds), *The Battle of Neville's Cross* (Stamford, 1998), contains a number of studies relating to the battle.

For the financing of the war in England, see G. L. Harriss, *King, Parliament and Public Finance to 1369* (Oxford, 1975), and the papers by E. B. Fryde, published in his *Studies in Medieval Trade and Finance* (London, 1983). For France, see John B. Henneman, *Royal Taxation in Fourteenth Century France: The Development of War Financing 1322–1356* (Princeton, NJ, 1971). J. R. Maddicott, *The English Peasantry and the Demands of the Crown, 1294–1341* (*Past and Present* Supplement 1, 1975) is essential for the burdens placed on England in the early stages of the war.

CHAPTER 4: POITIERS AND BRÉTIGNY

Richard Barber, *Edward Prince of Wales and Aquitaine* (Woodbridge, 1978), is a full biography of the prince. H. J. Hewitt provided a detailed study in *The Black Prince's Expedition of 1355–57* (Manchester, 1958), and for the culminating battle of the 1356 campaign, see David Green, *The Battle of Poitiers 1356* (Stroud, 2002). The prisoners taken there are discussed by C. Given-Wilson and F. Bériac, 'Edward III's Prisoners of War: the Battle of Poitiers and its Context', *English Historical Review* 116 (2001), pp. 802–33. English war aims were discussed by John Le Patourel in 'Edward III and the kingdom of France', reprinted in Rogers (ed.), *The Wars of Edward III: Sources and Interpretations*. For a recent analysis of the peace negotiations, see Clifford J. Rogers, 'The Anglo-French Peace Negotiations of 1354–1360 revisited', in J. S. Bothwell (ed.), *The Age of Edward III* (Woodbridge, 2001), pp. 193–213. The *Jacquerie* was studied by Siméon Luce, *Histoire de la Jacquerie d'apres des document inédits* (2nd edn, Paris, 1894), and far more recently by J. Firnhaber-Baker, 'Soldiers, Villagers and Politics: Military Violence and the Jacquerie of 1358'., in G. Pépin, F. Lainé and F. Boutoulle (eds), *Routiers et mercenaires pendant la guerre de Cent ans* (Bordeaux, 2016), pp. 101–14. The transformation of French finances is discussed by J. B. Henneman, *Royal Taxation in Fourteenth-Century France: The Captivity and Ransom of John II, 1356–1370* (Philadelphia, 1976).

CHAPTER 5: PEACE AND WAR, 1360–77
CHAPTER 6: NEW KINGS, 1377–99

For the *routiers*, see Kenneth Fowler, *Medieval Mercenaries* (Oxford, 2001). The Black Prince's role in Gascony is studied by G. Pepin, 'Towards a New Assessment of the Black Prince's Principality of Aquitaine: a Study of the Last Years (1369–72), *Nottingham Medieval Studies* 50 (2006), pp. 59–114. A. Goodman, *John of Gaunt: The Exercise of Princely Power in Fourteenth-Century Europe* (Harlow, 1992), is important for this period, as are J. W. Sherborne's papers in his *War, Politics and Culture in Fourteenth-Century England* (London, 1994). J. J. N. Palmer, *England, France and Christendom 1377–99* (London, 1972), remains somewhat controversial. For a French perspective there is J. B. Henneman, *Olivier de Clisson and Political Society in France under Charles V and Charles VI* (Philadelphia, 1996). R. Vernier, *The Flower of Chivalry: Bertrand du Guesclin and the Hundred Years War* (Woodbridge, 2003), provides an outline of the French hero's career. For John Hawkwood, see William Caferro, *John Hawkwood: An English Mercenary in Fourteenth-Century Italy* (Baltimore, MD, 2006), and his articles in Villalon and Kagay (eds), *The Hundred Years War*. A more popular treatment is provided by Frances Stonor Saunders, *Hawkwood, Diabolical Englishman* (London, 2004). The classic study of the war in the Iberian peninsula is P. E. Russell, *The English Intervention in Spain and Portugal in the Time of Edward III and Richard II* (Oxford, 1955). The Otterburn campaign and its context is discussed in A. Goodman and A. Tuck (eds), *War and Border Societies in the Middle Ages* (London, 1992). There is a valuable comparative analysis of the financial position in England and France in David Grummitt and Jean-François Lassalmonie, 'Royal Public Finance (c. 1290–1523)', in Christopher Fletcher, Jean-Philippe Genet and John Watts (eds), *Government and Political Life in England and France* c. *1300*–c. *1500* (Cambridge, 2015).

CHAPTER 10: AGINCOURT
CHAPTER 11: THE CONQUEST OF NORMANDY

Agincourt has attracted the attention of many historians. See above all, Anne Curry, *Agincourt: A New History* (Stroud, 2005). A more popular account was provided by Juliet Barker, *Agincourt* (London, 2005), and for different analyses, Clifford J. Rogers in 'The Battle of Agincourt', in Villalon and Kagan (eds), *The Hundred Years War (Part III)*, and Michael K. Jones, *Agincourt 1415* (Barnsley, 2005). The context for the killing of the prisoners is explained by Andy King, '"Then a great misfortune befell them": the laws of war on surrender and the killing of prisoners on the battlefield in the Hundred Years War', *Journal of Medieval History* 43 (2017), pp. 106–17. R. A. Newhall, *The English Conquest of Normandy* (New Haven, CT, 1924), provides the fullest account of Henry V's subsequent campaigns, and C. T. Allmand, *Lancastrian Normandy 1415–1450* (Oxford, 1983), discusses the English occupation. See also Juliet Barker, *Conquest: The English Kingdom of France, 1417–1450* (London, 2009). Henry's character is the subject of Malcolm Vale, *Henry V: The Conscience of a King* (London, 2016), and see also Craig Taylor, 'Henry V, Flower of Chivalry', in G. Dodd (ed.), *Henry V, New Interpretations* (Woodbridge, 2013). The royal shipbuilding programme is discussed by W. J. Carpenter Turner, 'The Building of the *Gracedieu*, *Valentine* and *Falconer* at Southampton, 1416–1420', *The Mariner's Mirror* 40 (1954), pp. 55–72, and more recently by Ian Friel, *Henry V's Navy: The Sea Road to Agincourt and Conquest 1413–1422* (Stroud, 2015).

An interesting analysis of Verneuil is provided by M. K. Jones, 'The Battle of Verneuil (17 August 1424): Towards a History of Courage', *War in History* 9 (2002), pp. 375–411. The occupation of Paris is discussed by G. L. Thompson, *Paris and its People under English Rule: The Anglo-Burgundian Regime 1420–1436* (Oxford, 1991). B. J. H. Rowe, 'John Duke of Bedford and the Norman "Brigands"', *English Historical Review* 47 (1932), pp. 545–67, discusses the breakdown of order in Normandy.

For the history of France in this period, in addition to Autrand on Charles VI, see B. Schnerb, *Armagnacs et Bourguignons: La maudite guerre 1407–1435* (Paris, 2001), and for the Burgundian dimension, R. Vaughan, *John the Fearless* (Woodbridge, 1973).

CHAPTER 12: THE MAID AND THE ENGLISH COLLAPSE

There is much written about Joan of Arc, but little of it concentrates on her role in war. Kelly DeVries, *Joan of Arc: A Military Leader* (Stroud, 1999), is an exception. Helen Castor, *Joan of Arc: A History* (London, 2014), provides a more general study of the Maid, as does Larissa J. Taylor, *The Virgin Warrior: The Life and Death of Joan of Arc* (London, 2009). A. J. Pollard, *John Talbot and the War in France 1427–1453* (2nd edn, Barnsley, 2005), is a classic study, while Juliet Barker, *Conquest*, also covers this later stage of the war. The reversal of alliances in 1435 was examined by J. G. Dickinson in *The Congress of Arras 1435: A Study in Medieval Diplomacy* (Oxford, 1955). Gerald Harriss's biography of *Cardinal Beaufort: A Study of Lancastrian Ascendancy and Decline* (Oxford, 1988) is important for the financial background. M. H. Keen discussed 'The End of the Hundred Years War: Lancastrian France and Lancastrian England', in M. Jones and M. Vale (eds), *England and her Neighbours 1066–1453: Essays in Honour of Pierre Chaplais* (London, 1989), and for the final debacle, see Craig Taylor, 'Brittany and the French Crown: the Aftermath of the Attack on Fougères', in J. R. Maddicott and D. M. Palliser (eds), *The Medieval State: Essays Presented to James Campbell* (London, 2000).

CHAPTER 7: ENGLISH FORCES IN THE FOURTEENTH CENTURY
CHAPTER 8: FRENCH FORCES IN THE FOURTEENTH CENTURY
CHAPTER 13: ARMIES IN THE FIFTEENTH CENTURY

The massive detailed study by P. Contamine, *Guerre, état et societé à la fin du moyen âge* (Paris, 1972), did much to transform understanding of late medieval armies. A summary account of English armies is provided by Michael Prestwich, *Armies and Warfare in the Middle Ages: The English Experience* (London, 1996), and for a comparative study of English and French armies there is a valuable essay by Steven Gunn and Armand Jamme, 'Kings, Nobles and Military Networks', in Christopher Fletcher, Jean-Philippe Genet and John Watts (eds), *Government and Political Life in England and France c. 1300–c. 1500* (Cambridge, 2015).

Pioneering work on English armies was done by A. E. Prince in his 'The Strength of English Armies under Edward III', *English Historical Review* 46 (1931), pp. 353–71. Andrew Ayton's book, *Knights and Warhorses: Military Service and the English Aristocracy under Edward III* (Woodbridge, 1994), did much to reveal the potential of record evidence. Recently, Adrian R. Bell, Anne Curry, Andy King and David Simpkin conducted a major research project, which led to *The Soldier in Medieval England* (Woodbridge, 2013), covering the period from 1369 to 1453. This showed the value of computer analysis of muster rolls and other records. The same project yielded two volumes of essays: Adrian R. Bell and Anne Curry (eds), *The Soldier Experience in the Fourteenth Century* (Woodbridge, 2011) and *Waging War in the Fourteenth Century, Journal of Medieval History*

37, no. 3 (2011). Andrew Ayton and Philip Preston, *The Battle of Crécy, 1346* (Woodbridge, 2005), contains important chapters on English and French armies by Ayton and Bertrand Schnerb. Anne Curry and Michael Hughes (eds), *Arms, Armies and Fortifications in the Hundred Years War* (Woodbridge, 1994), includes chapters by Andrew Ayton, 'English armies in the Fourteenth Century', pp. 21–38, and by Anne Curry, 'English Armies in the Fifteenth Century', pp. 39–68. Curry also wrote on 'The Organisation of Field Armies in Lancastrian Normandy', in Matthew Strickland (ed.), *Armies, Chivalry and Warfare in Medieval Britain and France* (Stamford, 1998). Nicholas A. Gribit, *Henry of Lancaster's Expedition to Aquitaine, 1345–46* (Woodbridge, 2016), provides a useful analysis of one English army. Andrew Ayton, 'The Military Careerist in Late Medieval England', *Journal of Medieval History* 43 (2017), pp. 4–23, is particularly useful for the late fourteenth century. Part of David Grummitt's *The Calais Garrison: War and Military Service in England, 1436–1558* (Woodbridge, 2008) is relevant to the Hundred Years War. The Welsh contribution to English armies is examined in Adam Chapman, *Welsh Soldiers in the Later Middle Ages 1282–1422* (Woodbridge, 2015). Chris Given-Wilson, *The Royal Household and the King's Affinity: Service, Politics and Finance in England 1360–1413* (London, 1986), is valuable for the king's household knights. Jon Andoni Fernández de Larrea Rojas, *El precio de la sangre: Ejércitos y sociedad en Navarra durante la Baja Edad Medie (1259–1450)* (Madrid, 2013), provided a valuable comparison with his work on Navarrese forces, and for Brabant, see S. Boffa, *Warfare in Medieval Brabant 1356–1406* (Woodbridge, 2004).

Recruitment, particularly the indenture system, was examined by A. E. Prince in 'The indenture system under Edward III', in J. G. Edwards, V. H. Galbraith and E. F. Jacob (eds), *Historical Essays in Honour of James Tait* (Manchester, 1933), pp. 283–97. Simon Walker, 'Profit and Loss in the Hundred Years War: the Subcontracts of Sir John Struther, 1374', *Bulletin of the Institute of Historical Research* 58 (1985), pp. 100–6, is valuable, as is A. Goodman, 'Responses to Requests in Yorkshire for Military Service under Henry V', *Northern History* 17 (1981), pp. 240–52. A detailed analysis of one early fifteenth-century retinue is provided by Gary Baker, 'To Agincourt and beyond! The martial affinity of Edward of Langley, second duke of York (*c*.1373–1415)', *Journal of Medieval History* 43 (2017), pp. 40–58. For the domestic background of the knightly class, see P. Coss, *The Knight in Medieval England 1000–1400* (Woodbridge, 1993).

For the archers (and much more besides), see Matthew Strickland and Robert Hardy, *The Great Warbow* (Stroud, 2005). For the problem of identifying their social background, see Gary Baker, 'Investigating the Socio-Economic Origins of English Archers in the Second Half of the Fourteenth Century', *Journal of Medieval Military History* 12 (2014), pp. 174–216. For controversy over the effectiveness of the longbow, see Kelly DeVries, 'Catapults Are Not Atomic Bombs: Towards a Redefinition of "Effectivenesss" in Premodern Military Technology', *War in History* 4 (1997), pp. 460–4; Clifford J. Rogers, 'The Efficacy of the English

Longbow: A Reply to Kelly DeVries', *War in History* 5 (1998), 233–42, and see also Clifford J. Rogers, 'The development of the longbow in late medieval England and "technological determinism"', *Journal of Medieval History* 37 (2011), pp. 321–41.

For mercenaries, see Kenneth Fowler, *Medieval Mercenaries* (Oxford, 2001), and the papers in G. Pépin, F. Lainé and F. Boutoulle (eds), *Routiers et mercenaires pendant la guerre de Cent ans* (Bordeaux, 2016). Scottish mercenaries are discussed by B. G. A. Ditcham, *The Employment of Foreign Mercenary Troops in the French Armies, 1416–1470* (PhD thesis, Edinburgh University, 1978).

Armour is discussed by Thom Richardson, *The Tower Armoury in the Fourteenth Century* (Leeds, 2016), and also in his 'Armour in England, 1327–99', *Journal of Medieval History* 37 (2011), pp. 304–20, and his 'Armour in Henry V's Great Wardrobe', *Arms and Armour* 12 (2015), pp. 22–9.

For the navy, see Graham Cushway, *Edward III and the War at Sea* (Woodbridge, 2011), and Craig L. Lambert, *Shipping the Medieval Military: English Maritime Logistics in the Fourteenth Century* (Woodbridge, 2011). See also Tony K. Moore, 'The Cost-Benefit Analysis of a Fourteenth-Century Naval Campaign: Margate/Cadzand 1387', in R. Gorski (ed.), *Roles of the Sea in Medieval England* (Woodbridge, 2012). For the French navy, C. de la Roncière, *Historie de la marine Française* (Paris, 1899–1932), remains useful, and see also *Documents relatifs au clos des galées de Rouen et aux armées de mer du roi de France de 1293 à 1418*, i and ii, ed. Anne Merlin-Chazelas (Paris, 1977–8).

There is a considerable literature on gunpowder artillery. For its impact on warfare, see Clifford J. Rogers, 'The Military Revolutions of the Hundred Years' War', *Journal of Military History* 57 (1993), pp. 241–78, and Malcolm Vale, 'New Techniques and Old Ideals: The Impact of Artillery on War and Chivalry at the End of the Hundred Years War', in C. T. Allmand (ed.), *War, Literature and Politics in the Late Middle Ages* (Liverpool, 1976). Vale also discussed the topic in his *War and Chivalry* (London, 1981). There is much information about Burgundian guns. See Robert D. Smith and Kelly DeVries, *The Artillery of the Dukes of Burgundy 1363–1477* (Woodbridge, 2005); J. Garnier, *L'artilllerie des ducs de Bourgogne d'après les documents conserves aux archives de la Côte d'Or* (Paris, 1895); Monique Sommé, 'L'armée Bourguignonne au siege de Calais de 1436', in P. Contamine, C. Giry-Deloison and M. H. Keen (eds), *Guerre et Société en France, en Angleterre, et en Bourgogne* (Villeneuve d'Ascq, 1991), pp. 204–5. English artillery is discussed by T. F. Tout, 'Firearms in England in the Fourteenth Century', in *The Collected Papers of Thomas Frederick Tout* (Manchester, 1932–4), ii, pp. 233–75, and for the fifteenth century, see Dan Spencer, '"The Scourge of the Stones", English Gunpowder Artillery at the Siege of Harfleur', *Journal of Medieval History* 43 (2017), pp. 59–73, and his 'The Provision of Artillery for the 1428 Expedition to France', *Journal of Medieval Military History* 13 (2015), pp. 179–92, and see also David Grummitt, 'The Defence of Calais and the Development of

Gunpowder Artillery in England in the Late Fifteenth Century', *War in History* 7 (2000), pp. 253–72.

CHAPTER 9: THE LOGISTICS OF WAR

H. J. Hewitt, *The Organization of War under Edward III* (Manchester, 1966), was a pioneering study of the logistics of war. Craig Lambert, *Shipping the Medieval Military: English Maritime Logistics in the Fourteenth Century* (Woodbridge, 2011), examines an important aspect of the way the English supplied their troops. Y. N. Harari, 'Strategy and Supply in Fourteenth-Century Western European Invasion Campaigns', *Journal of Military History* 64 (2000), pp. 297–333, challenged existing orthodoxies. For France, see M. Jusselin, 'Comment la France se préparait à la guerre de Cent ans', *Bibliothèque de l'école des chartes* 73 (1912), pp. 211–36.

CHAPTER 14: PROFIT AND LOSS

The economic effects of the war were debated by K. B. McFarlane, 'War, the Economy and Social Change: England and the Hundred Years War', *Past & Present* 22 (1962), pp. 3–13, and M. M. Postan, 'The Costs of the Hundred Years War', *Past & Present* 24 (1964), pp. 34–53. P. Contamine, 'La Guerre de Cent Ans en France: un Approche Économique', *Bulletin of the Institute of Historical Research* 47 (1974), pp. 125–49, provided a commentary from a French perspective. M. Jones, 'War and Fourteenth-Century France', in Anne Curry and Michael Hughes (eds), *Arms, Armies and Fortifications in the Hundred Years War* (Woodbridge, 1994), provides a valuable survey. For a classic regional analysis, see R. Boutrouche, *La Crise d'un société: Seigneurs et paysans du Bordelais pendant la Guerre de Cent Ans* (Paris, 1947). Nicholas Wright, *Knights and Peasants: The Hundred Years War in the French Countryside* (Woodbridge, 1998), examined late fourteenth-century evidence. The impact of war on the most important English export is evident from T. H. Lloyd, *The English Wool Trade in the Middle Ages* (Cambridge, 1977), and for the wine trade there is M. K. James, 'The Fluctuations of the Anglo-Gascon Wine Trade during the Fourteenth Century', *Economic History Review*, n.s., 4 (1951), pp. 170–96. M. Kowaleski puts forward interesting arguments in 'Warfare, Shipping and Crown Patronage: The Impact of the Hundred Years War on the Port Towns of Medieval England', in Lawrin Armstrong, Ivana Elbl and Martin M. Elbl (eds), *Money, Markets and Trade in Later Medieval Europe* (Leiden, 2006), pp. 233–56.

For discussion of mint activity and its implications, see J. L. Bolton, *Money in the Medieval English Economy: 973–1489* (Manchester, 2012), and H. A. Miskimin, *Money, Prices and Foreign Exchange in Fourteenth-Century France* (New Haven, CT, and London, 1963).

There is much information on the effects of war on individual fortunes. See for example K. B. McFarlane, 'The Investment of Sir John Fastolf's Profits of War', *Transactions of the Royal Historical Society,* 5th ser., 7 (1957), pp. 91–116, and Michael Jones, 'The fortunes of war: the military career of John, second lord Bourchier (d.1400)', *Essex Archaeology and History* 26 (1995), pp. 145–61. Henneman, *Olivier de Clisson and Political Society,* has much that is relevant.

CHAPTER 15: CHIVALRY AND WAR

Maurice Keen, *Chivalry* (London, 1984), is a classic study. More recent works include R. W. Kaeuper, *Chivalry and Violence in Medieval Europe* (Oxford, 1999), N. Saul, *Chivalry in Medieval England* (Cambridge, MA, 2011), and Craig Taylor, *Chivalry and the Ideals of Knighthood in France during the Hundred Years War* (Cambridge, 2013). The fifteenth century was examined by Malcolm Vale, *War and Chivalry* (London, 1981). Craig Taylor, 'English Writings on Chivalry and Warfare during the Hundred Years War', in P. Coss and C. Tyerman (eds), *Soldiers, Nobles and Gentlemen* (Woodbridge, 2009), pp. 64–84, looked at the literature of chivalry. The military orders were studied in detail by D'A. J. D. Boulton, *The Knights of the Crown* (Woodbridge, 1987); on the Garter in particular, see Richard Barber, *Edward III and the Triumph of England* (London, 2013). For the laws of war, see above all Maurice Keen, *The Laws of War in the Late Middle Ages* (London, 1965). An important aspect was examined by Rémy Ambühl, *Prisoners of War in the Hundred Years War: Ransom Culture in the Late Middle Ages* (Cambridge, 2013). For tournaments, see Juliet Barker, *The Tournament in England 1100–1400* (Woodbridge, 1986), and for discussion of jousts and deeds of arms in the later fourteenth century there is Steven Muhlberger's *Deeds of Arms* (Highland Village, TX, 2005). Crusading interests are the subject of T. Guard's *Chivalry, Kingship and Crusade: The English Experience in the Fourteenth Century* (Woodbridge, 2013).

CONCLUSION

There is a large literature on the concept of the early modern military revolution, originally put forward by Michael Roberts. For a convenient introduction, see G. Parker, 'The "Military Revolution," 1560–1660 – a Myth?', *Journal of Modern History* 48 (1976), pp. 195–214, and his *The Military Revolution* (London, 1988). Clifford Rogers looked at the medieval implications in 'The Military Revolutions of the Hundred Years War', *Journal of Military History* 57 (1993), pp. 241–78.

Notes

ABBREVIATIONS

CCR	*Calendar of Close Rolls* (London, 1900–49).
CPR	*Calendar of Patent Rolls* (London, 1906–66).
Froissart	Jean Froissart, *Chroniques de J. Froissart*, ed. Siméon Luce, Albert Mirot, Léon Mirot and Gaston Raynaud (Paris, 1869–).
Murimuth and Avesbury	Adam Murimuth and Robert of Avesbury, *Adae Murimuth, Continuatio Chronicarum: Robertus de Avesbury, De Gestis Mirabilibus Regis Edwardi Tertii*, ed. E. M. Thompson (Rolls ser., 1889).
Oeuvres de Froissart	*Oeuvres de Froissart: chroniques: publiées avec les variantes des divers manuscrits*, ed. J. B. M. C. Kervyn de Lettenhove (Brusssels, 1867–77).
TNA	The National Archives

PREFACE

1 *Joan of Arc: La Pucelle*, ed. Craig Taylor (Manchester, 2006), p. 240.
2 C. O. Desmichels and A. Trognon, *Tableau sommaire du cours d'histoire générale* (Paris, 1820), p. 28.

CHAPTER 1: THE CAUSES OF THE WAR

1 *Froissart*, i, part 2, p. 84.
2 Murimuth and Avesbury, p. 92.
3 *Chronique et annales de Giles le Muisit*, ed. Henri Lemaître (Paris, 1906), p. 111.

4 *The Wars of Edward III: Sources and Interpretations*, ed. Clifford J. Rogers (Woodbridge, 1999), p. 85.
5 Ibid., p. 125.
6 *Oeuvres de Froissart*, vol. 18, p. 171; Christopher Philpotts, 'The French Plan of Battle during the Agincourt Campaign', *English Historical Review* 99 (1984), p. 64.
7 W. Stubbs, *Select Charters* (9th ed., revised by H. W. C. Davis, Oxford, 1913), p. 480; *Parliament Rolls of Medieval England*, ed. Chris Given-Wilson et al. (Woodbridge, 2005, CD-Rom), 1343, m. 1; 1346, m. 1.
8 Guttiere Diaz de Gamez, *The Unconquered Knight: A Chronicle of the Deeds of Don Pero Niño*, ed. Joan Evans (London, 1928), pp. 104–5, 132–3.

CHAPTER 2: THE FIRST PHASE, 1337–45

1 Sir Thomas Gray, *Scalacronica, 1272–1363*, ed. Andy King (Surtees Society, 2005), p. 125.
2 *Chronique de Jean Le Bel*, ed. J. Viard and E. Déprez (Paris, 1904–5), i., p. 302.
3 *The Wardrobe Book of William de Norwell*, ed. Mary Lyon, Bryce Lyon and Henry S. Lucas (Brussels, 1983), p. 212.
4 *Scalacronica*, p. 127.
5 Murimuth and Avesbury, p. 304.
6 *Oeuvres de Froissart*, xviii, p. 90.
7 Murimuth and Avesbury, p. 306.
8 M. Jusselin, 'Comment la France se préparait à la guerre de Cent ans', *Bibliothèque de l'école des chartes* 73 (1912), pp. 228–32.
9 John B. Henneman, *Royal Taxation in Fourteenth Century France: The Development of War Financing 1322–1356* (Princeton, NJ, 1971), pp. 116–53.
10 *The Political Songs of England*, ed. Thomas Wright (Camden Society, 1839), pp. 182–7.
11 *Chronique de Jean le Bel*, i., pp. 308–9, 318.
12 *Parliament Rolls of Medieval England*, ed. Chris Given-Wilson et al. (Woodbridge, 2005, CD-Rom), 1345, section 1.
13 *CPR 1334–8*, pp. 502–4; *CCR 137–9*, p. 520.
14 *The Register of Ralph of Shrewsbury, bishop of Bath and Wells 1329–1363*, ed. T. S. Holmes (Somerset Record Society ix, 1896), pp. 324–6.
15 *The Political Songs of England*, pp. 182–7.
16 *CPR 1338–1340*, p. 371.

CHAPTER 3: CRÉCY AND CALAIS

1 J. F. Verbruggen, *The Art of Warfare in Western Europe During the Middle Ages: From the Eighth Century to 1340* (Woodbridge, 1997), p. 280.

2 Jonathan Sumption, *The Hundred Years War: Trial by Battle* (London, 1990), pp. 532–3; Clifford J. Rogers, *War Cruel and Sharp* (Woodbridge, 2000), pp. 217–37.
3 *The Wars of Edward III: Sources and Interpretations*, ed. Clifford J. Rogers (Woodbridge, 1999), p. 260.
4 *CCR 1346–9*, p. 57.
5 Murimuth and Avesbury, pp. 345–6.
6 *The Anonimalle Chronicle, 1333–1381*, ed. V. H. Galbraith (Manchester, 1927), p. 21; *The Wars of Edward III*, ed. Rogers, p. 130.
7 Andrew Ayton and Philip Preston, *The Battle of Crécy, 1346* (Woodbridge, 2005), pp. 109–37. The location of the battle has been challenged, unconvincingly, by Michael Livingston in *The Battle of Crécy: A Casebook*, ed. M. Livingstone and K. DeVries (Liverpool, 2015), pp. 415–38.
8 *The Battle of Crécy: A Casebook*, pp. 104, 116, 168, 218, 220.
9 L. Lacabane, 'De la poudre à canon et de sa introduction en France', *Bibliothèque de l'école des chartes* 6 (1845), p. 36.
10 Thom Richardson, *The Tower Armoury in the Fourteenth Century* (Leeds, 2016), pp. 136–7.
11 *Chronique de Jean le Bel*, ed. J. Viard and E. Déprez (Paris, 1904–5), ii, p. 152.
12 *CPR 1345–1348*, pp. 563–8.

CHAPTER 4: POITIERS AND BRÉTIGNY

1 *CCR 1349–1354*, p. 66.
2 *Calendar of Entries in the Papal Registers* (London, 1896–1989), i, p. 234.
3 Froissart, iv, pp. 88–97.
4 *Chronique et annales de Giles le Muisit*, ed. Henri Lemaître (Paris, 1906), pp. 274–9.
5 Ibid., pp. 299, 303.
6 *Chronique Normande du XIVe siècle*, ed. E. and A. Molinier (Paris, 1882), p. 101.
7 *Knighton's Chronicle 1337–1396*, ed. G. H. Martin (Oxford, 1995), p. 127; Murimuth and Avesbury, p. 421; Clifford J. Rogers, 'The Anglo-French Peace Negotiations of 1354–1360 revisited', in J. S. Bothwell (ed.), *The Age of Edward III* (Woodbridge, 2001), pp. 195–8.
8 *Oeuvres de Froissart*, xviii, p. 351.
9 Murimuth and Avesbury, p. 442.
10 J. F. Verbruggen, *The Art of Warfare in Western Europe during the Middle Ages: From the Eighth Century to 1340* (Woodbridge,1997), p. 307.
11 Murimuth and Avesbury, pp. 464–5.
12 Henri Denifle, *La guerre de cent ans et la desolation des* églises, *monastères et hôpitaux en France*, ii (Paris, 1899), pp. 123–7; Clifford J.

Rogers, *War Cruel and Sharp* (Woodbridge, 2000), pp. 361–72.
13 *Oeuvres de Froissart*, xviii, p. 387.
14 *Chronique Normande du XIVe siècle*, p. 114.
15 Froissart, v, p. 43.
16 *Oeuvres de Froissart*, xviii, pp. 391–2.
17 *La chronique du bon duc Loys de Bourbon*, ed. A.-M. Chazaud (Paris, 1876), pp. 4–5.
18 F. Bock, 'Some New Documents Illustrating the Early Years of the Hundred Years War', *Bulletin of the John Rylands Library* 15 (1931), pp. 98–9.
19 Rogers, 'The Anglo-French Peace Negotiations of 1354–1360 Reconsidered', pp. 199–208.
20 *Chronique des quatre premiers Valois*, ed. Siméon Luce (Paris, 1862), p. 73.
21 Froissart, v, pp. 166.
22 *The Chronicle of Jean de Venette*, ed. R. A. Newhall (New York, 1953), p. 95.
23 A. Chérest, *L'archiprêtre. Épisodes de la guerre de cent ans au xive siècle* (Paris, 1879), p. 389.
24 *The Chronicle of Jean de Venette*, p. 89.
25 TNA, C62/316, m. 2; *Foedera, Litterae & Acta Publica*, ed. T. Rymer et al., iii (i) (London, Record Commission, 1825), pp. 415, 428.
26 *Archives administratives de la ville de Reims*, ed. P. Varin (Paris, 1839–48), iii, pp. 137, 141.
27 Rogers, 'The Anglo-French Peace Negotiations of 1354–1360 Reconsidered', pp. 209–13.

CHAPTER 5: PEACE AND WAR, 1360–77

1 *Cronicas de los Reyes de Castilla*, i, ed. E. de Llaguno Amirola (Madrid, 1779), pp. 442–3.
2 *The Life and Campaigns of the Black Prince*, ed. Richard Barber (London, 1979), p. 126; *Chronique Normande du XIVe siècle*, ed. E. and A. Molinier (Paris, 1882), p. 184.
3 *Cronicas de los Reyes de Castilla*, i, p. 460.
4 *CCR 1354–60*, p. 481.
5 Froissart, viii, p. 161.
6 A. D. Carr, 'Sais, Sir Gregory', in H. G. C. Matthew, Brian Harrison and Lawrence Goldman (eds), *The Oxford Dictionary of National Biography* (Oxford, 2004, online version).
7 *Chronique des quatre premiers Valois*, ed. Siméon Luce (Paris, 1862), p. 234.
8 *Chronicon Angliae*, ed. E. M. Thompson (Rolls Ser., 1874), p. 143.

CHAPTER 6: NEW KINGS, 1377–99

1 *Parliament Rolls of Medieval England*, ed. Chris Given-Wilson et al. (Woodbridge, 2005, CD-Rom), 1378, m. 36.
2 *The* Chronica Maiora *of Thomas Walsingham 1377–1422*, ed. J. G. Clark, trans. D. Preest (Woodbridge, 2005), p. 97.
3 Froissart, ix, pp. 136–7; *The* Chronica Maiora *of Thomas Walsingham*, p. 104.
4 E. Perroy, *The Hundred Years War* (London, 1965), p. 140.
5 *La chronique du bon duc Loys de Bourbon*, ed. A.-M. Chazaud (Paris, 1876), p. 172.
6 *Knighton's Chronicle 1337–1396*, ed. G. H. Martin (Oxford, 1995), p. 325.
7 *Documents relatifs au clos des galées de Rouen et aux armées de mer du roi de France de 1293 à 1418*, ed. Anne Merlin-Chazelas (Paris, 1977–8), ii, p. 172.
8 *The Acts of the Parliaments of Scotland*, ed. C. Innes and T. Thomson (Edinburgh, 1844), i, p. 555.
9 *Knighton's Chronicle*, p. 349.
10 *La Chronique du bon duc Loys de Bourbon*, p. 185.
11 J. J. N. Palmer, *England, France and Christendom 1377–99* (London, 1972), pp. 142–65. For a considered assessment, see N. Saul, *Richard II* (London, 1997), pp. 205–34.
12 *Chronique du religieux de Saint-Denis*, ed. L. Bellaguet (Paris, 1839–52), i, p. 68.
13 David Grummitt and Jean-François Lassalmonie, 'Royal Public Finance (c. 1290–1523)', in Christopher Fletcher, Jean-Philippe Genet and John Watts (eds), *Government and Political Life in England and France,* c. *1300–*c. *1500* (Cambridge, 2015), p. 120.
14 *Fernão Lopes, Crónicas de D. Pedro e D. Fernando*, ed. Agostinho dos Campos (Lisbon, 1921), i, p. 205.
15 *Parliament Rolls of Medieval England*, October 1383, item 11.
16 Froissart, xii, p. 162.
17 A. do Paço, 'The Battle of Aljubarrota', *Antiquity* 37 (1963), pp. 264–9; Eugénia Cunha and Ana Maria Silva, 'War Lesions from the Famous Portuguese Medieval Battle of Ajubarrota', *International Journal of Osteoarchaeology* 7 (1997), pp. 595–9.
18 *Parliament Rolls of Medieval England*, 1385.
19 *Chronicles of the Revolution 1397–1400: The Reign of Richard II*, ed. C. Given-Wilson (Manchester, 1993), p. 241.

CHAPTER 7: ENGLISH FORCES IN THE FOURTEENTH CENTURY

1 S. Marshall, 'The Arms of Sir Robert Salle: An Indication of Social Status?', in J. S. Hamilton (ed.), *Fourteenth Century England* 8 (Woodbridge, 2014), pp. 86–7.

2 *Chronicon Galfridi le Baker de Swynbroke*, ed. E. Maunde Thompson (Oxford, 1889), p. 148.
3 TNA, E 101/25/19; E 101/32/30; E 101/33/25, E 101/509/12.
4 'Private Indentures for Life Service in Peace and War 1278–1476', ed. M. Jones and S. Walker, *Camden Miscellany* XXXII (London, 1994), pp. 70–1; TNA, E 101/68/5, no. 107.
5 *Laurence Minot Poems*, ed. T. B. James and J. Simons (Exeter 1989), p. 79.
6 *Sir Thomas Gray Scalacronica, 1272–1363*, ed. Andy King (Surtees Society, 2005), p. 181.
7 Froissart, vii, p. 23.
8 *Scalacronica*, p. 173.
9 TNA, E 101/28/70; *The Register of Edward the Black Prince*, ed. M. C. B. Dawes (London, 1930–3), iv., p. 441.
10 *Wardrobe Book of William de Norwell*, ed. Mary Lyon, Bryce Lyon and Henry S. Lucas (Brussels, 1983), pp. 326, 356.
11 *CPR 1343–5*, p. 516; *CPR 1345–8*, p. 113.
12 TNA, C 47/2/48, no. 13.
13 Kelly DeVries, 'Catapults Are Not Atomic Bombs: Towards a Redefinition of "Effectiveness" in Premodern Military Technology', *War in History* 4 (1997), pp. 460–4; Clifford J. Rogers, 'The Efficacy of the English Longbow: A Reply to Kelly DeVries', *War in His*tory 5 (1998), pp. 233–42.
14 *CPR 1338–40*, p. 124; Thom Richardson, *The Tower Armoury in the Fourteenth Century* (Leeds, 2016), pp. 111–12, 117.
15 *Register of Edward the Black Prince*, iii, p. 223; *Knighton's Chronicle 1337–1396*, ed. G. H. Martin (Oxford, 1995), p. 145.
16 *Wardrobe Book of William de Norwell*, p. 230.
17 W. Hudson, 'Norwich Militia in the Fourteenth Century', *Norfolk Archaeology* xiv (1901), pp. 303, 306–7.
18 TNA, C 47/2/58/18.
19 *CCR 1360–4*, p. 353.
20 *CPR 1381–5*, p. 457
21 *Wardrobe Book of William de Norwell*, p. 228.
22 TNA, C47/2/29.
23 TNA, C 61/68, m. 2.
24 TNA, E 101/68/5/112; E 101/68/6/134.
25 *Chronicon Galfridi le Baker*, p. 146.

CHAPTER 8: FRENCH FORCES IN THE FOURTEENTH CENTURY

1 *Chronique du religieux de Saint-Denis*, ed. L. Bellaguet (Paris, 1839–52), i, p. 206.
2 P. Contamine, *Guerre,* état *et societé à la fin du moyen* âge (Paris, 1972).
3 *Ordonnances des roys de France de la troisième race*, ed. Eusèbe Laurière et al. (Paris, 1723–1849), iv, pp. 67–8.

4 *Mémoires de servir de preuves à l'histoire ecclesiastique et civile de Bretagne*, ed. H. Morice (Paris, 1742–6), i., cols 1469, 1482–3; ii., cols 245–65.
5 M. Jones, 'Breton Soldiers from the Battle of the Thirty (26 March 1351) to Nicopolis (25 September 1396)', in Adrian R. Bell and Anne Curry (eds), *The Soldier Experience in the Fourteenth Century* (Woodbridge, 2011), pp. 165–6.
6 *Documents relatifs au clos des galées de Rouen et aux armées de mer du roi de France de 1293 à 1418*, ed. Anne Merlin-Chazelas (Paris, 1977–8), ii, pp. 170–1.
7 *Ordonnances des roys de France*, iv., pp. 658–61.
8 *Chronique du religieux de Saint-Denis*, p. 212.
9 L. Delisle, *Histoire du château et des sires de Saint-Sauveur-le-Vicomte* (Valognes, 1867), pp. 195, 209; ibid., pieces justificatifs, pp. 187–8.
10 *Documents relatifs au clos des galées de Rouen*, ii, pp. 157–8.
11 Michel Hébert, 'L'armée provençale en 1374', *Annales du Midi* 91 (1979), pp. 5–27.

CHAPTER 9: THE LOGISTICS OF WAR

1 Murimuth and Avesbury, pp. 371–2; K. Fowler, 'News from the Front in the Fourteenth Century', in P. Contamine, C. Giry-Deloison and M. H. Keen (eds), *Guerre et Société en France, en Angleterre, et en Bourgogne xive–xve siècle* (Villeneuve d'Ascq, 1991), p. 84.
2 TNA, C 47/2/31; *CPR 1350–1354*, p. 420.
3 *The Wardrobe Book of William de Norwell*, ed. Mary Lyon, Bryce Lyon and Henry S. Lucas (Brussels, 1983), pp. 363–86.
4 *CCR 1339–41*, p. 196; *CCR 1341–3*, p. 263; *CPR 1348–50*, p. 322.
5 TNA, E 101/26/25.
6 Y. N. Harari, 'Strategy and Supply in Fourteenth-Century Western European Invasion Campaigns', *Journal of Military History* 64 (2000), pp. 302–3; *Documents relatifs au clos des galées de Rouen et aux armées de mer du roi de France de 1293 à 1418*, ed. Anne Merlin-Chazelas (Paris, 1977–8), ii, p. 144.
7 TNA, C 47/2/29; TNA, E 101/20/4; E 101/569/9.
8 TNA, C 47/2/31, no. 2.
9 *CCR 1349–54*, p. 290.
10 *Statutes of the Realm* (London, 1810–28), i, p. 288.
11 TNA, E 101/21/38; *The 1341 Royal Inquest in Lincolnshire*, ed. B. W. McLane (Woodbridge, 1988), p. 42; TNA, E 101/569/9; *CPR 1345–48*, p. 535; *Calendar of Fine Rolls 1347–56* (London, 1921), pp. 273–7, 288–91.
12 *Foedera, Litterae & Acta Publica*, ed. T. Rymer et al. (London, Record Commission, 1825), iii (i), p. 448; *CCR 1349–54*, p. 293; *CCR 1354–60*, pp. 604, 647; S. J. Burley, 'The Victualling of Calais', *Bulletin of the Institute of Historical Research* 31 (1958), pp. 53–4.
13 TNA, C 61/68, m. 6; *CCR 1354–60*, p. 402.

14 *Statutes of the Realm*, i. p. 371.
15 A. le Moigne de la Borderie, *Histoire de Bretagne* (Paris and Rennes, 1898–1915), iii, p. 474.
16 M. Jusselin, 'Comment la France se preparait à la guerre de Cent ans', *Bibliothèque de l'école des chartes* 73 (1912), pp. 220–1; *Les Journaux du trésor de Philippe VI de Valois*, ed. J. Viard (Paris, 1899), pp. 216, 218; *Ordonnances des roys de France, de la troisième race*, ed. Eusèbe Laurière et al. (Paris, 1723–1849), ii, p. 567–70.
17 *Chronique du religieux du Saint-Denis*, ed. L. Bellaguet (Paris, 1839–52), i., pp. 264, 532.
18 Harari, 'Strategy and Supply in Fourteenth-Century Western European Invasion Campaigns', p. 314.
19 *Knighton's Chronicle 1337–1396*, ed. G. H. Martin (Oxford, 1995), p. 137.
20 Murimuth and Avesbury, pp. 203, 212–13.
21 *Chronicon Galfridi le Baker de Swynbroke*, ed. E. Maunde Thompson (Oxford, 1889), pp. 129, 134.
22 *Archives administratives de la ville de Reims*, ed. P. Varin (Paris, 1839–48), iii, pp. 151–2.
23 *Sir Thomas Gray Scalacronica, 1272–1363*, ed. Andy King (Surtees Society, 2005), pp. 175, 183, 185, 188 (my translation).
24 R. Boutrouche, *La Crise d'un société. Seigneurs et paysans du Bordelais pendant la Guerre de Cent Ans* (Paris, 1947), p. 174.
25 Froissart, viii, pp. 163–4.
26 *The Chronicle of Jean de Venette*, ed. R. A. Newhall (New York, 1953), p. 131.
27 *The Register of Edward the Black Prince*, ed. M. C. B. Dawes (London, 1930–3), iii, pp. 331, 350.
28 *CCR 1354–60*, p. 601.
29 Thom Richardson, *The Tower Armoury in the Fourteenth Century* (Leeds, 2016), pp. 198–9; TNA E 372/198, rot. 34 d.
30 Froissart, v, p. 200.

CHAPTER 10: AGINCOURT

1 Froissart, x, p. 254.
2 *Chronique du religieux de Saint Denis*, ed. L. Bellaguet (Paris, 1839–52), i, p. 564.
3 *Journal d'un bourgeois de Paris*, ed. A. Tuetey (Paris, 1881), p. 53.
4 Quoted by P. S. Lewis, 'War Propaganda and Historiography in Fifteenth-Century France and England', *Transactions of the Royal Historical Society*, 5th series, 15 (1965), p. 6.
5 G. Pepin, 'The French Offensives of 1404–1407 against Anglo-Gascon Aquitaine', *Journal of Medieval Military History* ix (2011), pp. 1–40.
6 *Chronique du religieux de Saint Denis*, iii, pp. 224.
7 Guttiere Diaz de Gamez, *The Unconquered Knight: A Chronicle of the Deeds of Don Pero Niño*, ed. J. Evans (London, 1928), pp. 112–30

(quotation on p. 127).
8 M. G. A. Vale, *English Gascony 1399–1453* (Oxford, 1970), pp. 72–3.
9 *The Battle of Agincourt: Sources and Interpretations*, ed. A. Curry (Woodbridge, 2000), p. 445.
10 *Chronique du religieux de Saint Denis*, v., p. 536.
11 'Le procés de Maître Jean Fusoris, chanoine de Notre Dame de Paris (1415–1416)', ed. L. Mirot, *Mémoires de la société de l'histoire de Paris et de l'Ile de France* 27 (1900), pp. 140, 208.
12 *Gesta Henrici Quinti*, ed. Frank Taylor and John S. Roskell (Oxford, 1975), p. 59.
13 Ibid., p. 61.
14 A. Curry, *Agincourt: A New History* (Stroud, 2005), p. 110; Clifford J. Rogers, 'Henry V's Military Strategy in 1415', in L. J. Andrew Villalon and D. J. Kagay (eds), *The Hundred Years War (Part III): A Wider Focus* (Leiden, 2005), p. 422.
15 *Gesta Henrici Quinti*, p. 75.
16 Christopher Phillpotts, 'The French Plan of Battle during the Agincourt Campaign', *English Historical Review* 99 (1984), p. 66.
17 Curry, *Agincourt: A New History*, pp. 113–31; Clifford J. Rogers, 'The Battle of Agincourt', in L. J. Andrew Villalon and D. J. Kagay (eds), *The Hundred Years War: A Wider Focus* (Leiden, 2005), *Part II*, pp. 114–21.
18 Curry, *Agincourt: A New History*, pp. 185–7; Rogers, 'The Battle of Agincourt', pp. 57–63.
19 *The Battle of Agincourt*, ed. Curry, pp. 105, 115, 154.
20 Ibid., pp. 181–2.
21 Ibid., p. 164.
22 Ibid., p. 134.
23 Ibid., p. 132.
24 Ibid., p. 155.
25 Ibid., p. 348.
26 *Oeuvres de Ghillebert de Lannoy*, ed. C. Potvin (Louvain, 1878), p. 460.
27 Rémy Ambühl, *Prisoners of War in the Hundred Years War: Ransom Culture in the Late Middle Ages* (Cambridge, 2013), p. 74.
28 *Oeuvres de Ghillebert de Lannoy*, p. 50.

CHAPTER 11: THE CONQUEST OF NORMANDY

1 *Proceedings and Ordinances of the Privy Council*, ed. N. H. Nicolas (London, 1834–7). ii, p. 196; *CPR 1416–22*, pp. 7–8.
2 *The Brut, or The Chronicles of England*, ed. Friedrich W. D. Brie (Early English Text Society, 1906), ii, p. 400.
3 *Proceedings and Ordinances of the Privy Council*, ii, p. 314.
4 R. A. Newhall, *The English Conquest of Normandy* (New Haven, CT, 1924), p. 263.
5 *Thomae Walsingham, Historia Anglicana*, ed. H. T. Riley (Rolls ser., 1863–4), ii, p. 327.

6 *Original Letters illustrative of English History,* ed. H. Ellis (London, 1824–46), i, pp. 69–70.
7 David Grummitt and Jean-François Lassalmonie, 'Royal Public Finance (c. 1290–1523)', in Christopher Fletcher, Jean-Philippe Genet and John Watts (eds), *Government and Political Life in England and France* c. *1300*–c. *1500* (Cambridge, 2015), p. 120.
8 *Parliament Rolls of Medieval England*, ed. C. Given-Wilson et al. (Woodbridge, 2005, CD-ROM), 1420, no 25.
9 *Journal d'un bourgeois de Paris*, ed. A. Tuetey (Paris, 1881), p. 136.
10 *Histoire de Charles VI*, cited by R. Ambühl, 'Henry V and the administration of justice: the surrender of Meaux (May 1422)', *Journal of Medieval History* 43 (2017), p. 87.
11 *Paris pendant la domination Anglaise (1420–1436)*, ed. A. Lognon (Paris, 1878), pp. 142–3.
12 *Recueuil des croniques et istoires anciennes de la Grant Bretagne, a present nome Engleterre, par Jehan de Waurin*, ed. W. Hardy (Rolls ser., 1864–91), iii, p. 109.
13 *Actes de la chancellerie d'Henri VI concernant la Normandie sous la domination anglaise (1422–1435),* ed. P. le Cacheux (Rouen, 1907–8), i., p. 174.
14 Newhall, *The English Conquest of Normandy*, p. 320.
15 *Histoires des règnes de Charles VII et de Louis XI par Thomas Basin*, ed. J. Quicherat (Paris, 1855–9), i., p. 52.
16 'Journal du siege d'Orléans', *Procès de condemnation et de rehabilitation de Jeanne d'Arc dite la Pucelle*, ed. J. Quicherat (Paris, 1841–9), iv., p. 100.

CHAPTER 12: THE MAID AND THE ENGLISH COLLAPSE

1 *Joan of Arc: La Pucelle*, ed. Craig Taylor (Manchester, 2006), pp. 148–9.
2 *Recueuil des croniques et istoires anciennes de la Grant Bretagne, a present nome Engleterre, par Jehan de Waurin*, ed. W. Hardy (Rolls ser., 1864–91), iii, p. 301.
3 *Journal d'un bourgeois de Paris*, ed. A. Tuetey (Paris, 1881), pp. 244, 246.
4 *Procès de condamnation et de rehabilitation de Jeanne d'Arc*, ed. J. Quicherat (Paris, 1841–9), iii., p. 85.
5 *Joan of Arc: La Pucelle*, p. 310.
6 *Procès de condamnation et de rehabilitation*, iii, p. 212.
7 *Joan of Arc: La Pucelle*, p. 113.
8 *Procès de condamnation et de rehabilitation*, iii, p. 130.
9 *Journal d'un bourgeois de Paris*, p. 279.
10 Ibid., pp. 280, 283, 286.
11 *The Brut, or The Chronicles of England*, ed. Friedrich W. D. Brie (Early English Text Society, 1906), ii, p. 571.
12 Sir John Fortescue, *The Governance of England*, ed. C. Plummer (2nd edn, Oxford, 1926), p. 141.

13 L. de La Trémoille, *Les La Trémoille pendant cinque siècles* (Nantes, 1890), i, p.195.
14 *Journal d'un bourgeois de Paris*, p. 375.
15 *Letters and Papers Illustrative of the Wars in France during the reign of King Henry VI of England*, ed. J. Stevenson (Rolls Ser., 1861–4), ii, part 2, pp. 575–96.
16 Kelly DeVries, 'Calculating Profits and Losses during the Hundred Years War', in L. Armstrong, I. Elbl and M. M. Elbl (eds), *Money, Markets and Trade in Later Medieval Europe: Essays in Honour of John H. A. Munro* (Leiden, 2007), pp. 199, 202, 207.
17 P. Champion, *Guillaume de Flavy, capitaine de Compiègne* (Paris, 1906), p. 155.
18 *Chronique d'Arthur de Richemont, connétable de France, duc de Bretagne (1393–1458)*, ed. G. Gruel (Paris, 1890), p. 260.
19 *Journal d'un bourgeois de Paris*, p. 363.
20 *Letters and Papers Illustrative of the Wars in France*, ii., part 2, pp. 605–6.
21 Ibid., i, pp. 216, 219–20.
22 *Chronique du Mont-Saint-Michel*, ed. S. Luce (Paris, 1879), ii, p. 93.
23 P. Contamine, *La France au XIVe et XVe siècles: Hommes, mentalités, guerre et paix* (London 1981), p. 267.
24 'Le livre des trahisons de France envers la maison de Bourgogne', in Kervyn de Lettenhove (ed.), *Chroniques relative à l'histoire de Belgique* (Brussels, 1873), pp. 215–6.
25 *Chronique de Mont-Saint-Michel*, i, p. 133.
26 *Actes de la chancellerie d'Henri VI concernant la Normandie*, ed. Paul le Cacheux (Rouen, 1907–8), ii, pp. 258–60.
27 Ibid., ii, pp. 114–6.
28 *Chronique de Mont-Saint-Michel*, i, pp. 300–1.
29 *Letters and Papers Illustrative of the Wars in France*, i, pp. 503–8.
30 *Chronique de Charles VII par Jean Chartier*, ed. A. Vallet de Viriville (Paris, 1858), ii, pp. 237–8.
31 *La Cronique de Mathieu d'Escouchy*, ed. G. du Fresne de Beaucourt (Paris, 1863–4), i, pp. 281–4.
32 Ibid., iii, p. 387.
33 *Memorials of the Reign of Henry VI: Official Correspondence of Thomas Beckyngton*, ed. G. Williams (Rolls ser., 1872), ii, p. 214.
34 *Chronique de Charles VII par Jean Chartier*, ii, pp. 254–91.
35 M. G. A. Vale, 'The Last Years of English Gascony', *Transactions of the Royal Historical Society*, 5th ser., 19 (1969): 219–38.
36 P. S. Lewis, 'War Propaganda and Historiography', *Transactions of the Royal Historical Society* 15 (1965), pp. 2–3; Craig Taylor, 'War, Propaganda and Diplomacy in Fifteenth-Century France and England', in C. Allmand (ed.), *War, Government and Power in Late Medieval France* (Liverpool, 2000), pp. 70–91.
37 *Gesta Henrici Quinti*, ed. Frank Taylor and John S. Roskell (Oxford, 1975), p. 94.

38 *Chronique du Mont-Saint-Michel*, p. 98.
39 Lewis, 'War Propaganda and Historiography', p. 6.

CHAPTER 13: ARMIES IN THE FIFTEENTH CENTURY

1 David Grummitt, *The Calais Garrison: War and Military Service in England, 1436–1558* (Woodbridge, 2008), pp. 84, 190.
2 *Chronique du Mont-Saint-Michel*, ed. S. Luce (Paris, 1879), p. 84.
3 Adrian R. Bell, Anne Curry, Andy King and David Simpkin, *The Soldier in Later Medieval England* (Woodbridge, 2013), pp. 38–9, 42.
4 A. Goodman, 'Responses to Requests in Yorkshire for Military Service under Henry V', *Northern History* 17 (1981), pp. 240–52.
5 P. Coss, *The Knight in Medieval England 1000–1400* (Woodbridge, 1993), pp. 133–4.
6 Robert Hardy, quoted in Bell, Curry, King and Simpkin, *The Soldier in Later Medieval England*, p. 143.
7 *Recueil des croniques et istoires anciennes de la Grant Bretagne, a present nome Engleterre, par Jehan de Waurin*, ed. W. Hardy (Rolls ser., 1864–91), iii, p. 173.
8 Anne Curry, 'The Military Ordinances of Henry V: Texts and Contexts', in Chris Given-Wilson, Ann Kettle and Len Scales (eds), *War, Government and Aristocracy in the British Isles c. 1150–1500: Essays in Honour of Michael Prestwich* (Woodbridge, 2008), pp. 214–49.
9 R. A. Newhall, *The English Conquest of Normandy* (New Haven, CT, 1924), p. 233–6.
10 *Chronique du Mont-Saint-Michel*, i, pp. 137, 145.
11 *Ordonnances des roys de France de la troisième race*, ed. Eusèbe Laurière et al. (Paris, 1723–1849), iii., pp. 306–11.
12 *Chronique d'Arthur de Richemont, connétable de France, duc de Bretagne (1393–1458)*, ed. G. Gruel (Paris, 1890), pp. 188–9.
13 *Chronique de Charles VII par Jean Chartier*, ed. A. Vallet de Viriville (Paris, 1858), ii., pp. 235–6.
14 Thom Richardson, 'Armour in Henry V's Great Wardrobe', *Arms and Armour* 12 (2015): 22–9.
15 *Chronique de Charles VII par Jean Chartier*, ii, pp. 25–6.
16 J. R. Hale, *Renaissance War Studies* (London, 1983), pp. 1–29; J. Mesqui, *Châteaux et enceintes de la France médiévale: De la défense à la residence* (Paris, 1991), i, pp. 89–92.
17 *Actes de la chancellerie d'Henri VI concernant la Normandie*, ed. Paul le Cacheux (Rouen, 1907–8), i, pp. 82–7.

CHAPTER 14: PROFIT AND LOSS

1 Gutierre Diaz de Gamez, *The Unconquered Knight: A Chronicle of the Deeds of Don Pero Niño*, ed. J. Evans (London, 1928), p. 13.

2 *Sir Thomas Gray Scalacronica, 1272–1363*, ed. Andy King (Surtees Society, 2005), p. 153.
3 *The Chronicle of Jean de Venette*, ed. R. A. Newhall (New York, 1953), p. 104.
4 Froissart, vi, p. 159.
5 *Le livre de la description des pays de Gilles le Bouvier, dit Berry*, ed. E.-T. Hamy (Paris, 1908), p. 120.
6 *CPR 1345*–1348, pp. 226, 438, 546; M. Jones, 'Audley, Sir James', *Oxford Dictionary of National Biography* (Oxford, 2004).
7 A. J. Pollard, *John Talbot and the War in France 1427–1453* (2nd edn, Barnsley, 2005), p. 17.
8 De La Trémoille, *Les La Trémoille pendant cinque siècles* (Nantes, 1894), i, p. 165.
9 *The Battle of Crécy: A Casebook*, ed. Michael Livingston and Kelly DeVries (Liverpool, 2015), p. 104 (my translation).
10 *Registre criminel du Châtelet de Paris, du 6 septembre 1389 au 18 Mai 1392*, ed. H. Duplès-Agier (Paris, 1861–4), i, p. 383.
11 *Oeuvres de Froissart*, xviii, pp. 484, 555.
12 L'abbé Galabert, *Désastres causes par la guerre de cent ans au pays de Verdun-sur-Garonne* (Paris, 1894), p. 10.
13 J. Quicherat, *Vie de Rodrigue de Villandrando* (Paris, 1879), p. 316.
14 *Thomae Walsingham, Historia Anglicana*, ed. H. T. Riley (London, 1864), i., p 272.
15 TNA, E 101/354/2.
16 Murimuth and Avesbury, p. 465.
17 *Knighton's Chronicle 1337–1396*, ed. G. H. Martin (Oxford, 1995), p. 165.
18 *Chronicles of England, France, Spain ... by Sir John Froissart*, trans. Thomas Johnes (London, 1839), ii, p. 450. For Mérigot, see H. Moranvillé, 'La fin de Mérigot Marchès', *Bibliothèque de l'école des chartes* 53 (1892), pp. 77–84.
19 J.-L. Lemaitre, 'Miracles de guerre, miracles de paix en Limousin d'aprés les miracles de saint Martial (1388)', in Michel Sot (ed.), *Médiation, paix et guerre au Moyen* Âge (Paris, 2012), pp. 63–73.
20 *Knighton's Chronicle*, p. 164.
21 *CPR 1441–46*, p. 315.
22 *Froissart Chronicles*, ed. and trans. G. Brereton (Harmondsworth, 1968), p. 288.
23 K. B. McFarlane, 'War, the Economy and Social Change: England and the Hundred Years War', *Past & Present* 22 (1962), pp. 3–13; M. M. Postan, 'The Costs of the Hundred Years War', *Past & Present* 24 (1964), pp. 34–53; P. Contamine, 'La Guerre de Cent Ans en France: un Approche Économique', *Bulletin of the Institute of Historical Research* 47 (1974), pp. 125–49.
24 Alain Chartier, *Le quadrilogue invectif*, ed. E. Droz (Paris, 1923), p. 30.
25 A. Tuetey, *Les* écorcheurs *sous Charles VII* (Paris, 1874), ii, p. 403.
26 *The Libelle of Englyshe Polycye*, ed. George Warner (Oxford, 1926), p. 21.
27 Chartier, *Le quadrilogue invectif*, pp. 18–19.

CHAPTER 15: CHIVALRY AND WAR

1 *The Book of Chivalry of Geoffroi de Charny*, ed. R. W. Kaeuper and E. Kennedy (Philadelphia, 1996), p. 98 (my translation).
2 Cited by Malcolm Vale, *War and Chivalry* (London, 1981), p. 15.
3 *Oeuvres de Froissart*, xviii, p. 507.
4 D'A. J. D. Boulton, *The Knights of the Crown* (Woodbridge, 1987), p. 185.
5 Guttiere Diaz de Gamez, *The Unconquered Knight: A Chronicle of the Deeds of Don Pero Niño*, ed. J. Evans (London, 1928), p. 11.
6 T. Guard, *Chivalry, Kingship and Crusade: The English Experience in the Fourteenth Century* (Woodbridge, 2013), pp. 10, 37.
7 *La chronique du bon duc Loys de Bourbon*, ed. A.-M. Chazaud (Paris, 1876), p. 238.
8 *Anonimalle Chronicle, 1333 to 1381*, ed. V. H. Galbraith (Manchester, 1927), p. 22.
9 *The Book of Chivalry of Geoffroi de Charny*, pp. 95, 193.
10 *Laurence Minot Poems*, ed. T. B. James and J. Simons (Exeter, 1989), p. 75; Froissart, v, p. 166; *Chronique des quatre premiers Valois*, ed. Siméon Luce (Paris, 1861), pp. 230–1.
11 *Chronique de Jean le Bel*, ed. Jules Viard and Eugène Déprez (Paris, 1862), i, p. 83.
12 Froissart, viii, pp. 159–60.
13 Monstrelet, cited by A. J. Pollard, *John Talbot and the War in France 1427–1453* (2nd edn, Barnsley, 2005), p. 126.
14 *Letters and Papers Illustrative of the Wars of the English in France*, ed. J. Stevenson (London, 1861), ii, p. 580.
15 D. Lalande, *Jean II le Meingre, dit Boucicaut (1360–1421)* (Geneva, 1988), p. 94.
16 *Mort Artu*, http://everything2.com/title/Mort+Artu+1 (accessed 17 March 2017).
17 R. W. Kaeuper, *Chivalry and Violence in Medieval Europe* (Oxford, 1999), pp. 228–9.
18 Honoré Bonet, *L'arbre des batailles*, ed. E. Nys (Brussels, 1883), pp. 121, 141.
19 Nigel Saul, *Chivalry in Medieval England* (Cambridge, MA, 2011), pp. 128–34. I have modernized the quotation given on p. 130.
20 Jules Quicherat, *Vie de Rodrigue de Villandrando* (Paris, 1879), pp. 209–10.
21 Richard Vaughan, *Philip the Good* (Woodbridge, 2002), pp. 144–9, 160–3.
22 P-M. Vicomte du Breil de Pontbriand, 'Maurice de Trésguidi', *Revue Historique de l'Ouest* 15 (1899), pp. 372–8.

CONCLUSION

1 E. Perroy, *The Hundred Years War* (London, 1951), p. xxviii.
2 A. Ayton, 'Hastings, Sir Hugh', *Oxford Dictionary of National Biography* (Oxford, 2004); *Original Letters illustrative of English History*, ed. H. Ellis (London, 1827), 2nd series, i, p. 78; *Letters and Papers Illustrative of the English Wars in France*, ed. J. Stevenson (London, 1861), i, p. 421; *CPR 1441–46*, p. 170.

Index

Italic denotes a reference to an illustration

Agenais 2, 12, 91
Agincourt, Battle of 6, 119–24, 126, 178, 184, 193
Aiguillon, siege of 22
Albret, Charles d' 114, 124
Alençon, Jean, duke of 123, 140–1, 144, 174
Aljubarrota, Battle of 72–3, *73*, 122
Álvares Pereira, Nuno 73
appatis 34, 147, 171
archers
  in battle 14–15, 21, 26, 28–9, 35, 40, 44, 52, 121, 123, 134–6
  recruitment and origins of 84, 87, 157–8
Archpriest (Arnaud de Cervole) 44–5, 49–50, 110
Armagnac, Bernard count of (d. 1418) 114, 131
Armagnacs 114, 116–17, 126, 132, 149
armour 76, 78, 93, 97, 110, 162–5, 190
Arras, Congress of 143
Arthur, legendary king of Britain 181, 186
Artois, Robert of 4, 15
Arundel, earls of
  John d'Arundel (d. 1435) 143
  Richard FitzAlan (d. 1376) 89
  Richard FitzAlan (d. 1397) 67–9, 81
  Thomas FitzAlan (d. 1415) 116, 119–20
Arundel, John 62
atrocities 18, 57, 122, 185–6
  see also rape
Auberoche, Battle of 21
Audrehem, Arnoul d' 53, 95
Auray, Battle of 51–2, 168
Avignon 17, 32, 35–6, 61
Ayala 52
Ayton, Andrew 83

Baker, Geoffrey le 39, 77, 90
Balliol, Edward, titular king of Scots 3, 29, 37
Bannockburn, Battle of 2, 25
Bardi and Peruzzi 13, 19, 173
Bascot de Mauléon 176
Basin, Thomas 136, 150
Battle of the Thirty 34
Baugé, Battle of 132, 169–170
Bayonne 115, 130
Beauchamp, Richard, earl of Warwick *see* Warwick, earls of
Beauchamp, Thomas, earl of Warwick *see* Warwick, earls of
Beaufort, Cardinal Henry 144, 149
Beaufort, Edmund, duke of Somerset *see* Somerset, dukes and earls of
Beaufort, John, duke of Somerset *see* Somerset, dukes and earls of
Bedford, John duke of (d. 1435) 128, 134–7, *135*, 142–3, 147, 154

Bentley, Walter 34, 35, 77, 109, 171, 174
Berwick 37, 104
Black Death xv, 6, 32, 180, 191
Black Prince *see* Edward, the Black Prince
Blois, Charles of 29, 48, 51
bombards 114, 132, 145, 152, 164–6, *165*, *166*, 190
Bordeaux 12, 37, 38, 103, 109, 110, 153, 178
Bosquet, Jean 100
Boucicaut (Jean le Meingre) 65, 119, 123–5, 164, 181–2, 184, 186
boulevards 139, 167
Bourbon, dukes of
  Charles (d. 1456) 144, 161
  John (d. 1434) 114, 123,
  Louis (d. 1410) 42, 62, 65, 68, 181, 183
  Peter (d. 1356) 41
Bourchier, John 175–6
Bourg, siege of 115
Bourges 38, 114, 132, 160
Bovet, Honorat 181, 186
Brest 61, 69
Brétigny, Treaty of 47–9, 54
Brignais, Battle of 49
Brittany 16–17, 20, 29, 31, 34–5, 38, 47, 51, 55, 59, 84, 171, 173–4
Brittany, dukes of
  Francis (d. 1450) 150
  John (d. 1341) 16, 20
  John de Montfort (d. 1345) 51
  John de Montfort (d. 1399) 58, 62
Bruges, Truce of 59
Buckingham, Thomas, earl of (d. 1397) 89
Buironfosse, abortive battle at 11
Bureau, Jean 146, 150, 152, 166
  Gaspard 150, 160, 166
Burghersh, Bartholomew 22–3, 40, 41
Burgundy, dukes of
  John the Fearless (d. 1419) 116, 131
  Philip the Bold (d. 1404) 68, 113–5
  Philip the Good (d. 1467) 131–2, 143, 146, 166, 170, 187
Burnt Candlemas 38
Cadzand, Battle of 10
  naval battle near 67
Caen 23–4, *24*, 28, 128–31, 185
Calais xiii, 24, 31–2, 34–7, 42, 46–7, 61, 64, 69, 80, 102–3, 105–8, 111, 129, 142, 155–6, 177, 183–4
  sieges of 20, 28–30, 106, 145, 166
Calveley, Hugh 34, 51–2, 55, 62, 65
Camoys, Thomas lord 123
Castagnaro, Battle of 71
Castile 52–3, 72, 74, 99
Castillon, Battle of 152–3, *152*, 156
Catherine, queen of England 117, 131
Chandos, John 33, 41, 51, 56, *57*, 168, 170, 188
Charles of Blois *see* Blois, Charles of
Charles, duke of Bourbon *see* Bourbon, dukes of
Charles, duke of Orléans *see* Orléans, dukes of
Charles, king of Navarre (1349–87) 36–8, 42, 43–4, 46, 50–2, 54, 57, 61
Charles V, king of France (1364–80) 70, 95, 99, 170, 174
  death of 64, 98
Charles VI, king of France (1380–1422) 64, 68–70, 97, 112–14, *113*, 117, 132, 134, 184
  character of 112
Charles VII, king of France (1422–61) 131, 134, 138–9, 140, 142–4, 146, 147, 149–151, 159–60, 166, 169
Charny, Geoffroi de 41, 181, 185
Chartier, Alain 124, 177, 180
Chartier, Jean 150, 162
Chaucer, Geoffrey 187
Cherbourg 61, 69, 128
chevauchée 22, 64, 69, 81–2, 128, 172–3, 178, 185
chivalry xiv–xv, 7, 28, 32–33, 65, 146, 151–2, 181–8, 193
Chronique Normande 26, 40
Clanvowe, John 186–7
Clarence, Thomas duke of 116, 132
Clement VII, pope 61, 65
Clisson, Olivier de 51, 55, 58, 64–5, 68, 96, 110, 174–5, *175*, 185, 188

Cocherel, Battle of 50
coinage, debasement of 7, 12, 31, 33–4, 70, 131, 134, 177, 180
Colville, Thomas 183
compagnies d'ordonnance 162
Company of the Star 33, 35, 182
Constables of France 33, 36, 41, 63, 93, 95, 122–3, 144, 151
Contamine, Philippe xiv, 91, 176
contracts, military 79–81, 87–9, 92, 156
Coupland, John de 169
Courtrai, Battle of 3, 91, 191
Cravant, Battle of 134
Crécy, Battle of 20, 23, 25–8, *27*, 43, 84, 92, 95, 170
Crispin and Crispinianus, saints 122
crossbowmen 27, 92–3, 158, 160
crusade 4, 5, 65, 68, 183, 187, 190
Curry, Anne 119–20

Dagworth, Thomas 34, 77, 79
d'Arundel, John *see* Arundel, earls of
d'Auberchicourt, Eustace 44, 51–2, 185
Dauphin, Louis 117–8
David II, king of Scots (1329–71) 3, 29, 31, 37, 42, 48, 66, 85
de la Pole, Michael, earl of Suffolk *see* Suffolk, earls of
de la Pole, William 173
de la Pole, William, duke, marquess and earl of Suffolk *see* Suffolk, earls of
de Montfort, John, duke of Brittany (d. 1345) *see* Brittany, dukes of
de Montfort, John, duke of Brittany (d. 1399) *see* Brittany, dukes of
Denia, count of 53
Deschamps, Eustace 186
desertion 118, 136, 159
DeVries, Kelly 85
Diaz de Gamez, Guttiere 168, 183
discipline 51, 89, 98, 124, 133, 159
Dordrecht bonds 13
Douglas, James 67
Douglas, William 39
Du Guesclin, Bertrand 34, 50–2, 55, 57–9, 63, *63*, 95, 110, 170, 184
  death and reputation of 63
Dupplin Moor, Battle of 3, 11, 25

écorcheurs 144, 160–1, 178, 191
Edmund, duke of York *see* York, dukes of
Edward I, king of England (1272–1307) 2, 189
Edward II, king of England (1307–27) 2, 10
Edward III, king of England (1327–77) 1– 7, 9–12, 14, 17–18, 20, 28, 30, 33–4, 36–8, 41–2, 46–8, 59–60, 88, 183–4, 187
  character and death of 59
  claim to the French throne xiii, 3–4, 13, 35–6, 42, 46–8
Edward, the Black Prince 5, 28, 36–8. 40–1, 52–5, 57–8, *57*, 81, 90, 102, 108
  character 59–60
Edward, duke of York *see* York, dukes of
English character 8
English language 7, 18, 117
Enrique of Trastamara, king of Castile (1369–79) 52–3, 72
Erpingham, Thomas 121
Esplechin, Truce of 15
estates-general 33, 42, 46, 191

Falaise 128–9, 148
Fastolf, John 137, 139, 141, 145, 174, 182, 186
Felton, Thomas 62, 170
Felton, William 82, 183
Fernando I, king of Portugal 72
feudal service 66, 78
  French 91–2
  in Normandy 131
Flanders 13, 20, 28, 64, 72, 83, 113
Formigny, Battle of 150
Fougères 150
franc-archers 162
Francis, duke of Brittany *see* Brittany, dukes of
French character 8
Froissart, Jean 1, 26, 33–4, 40, 43, 111–12, 176

Garter, Order of the 30, 33, 44, 89, 182
Gascony 1–5, 8–11, 18, 20–2, 26, 31, 35, 37, 39, 61–2, 79, 102–4, 106, 108–10, 115, 117, 151, 153, 158
Gaunt, John of *see* Lancaster, dukes and earls of
Genoa 68, 99
George, St 6, 40, 44, 136, 149, 152, 187
Gesta Henrici Quinti 118, 119, 121, 153
Ghent 3–4, 13, 21, 64, 67
Gloucester, Humphrey duke of (d. 1447) 136, 144, 155
Good Parliament *see* parliament
Gower, John 186
Grailly, Jean de, Captal de Buch 40, 50
Gray, Thomas 10, 109, 168
Great Company 44, 49
Gressart, Perrinet 169
Gribit, Nicholas 80
Grosmont, Henry of, *see* Lancaster, dukes and earls of
guns 26, 98–9, 117, 129, 151–2, 164–5
  see also bombards; ribalds

Hale, J. R. 166
Halidon Hill, Battle of 11, 25, 84
Harari, Yuval 108
Harcourt, Godfrey of 22
Harfleur 120, 124, 127–8, 130–1, 158, 171, 193
  siege of 117–9, 146, 158, 164
Hawkwood, John 50, 71–2
Hennebont 16
Henry IV, king of England (1399–1413) 75, 114, 116
Henry V, king of England (1413–22) 6, 85, 116–34, *125*, 137, 185, *192*
  character and death of 133
  claim to the French throne 117, 122, 132, 134
Henry VI, king of England (1422–61, 1470–1) 142, 143, 145, 147, 151, 154, 186
  character of 144
Herrings, Battle of the 137, 158
herse 26
Holland, Thomas 169, 185
honour 7, 124, 181, 182
horses 38, 58, 83, 85, 98, 109–8,128, 148, 172
  compensation for lost 83, 169
  types and value of 82–3, 93, 96–7
Huntingdon, John Holand, earl of 133, 170

Ingham, Oliver 10, 12
intelligence 3, 22, 46, 71, 129
Isabeau of Bavaria, queen of France *113*, 132, 184
Isabella of France, queen of England 1, 3

Jacquerie 43–4, 43
James I, king of Scots (1406–37) 116
Jeanne de Montfort, countess 16–17
Joan of Arc 138–142, 154, 193
John, duke of Bourbon *see* Bourbon, dukes of
John, duke of Brittany *see* Brittany, dukes of
John II, king of France 33, 38, 40, 42, 45, 49, 93, 191
  as duke of Normandy 14, 20, 22
John the Fearless, duke of Burgundy *see* Burgundy, dukes of
John of Luxembourg, king of Bohemia 27, 28, 92, 95
Journal d'un bourgeois de Paris 140, 144, 180

Knollys, Robert 34, 51, 55–7, 65, 77, 79, 82, 171–3, 185

Lancaster, dukes and earls of
  Henry of Grosmont (d. 1361) 6, 20–2, 29, 31–2, 35, 36–8, 46, 77, 80, 109, 183, 188
  John of Gaunt (d. 1399) 56, 58–9, 62, 69, 72, 74–5, 79, 81–3, 109, 157, 172
Lannoy, Ghillebert de 124, 126, 182
La-Roche-Derrien, Battle of 29, 34
La Rochelle, Battle of 58

laws of war 57, 139, 146, 186
le Bel, Jean 22, 39, 78
le Muisit, Gilles 5, 33
Libelle of Englyshe Polycye 179
Limoges 57, 117, 173
living off the land *see* victualling
Lointren, Gilles de 167
longbow xiv, 84–55, 90
Louis, duke of Bourbon *see* Bourbon, dukes of
Louis, duke of Orléans *see* Orléans, dukes of

Malestroit, Truce of 17–18
Marcel, Étienne 42, 43–4
Marchès, Mérigot 172, *172*
Margaret of Anjou, queen of England 147
marmousets 68–9
Marshals of France 41–2, 63, 93–5, 119, 123, 125, 160
Martial, St 173
Mauny, Walter 10, 16, 29, 32, 169
Mauron, Battle of 35, 39
McFarlane, K. B. 176–9
Meaux *43*, 133, 146
mercenaries 92, 100, 160
  Scots 116, 135–6, 160
merchants 14, 92, 105–7, 129, 131, 173
  Gascon 2
  Italian 12–13
  see also Bardi and Peruzzi
Merciless Parliament *see* parliament
military revolutions xiv, 190–1
Montereau 131–2, 134, 146
Mont-Saint-Michel 149, 158
Morlaix, Battle of 17

Nájera, Battle of 52–3, 59
navy
  English 65, 88–9, 130
  French 99–100
  see also shipping
Neville's Cross, Battle of 29, 169
Nicopolis, Battle of 68, 96, 114, 119, 121
Normandy 22–4, 33, 35–6, 38, 42, 47, 105, 135, 137, 139–40, 143, 154–6, 162, 167, 191, 193
  defence and occupation of 146–51, 154, 156
  English conquest of 127–32
Northampton, William de Bohun, earl of (d. 1360) 20
nuns 45, 62, 88, 132

Orléans, dukes of
  Charles (d. 1465) 114, 125, 139
  Louis (d. 1407) 75, 114–5, 131
  Philip (d. 1375) 41
Orléans, siege of 137–9, 141, 160
Otterburn, Battle of 67

Palmer, John 69
pardons 45, 88, 114, 142–3, 148, 167, 171
Paris, 114, 116–7, 131–4, 137, 140, 142, 146, 153
parlement of Paris 2, 54, 62, 184
parliament 7, 13, 16–17, 30, 34–5, 54, 61, 65, 69, 72, 74, 78, 106, 132, 149, 191
  Good 68
  Merciless 67–8
Patay, Battle of 139, 158, 169
pavises 86
Peasants Revolt 71
Pedro the Cruel, king of Castile (1335–69) 52–3
Pembroke, John Hastings, earl of (d. 1375) 58
Perroy, Edouard 63, 189
Peter, duke of Bourbon *see* Bourbon, dukes of
Philip, duke of Orléans *see* Orléans, dukes of
Philip IV, king of France (1285–1314) 1, 3, 20, 37, 132, 189
Philip VI, king of France (1328-50) 1, 3–4, 7, 11, 12–13, 15, 22–3, 27, 29, 31, 33, 85, 92, 187
Philip the Bold, duke of Burgundy *see* Burgundy, dukes of
Philip the Good, duke of Burgundy *see* Burgundy, dukes of
Philippa of Hainault, queen of England 3, 10

Plymouth 11, 66
Poitiers, Battle of 38, 42, 77, 85, 90
Portsmouth 3, 11, 21, 37, 103, 118
Portugal 72–4
Postan, M. M. 176, 179
Praguerie 144
propaganda 5, 7, 18, 23–4, 38
prostitutes 92, 134, 141, 148, 159

ransoms 41, 45, 53, 126, 167, 169–70, 173–6, 178–9
  of David II 29, 66
  of John II 42, 47–9
rape 24, 43, 45, 72, 122, 132, 159, 185
recruitment
  English 10, 46, 65, 79–81, 84
  French 91–2, 160-2
regard 79, 169
Reims 15, 46–7, 139, 140
ribalds 26
Richard II, king of England (1377–99) 61–2, 65–6, 67–9
  character of 74–5
Richemont, Arthur de 122, 125, 144, 146, 151, 162, 183
Rinel, Jean de xiii
Rogers, Clifford 23, 39, 85, 119–20
Roosebeke, Batttle of 65, 70, 91–2, 96–8, 107, 119
Rouen 24, 117, 128, 133, 146
routiers 44, 49, 52–3, 62, 96, 110, 115, 169, 171, 178, 191
royal household 76, 79–80, 121, 155

St Albans, chronicle 59
Saint-Denis, monk of 117
Saint-Inglevert, jousts 184
Saint-Sauveur-le-Vicomte 59, 98
Saint-Vaast-la-Hougue 22, 116
Salisbury, earls of
  Thomas Montague (d. 1428) 134, 137, 155
  William Montague (d. 1344) 9, 14, 69, 185
  William Montague (d. 1397) 79–80
Salle, Robert 76
schism, papal 61, 65, 74
Scotland 2–5, 29, 37–8, 66, 104, 116, 171
Scrope and Grosvenor dispute 81
Shakespeare, William 192–3
Sherborne, James 69
shipping 7, 88–9, 99, 101–3, 177
  see also navy
Shrewsbury, Battle of 116
Shrewsbury, John Talbot, earl of 139, 146, 151–4, 156, 169, 186
Sluys, Battle of 5, 14–15
Soissons 114
Somerset, dukes and earls of
  Edmund Beaufort (d. 1455) 132, 144–5, 147, 150–1
  John Beaufort (d. 1444) 147, 155–7, 170
Southampton 11, 66, 102, 116
Spain 51–3, 72, 74, 82, 184
  see also Castile
spies 87, 129, 183
squires, status of 77–8, 157
Stafford, Ralph, earl of (d. 1372) 103
strategy
  English xv, 9, 15–16, 22, 37–8, 61, 64, 128, 139, 145, 147, 190
  French 46, 54, 191
Stratford, John, archbishop of Canterbury 13, 15
Suffolk, duke, marquess and earls of
  Michael de la Pole (d. 1389) 173
  Robert Ufford (d. 1369) 14, 106, 169
  William de la Pole (d. 1450) 144, 150, 157
Sumption, Jonathan xv, 23
Surienne, François de 150

tactics 17, 25–7, 34–5, 40–1, 51, 55, 65, 71, 120–1, 141, 191
Talbot, John, earl of Shrewsbury *see* Shrewsbury, John Talbot, earl of
taxation
  English 5, 13–14, 16, 30, 70, 149
  French 33, 48–9, 68, 70, 107, 177
Thirty, Battle of the *see* Battle of the Thirty
Tournai, siege of 15, 18, 81
tournaments 30, 184–5, 187
  see also Saint Inglevert, jousts
Tours, Truce of 147

training 86, 182, 184
Trésiguidi, Morice de 96, 188
Troyes 140
  Treaty of 131–2, 134

Ufford, Robert, earl of Suffolk *see* Suffolk, earls of
Urban VI, pope 61, 65

van Artevelde, Jacob 13, 21
van Artevelde, Philip 64–5, 91
Vannes 110
Vegetius 95, 162
Venette, Jean de 44, 110, 168
Verneuil, Battle of 135–6, 141, 158, 160, 174, 178
victualling 101, 103–7, 127–30
  living off the land 103, 108–10
Vienne, Jean de 66
Villandrando, Rodrigo de 144, 171, 187
Villani 26
Vincennes 44, *45*

wages 10, 16, 33, 46, 78–81, 87, 93, 104, 169, 174
Walsingham, Thomas 62
Walton Ordinances 13
Warwick, earls of
  Richard Beauchamp (d. 1439) 116
  Thomas Beauchamp (d. 1369) 79–80, 88–9
Waurin, Jean 136, 159
weather 6, 47, 142, 148, 180
Wesenham, John 106
White Company 71
Winchelsea 47, 66
  Battle of 33
Wingfield, John 37
wool 3, 7, 12–14, 16, 18, 34, 143, 177–8
Wykeham, William, 65

York, dukes of
  Edmund (d. 1402) 72
  Edward (d. 1415) 122